Religious Issues

In Nineteenth Century Feminism

Religious Issues

In Nineteenth Century Feminism

by

Donna A. Behnke

The Whitston Publishing Company
Troy, New York
1982

Library of Congress Catalog Card Number 80-52544

ISBN 0-87875-203-X

Printed in the United States of America

Dedication

This book is dedicated to the women of the nineteenth century whose courage and tenacity I found fascinating and a source of inspiration.

It is also dedicated affectionately to the women who continue that legacy of stubborn refusal to surrender the dignity of their sex.

Contents

Introduction

The difficulties involved in writing a history of women are already a matter of record. The chief reason cited is always the fact that so few women took pen in hand to record or interpret significant or crucial events. When they did, it was often only to find that they either lacked the literary skills to write well or had not been provided with the prerequisite knowledge necessary to comment intelligently on the social, political, or economic events surrounding them. More often than not, they had to content themselves with commentaries on limited personal worlds in the form of diaries, travel journals, works on etiquette, and the like. While such works are of immeasurable importance to modern day historians, they are for women yet another bold reminder of their historical subjection— a testimony to their inability to affect choice, action, and idea in the arenas where history is made.

The nineteenth century, however, was to bring about significant changes, for in that century woman's restlessness and dissatisfaction with her subject status reached a highwater mark. Dissatisfied with her subordinate position, she challenged it—in literature, politics, economics, education, religion, medicine, the sciences and all those so-called masculine spheres previously closed to her.

A great deal has already been written about the sociological, economic and political aspects of the nineteenth century woman's rights movement. So much, in fact, that it has dwarfed an equally important aspect of the movement—its concern for religious and theological issues. To ignore this element is to overlook much of the profundity of feminist efforts.

Throughout the nineteenth century, feminists showed an intense interest in the theological and ecclesiastical barriers which were reared before them; and, spurred by religious insights of their own, they developed an impressive theological rationale for their movement. While the early decades of the century provided few women articulate enough to present bold, well-reasoned arguments intent upon reversing theological prejudices adverse to women, the Abolitionist Movement and other reform movements which gripped the century would bring strong-willed, well-educated women into the public arena. As women became active in the abolitionist crusade, they were repeatedly called upon to justify their public role against seasoned arguments for their divinely ordered subjection and exclusion from public life.

The women rose to the challenge, and by the 1830s women like the Grimke sisters, Sarah and Angelina, from South Carolina had produced a theological defense for woman's equality which contained ideas and insights that were to echo and re-echo throughout the remaining decades of the nineteenth century.

From the initial woman's rights convention in Seneca Falls, New York, women's rights conventions became open forums for the debate of crucial issues. While their main thrusts were for political privileges, legal rights and economic and educational equality, they also recognized one other important factor. If women were to reverse centuries of social and political suppression and conditioning, they would have to confront the ideological bases supportive of their subordination. The women were quick to see that theology, reinforced throughout centuries of church history, had provided the main argument for woman's subjection by insisting that woman was man's divinely ordered subordinate and convicted introducer of sin into God's perfect world. Thus, theological and ecclesiological questions were readily debated, and conventions continually acknowledged the priority and importance of religious prejudice. Succinctly worded resolutions were drawn up and passed, setting forth the injustices thought to proceed directly from male-dominated biblical and theological scholarship.

Their chief enemy was tradition; centuries of biblical scholarship had labored, intentionally and unintentionally, to delineate woman's place in the created order of things—a place which was

always envisioned far below that of the male and equally far removed from public life and the arenas of authority.

If woman's chief enemy was tradition and the men and women
who upheld it, her chief weapons were faith, reason and the finest
arguments the democratic mind could muster. Reason and justice,
they charged, were antithetical to claims demanding half of the human race's submission to the dictates of the other half. Such reasoning was similarly opposed to the spirit of the Christian gospel and the
Judeo-Christian testimony that God was a god of love and all persons
children of that love.

The women who championed the woman's struggle prior to
Seneca Falls knew the power of this argument and the influential
position it held among their avowed opponents. The women of
Seneca Falls acknowledged it and it reverberated throughout the
succeeding decades. It surfaced as an abiding concern in national and
state conventions and supplied fuel for many convention orations
and floor arguments. It caused many in the struggle to sharpen their
theological wits and produced in its wake numerous journal articles
and several books by movement leaders. Each was intent upon reduc-
ing theology's stranglehold on the present liberation effort.

Convention debate and resolution was not the only way women sought to reverse centuries of theological discrimination; some
sought to attack the issues involved in an even more direct way
than the means provided by women's conventions and conferences.
They become biblical scholars and sought to expound biblical and
theological alternatives to current exegesis. A few women, like
Frances E. Willard, Anna Howard Shaw and, to some extent, Elizabeth Cady Stanton, became accomplished biblical scholars, effectively exposing texts thought mistranslated or misappropriated by their
male counterparts.

Still other women in the movement turned their attention to
a critique of church history. Among their number stood Ellen B.
Dietrick, an early church historian who chose to base her claim for
feminine equality on precedence, assuring readers that women had
participated freely and responsibly in the ministry of the early

church. Matilda J. Gage, another female historian of note, chose a somewhat different approach with her penetrating, often blistering, attack on church practices, i. e., celibacy and witch-hunting, which she thought conscious attempts to depreciate and oppress women.

Nineteenth century feminist materials reveal that not all feminists faced the religious questions in the same way or with the same frame of mind. In fact, there was much disagreement, particularly on questions of emphasis and methodology. Some ridiculed the religious issue while, at the same time, acknowledging its potency. For them, anti-feminist theology was nothing more than the pompous sputterings of ancient ecclesiastics intent upon consolidating and securing their own power. Some of these women, like Stanton, attacked ecclesiastical barriers with a vengence, sparing few words of consolation or sympathy and never hesitating in disregard for the traditionally sacred. Like the proverbial bull in the China shop, Stanton shattered devoutly held beliefs, challenged the sincerity of opponents arguments and, at times, discredited the biblical record itself. Her elan often proved an embarrassment to others in the movement and brought forth numerous statements of disapproval from fellow feminists.

At the opposite end of the spectrum, however, stood men and women deeply committed to the Christian gospel who proposed to meet theological arguments against them with persuasive theological arguments of their own. Best represented by Frances Willard, they faced the issues with force, but a force which presented itself in well-reasoned arguments springing from minds which never wavered in their Christian commitment. They thought the question of woman's subjection best answered by persuasion, utterly convinced that political ideals and divine will stood unopposed to their demands.

These feminists, who retained an appreciation for the biblical record, thought theologically-reckoned arguments for their subordination essentially a product of male dominated biblical and historical scholarship. They themselves found no rigid pronouncements for their inferior station in the testamental records. Questionable passages could be explained any of a number of ways—mistranslation, misinterpretation or falsely universalizing a parochial restriction.

As the women became more outspoken and self-assured on theological issues and as their arguments grew increasingly bolder with the development of their oratorial skills and literary abilities, their opposition was forced to pass beyond simple ridicule and now counter feminist scholarship by employing their best biblical and ecclesiastical arguments.

Theologians, biblical scholars and even laymen quickly jumped to the defense against these insistent women with their liberal theologies. Throughout the century denominational journals resounded with criticism as they devoted an impressive amount of space to refutation and warning. Indeed, some of the richest theological minds in America expended time and energies developing defensive exegeses against these female insurgents.

Whether women denounced religion and the church to embrace atheism or whether they sought to meet religious opposition on the appropriate battlefield of biblical and historical scholarship, their opposition was awesome. Amateur and professional alike reared their heads to quote biblical passage after biblical passage condemning women to social and ecclesiastical serfdom. Anathemas were hurled from pulpits and echoed in the halls of the nation's legislatures. Figureheads among America's theologians and politicians wrote erudite treatises chiding female demands.

Biblical opposition cut across denominational and social class barriers, and it was not uncommon to find denominational bishops and clerics ranging themselves on opposite sides on the issue. While certain denominations did soften in their opposition as the century drew to a close, e. g., Methodist, Baptist and Congregational, and a definite trend may be discerned tending toward a liberalizing regard for woman's service in state and church, it behooves this writer to conclude anything other than the fact that individual conscience played the most decisive role determining clerical support or non-support. This especially among mainline Protestant bodies— the major concern of this work. It might fairly be said that it was primarily an era of single champions resolutely declaring the messages of their consciences and intellects.

By the end of the century, many strides had indeed been taken. Female scholarship showed real growth. It had matured significantly and noticeably, reflecting a greater breadth of concern and a greater depth of argument. Naive presentations had gained sophistication. The biblicists and historians among the feminists had become a force to be reckoned with. Former skeptics sensed as much and were forced to admit the integrity of feminine arguments and scholarship, while die-hard opponents were pressured into constructing more comprehensive arguments to remain convincing.

Although the century did not bring total victory for feminist theology (indeed, such is not the case even today), it did succeed in outlining the crucial issues and shaping those theological and biblical foundational arguments which remain valid and vital today.

It is my purpose in this work to investigate but one aspect of a rather comprehensive challenge by nineteenth century women in America. Though only part of the struggle to attain equality for women in all spheres of human endeavor, it is woman's attempt to topple religious prejudices, and thus weaken ideological foundations, that commands attention here.

Such intent necessitates a thorough investigation of convention deliberations, careful perusal of feminist literature and an equally conscientious look at theological and denominational literature written against the woman's movement.

Time and good sense have imposed certain limitations on the scope of my research. I have restricted my investigation to the nineteenth century American scene, though I realize that the woman's movement and its attendant religious concerns were most definitely transatlantic in scope. It also must be noted that although I have recorded feminist arguments regardless of the debater's religious preferences, or lack of them, I have, with a few necessary exceptions, limited my investigation of opposition arguments to what is often referred to as "mainline Protestantism". Much might have been said about Roman Catholic contributions to the debate, the participation of Black women or the activities of America's sect groups. However, these aspects and areas seemed best left to future scholars competent to deal with them.

I have willingly contented myself with but a small section of a very complex and comprehensive area of study, i. e., the White, American, Protestant woman's confrontation with biblical, ecclesiastical and historical material which she felt deterimental to her hope of sexual equality. Her biblical exegeses, her historical analyses and her penetrating defense of her integrity amid the outcries of ecclesiastical and lay opponents is the subject of this work.

Chapter I

True Pioneers

Although the Woman's Rights Convention held in Seneca Falls, New York in July of 1848 is often heralded by historians as the beginning of the woman's rights movement in America, to begin here is to miss the very roots of the movement and to seriously neglect some of the real pioneers of feminist rights in this country. Not only was the issue of woman's rights a subject of fiery controversy prior to the Seneca Falls convention, but many arguments, which would later occupy the attention of movement leaders throughout the nineteenth and into the twentieth century, were already exceedingly well-defined. Such was certainly evident with regard to theologically based arguments devised to deter woman's entrance into public life.

As early as 1790 a two-part article appeared in the March and April issues of *The Massachusetts Magazine* entitled "On the Equality of the Sexes." The articles were written by a young woman who retained her anonymity by publishing under the pseudonym "Constantia." The articles were primarily concerned with affirming the intellectual equality of men and women and the benefits to be derived from the formal education of women in disciplines then closed to her, yet the author was fully aware that the traditional arguments for woman's inferior station in life were based on the theological pronouncements regarding her creation.

To those who argued that woman was incapable of rational pursuits and fit only for the more domestic tasks of society, Constantia responded with biting satire.

Should it be vociferated, "Your domestick employments are sufficient"—I would calmly ask, is it reasonable, that a candidate for immortality, for the joys of heaven, and intelligent being, who is to spend eternity in contemplating the works of Deity, should at present be so degraded, as to be allowed no other ideas, than those which are suggested by the mechanism of a pudding, or the sewing of the seams of a garment? Pity that all such censurers of female improvement do not go one step further, and deny their future existence; to be consistent they surely ought.[1]

Constantia continued her argument by insisting that a woman's soul is by nature equal to that of a man; the "fall" did not result in one sex falling lower than the other to now occupy an inferior position in life. Judith Sargent Murray (Constantia), like others who would follow and well before most of her sex dared openly voice the sentiment, maintained that woman was mentally, emotionally and spiritually the equal of the male sex.

Although her thoughts were not published until they appeared in *The Massachusetts Magazine* in the spring of 1790, her religious convictions in the matter were formulated at least a decade earlier. A letter appended to the magazine articles, dated December, 1780 and penned to a friend identified only as Mr. P. evidences her deep convictions on the issue of the equality of women.

Mr. P. is quite obviously concerned about the religious consequences of Miss Murray's feminist beliefs. Yet when he confronted her with the charge, which will so often be repeated in the following decades, that Eve was the first in transgression, a subtle warning, Murray countered by accusing him and his sex of self-love. With but a modicum of theological insight and exegetical skill, she tackled the problem which was later to plague the woman's movement.

It is true some ignoramuses have, absurdly enough informed us, that the beauteous fair of paradise, was seduced from her obedience, by a malignant demon, *in the guise of a baleful serpent* (her emphasis); but we, who are better informed, know that the fallen spirit presented himself to her view, *a shining angel still*; for thus, saith the criticks in the Hebrew tongue, ought the word to be rendered.[2]

Her caustic response foreshadows the healthy skepticism which will continue to characterize many women in the later woman's movement when they too were presented with supposed biblical sanctions against their feminist ideas and activities.

It is apparent that Murray saw the transgression drama in the Garden almost exclusively in terms of her contemporary interests and concerns. Thus, the transgression of Eve was not based on lust, ambition or haughtiness, but rather on woman's thirst for knowledge. In comparison, Murray found that Adam had no such noble reasoning for his disobedience. In Eve he should have seen the results of disobedience, or, in the words of Murray, ". . . he had proof positive of the fallacy of the argument, which the deceiver had suggested."[3] Yet Adam, according to Murray, directly and wilfully entered into disobedience although *he* knew firsthand the consequences of his act. In Eve he could see, or should have seen, that the price of wisdom was too great a price.

Murray concluded her argument and declaration to Mr. P. with these rather acid comments:

> Blush, ye vaunters of fortitude; ye boasters of resolution; ye haughty lords of creation; blush when ye remember, that he (Adam) was influenced by no other motive than a bare pusillanimous attachment to a woman! by sentiments so exquisitively soft, that all his sons have, from that period, when they have designed to degrade them, described as highly feminine. Thus it should seem, that all the arts of the grand deceiver (since means adequate to the purpose are, I conceive, invariably pursued) were requisite to mislead our general mother, while the father of mankind forfeited his own, and relinquished the happiness of posterity, merely in compliance with the blandishments of a female.[4]

Two years after the Murray articles appeared in Massachusetts, Mary Wollestonecraft Godwin's book *A Vindication of the Rights of Women* appeared in England. Although its bold ideas and brusque style and presentation created great sensation in some branches of the reading public, American women read it with reservation. Wollestonecraft's reputation for promiscuous living had preceded the publication and proved decisive. The book did not gain immediate appeal among women readers, especially in the United States. Decades later, however, American feminists were to repeatedly refer to and quote from its text without hesitation or embarrassment.

Wollestonecraft was not recognizably sympathetic to religion and often showed suspicion toward religious institutions and clerical intent. Such attitudes led to repeated denunciations, and she was often labelled an atheist or heretic by the more conventional.

Despite such charges, Wollestonecraft possessed an insight into religious matters which was more penetrating and far outdistanced her more religiously-shackled female contemporaries. Like Judith Sargent Murray, she was quick to recognize that if women were ever to shed the chains of suppression and traditionalism, they would have to confront the ideological bulwark, and thus the religious questions, which had been raised against them. To ignore or discount them was folly. Also like Murray, she addressed the creation account in Genesis. But in contrast to Murray's approach, she did not accept the account first in order to deal with it, but instead sought to openly discredit it. She eschewed biblical literalism and traced the promulgation of the doctrine of female suppression to the exercise of male domination throughout history.

> Probably the prevailing opinion that woman was created for man, may have taken its rise from Moses' poetical story; yet as very few, it is presumed, who have bestowed any serious thought on the subject ever supposed that Eve was, literally speaking, one of Adam's ribs, the deduction must be allowed to fall to the ground, or only be so far admitted as it proves that man, from the remotest antiquity, found it convenient to exert his strength to subjugate his companion, and his invention to show that she ought to have her neck bent under the yoke, because the whole creation was only created for his convenience or pleasure.[5]

So adamant was Wollestonecraft in her stance, she affirmed that she would not only doubt a belief which insisted woman was made for man, but ". . . though the cry of irreligion, or even atheism, be raised against me, I will simply declare that were an angel from Heaven to tell me that Moses' beautiful poetical cosmogony, and the account of the fall of man, were literally true, I could not believe what my reason told me was derogatory to the character of the Supreme Being; . . ."[6]

She argued instead that the qualities presently thought advantageous to the female sex essentially worked at cross purposes to the Christian vision of eternity. With this idea clearly in mind, she insisted woman was woefully untrained for a future life. She had been effectively conditioned to serve as a present amusement for man and little else.

> How women are to exist in that state where there is neither to be marrying nor giving in marriage, we are not told. For though moralists have agreed that the tenor of life seems to prove that man is prepared by various circumstances for a future state, they constantly concur in advising woman only to provide for the present. Gentleness, docility, and a spaniel-like affection are, on this ground, consistently recommended as the cardinal virtues of the sex;. . . .[7]

Wollestonecraft was very much a child of the Englightenment, and with her, as well as many of her contemporaries, reason ranked supreme. She would submit, if such was ever required, only to reason. "I love man as my fellow; but his scepter, real or usurped, extends not to me, unless the reason of an individual demands my homage; and even then the submission is to reason, and not to man. In fact, the conduct of an accountable being must be regulated by the operations of its own reason; or on what foundation rests the throne of God?"[8]

For almost three decades following the Wollestonecraft publication and the Murray articles, American women were notoriously silent on the issue of women's rights. Few articles raised the issue of religious prejudice as it related to the question of sexual equality. There were some exceptions no doubt, but those have not faired well amidst the ravages of time and history.

One notable publication which does survive and which certainly did interrupt these years of otherwise ominous silence was written not by a woman, but a man, the poet Thomas Branagan of Philadelphia. His work, whose full title read *The Excellency of the Female Character Vindicated; Being an Investigation Relative to the Cause and Effects of the Encroachments of Men Upon the Rights of Women and the Too Frequent Degradation and Consequent Misfortunes of the Fair Sex*, was ostensibly an attempt by its author to reveal the growing moral decadence of American society and rescue its chief victim—woman. Beyond its claim that the female mind was equal to, if not superior to, that of the male and its consistent warnings that young women beware of libertines and those practiced in the arts of seduction, the book reveals a decidedly liberal stance regarding woman's participation in the church. Arguing that the Christian, as well as the pagan, had imprisoned the female mind, Branagan maintained that

> In ancient times, prophetesses as well as prophets were allowed and encouraged to preach, or as it was then called prophesy; but in modern times, a holy and almost seraphic female, the favourite of heaven, the child of God, if her heavenly Father should move her by his spirit, to bear a testimony for him to his guilty creatures, the clergy are up in arms and unanimously say it shall not be so. Thus we see, even the will of Heaven is counteracted by the tyranny of custom.[9]

Branagan's "tyranny of custom" charge, like Wollestonecraft's attack on biblical literalism would become common approaches in later decades. To what extent succeeding feminists were influenced by such writers is difficult to assess, yet it is quite possible that the popularity of both works assured a reading by early feminists.

Almost thirty years after Murray and Wollestonecraft published, Hannah Mather Crocker, granddaughter of Cotton Mather, published her essay "Observation on the Real Rights of Women, with their appropriate duties agreeable to Scripture, reason and common sense." The essay, which appeared in 1818, was regarded by many as a step backward rather than forward.

At the beginning of her essay, Crocker made it clear that her intent was not to "dispute respecting superiority or inferiority, of the sexes; but the aid will be to prove, in a pleasant manner, and we hope, to even demonstration, that though there are appropriate duties peculiar to each sex, yet the wise Author of nature has endowed the female mind with equal powers and faculties, and given them the same right of judging and acting for themselves, as he gave to the male sex; . . . .[10] On the surface, the statement appears to be a strong one, even revolutionary for its time. Only later in the essay do we find that she qualifys much and backs away from some crucial insights which her initial statement of intent leads us to anticipate.

While affirming equality of faculties for the sexes, she still did not question the proposed and traditional interpretation of Genesis 2 and 3. Woman, for Crocker, was judged guilty as the first transgressor, thereby forfeiting her right to equality. Crocker's only challenge to existent and accepted exegesis was her insistence that the humiliation of women consequent to transgression was not to last.

In this view she provided a third alternative to those views already presented by Murray and Wollestonecraft. Whereas Murray had opted for justifying Eve's behavior and, at the same time, discrediting Adam's similar act, Crocker made no attempt to justify Eve. And whereas Wollestonecraft had seriously questioned the literalism employed by translators and considered the account a mere construction or tool designed and invented by man to insure him the reins of power, Crocker raised no serious exegetical questions. She alined with neither of the previous arguments, but simply insisted that although woman's subordination was fact and even biblically justified, such was no longer valid. For Crocker, the Christ event had broken "the yoke of bondage."

> We shall consider woman restored to her original right and dignity at the commencement of the christian dispensation, although there must be allowed some moral and physical distinction of the sexes agreeably to the order of nature, and the organization of the human frame, still the sentiments must predominate, that the powers of the mind are equal in the sexes . . . .[11]

As can be seen, Hannah Crocker remained a conservative, somewhat confusing spokesperson. And lest her more liberal-sounding statements be misunderstood, she further beclouded the issue by insisting that although male and female judgment may be equal in law, politics or religion, "it would be morally improper, and physically very incorrect, for the female character to claim the statesman's birth (sic), or ascend to the rostrum to gain the loud applause of men, although their powers may be equal to the task . . . ."[12] Still evidencing a deeply ingrained traditionalism, Crocker appears to be arguing that women were the mental, emotional and even spiritual equals of men, but that such equality should have little, if any, social affect. Women should still occupy an inferior social station, limited to previous social roles.

Crocker was also careful to segregate herself from the views of the more radical Mary Wollestonecraft. Though praising Wollestonecraft's great energy and independent mind and noting the "fine sentiments" of her book, she concluded, "we do not coincide with her opinion respecting the total independence of the female sex. We must be allowed to say, her theory is unfit for practice, though some of her sentiments and distinctions would do honour to the pen, even of a man (!) . . . ."[13]

One is left with the decided impression that Crocker was amazingly adept at entertaining contradictory ideas while totally oblivious of doing so and, at the same time, possessed of a timidity which would not allow her to carry either idea to its logical conclusion. Women were equal but to no affect. The christ event had reversed the sentence of subordination, but the social impact of such a reversal was negligible.

It is a good thing for the female half of the human race that those who followed a decade later, now spurred by the abolitionist movement, were not possessed of the same confusion and timidity.

Notes

[1]Judith Sargent Murray, "On the Equality of the Sexes" *The Feminist Papers*, ed. Alice S. Rossi (New York: Columbia University, 1973), p. 21. [The article is a reprint which originally was published in *The Massachusetts Magazine*, March and April, 1790.]

[2]*Ibid.*, p. 23.

[3]*Ibid.*

[4]*Ibid.*, p. 24.

[5]Mary Wollestonecraft Godwin, *A Vindication of the Rights of Women* (1792; rpt. New York: E. P. Dutton, 1929), pp. 30-31. [The 1929 reprint is published together with John Stuart Mills *On the Subjection of Women*.]

[6]*Ibid.*, p. 87.

[7]*Ibid.*, p. 38.

[8]*Ibid.*, p. 41.

[9]Thomas Branagan, *The Excellency of the Female Character Vindicated* (1808; rpt. New York: Arno, 1972), pp. 121-22.

[10]Hannah Mather Crocker, "Observation of the Real Rights of Women" in *Up From the Pedestal: Selected Documents From the History of American Feminism*, ed. Aileen Kraditor (Chicago: Quadrangle, 1968), p. 40. [The essay was originally published in Boston in 1818. An abbreviated text is also found in Harriet Robinson's *Massachusetts in the Woman Suffrage Movement* (Boston: Roberts, 1881), Appendix A.]

[11]*Ibid.*

[12]*Ibid.*, p. 41.

[13]*Ibid.*, p. 43.

Chapter II

The Right to Speak Publicly

The century evidenced a slow start for woman's rights. Only a few spoke out publicly to question the subordinate status of women. Matters were to change dramatically with the 1830s and the advent of the public crusade for the abolition of slavery. In point of fact, the cause of woman's rights did not fully blossom in this country until it became linked to and nourished by the great humanitarian movement of the nineteenth century—abolition. As women entertained an ever-broadening interest and participation in the reform, they were repeatedly challenged to justify their public activities.

This they did, and the decades preceding the outbreak of the Civil War provided the woman's movement with new and decidedly more capable champions. These women no longer possessed the hesitancy and timidity which had characterized their immediate predecessors. They spoke with a new sense of boldness, conviction and even anger. Their ability to articulate their concerns was enhanced with continued practice; their confrontations with critics, religious and otherwise, helped them to sharpen their newly acquired oratorial skills and furthered development of carefully researched arguments.

As male abolitionists stumped the country delivering impassioned oratories against slavery and facing the enraged mobs who opposed them, women with similar convictions also felt compelled to voice their concerns on the public platform. Among their ranks stood such women as the Hicksite Quaker Lucretia Mott; the beautiful Anna Dickinson; Mary A. Livermore, wife of a Unitarian minister; Abby Kelley; recent Oberlin graduate Lucy Stone; and, of course, the Grimke sisters Angelina and Sarah of South Carolina.

All were to become outspoken not only on the anti-slavery issue, but also on the mushrooming issue of woman's rights. As the women openly faced irate mobs and publicly denounced the institution of slavery, they produced a reaction founded not only in response to their anti-slavery views, but also in response to their alleged defiance of "public decency." To speak from a public platform to mixed assemblies of men and women was unheard of behavior on the part of women. Opponents raised not only their eyebrows at such wanton behavior on the part of female abolitionists, but also the question of their right to disgrace themselves in such unseemly activity. Such activity on the part of women, together with opposition to it, served subsequently to link the issue of abolition to that of woman's rights, a link which was not to be broken until after the Civil War and the passage of the Thirteenth and Fourteenth Amendments to the United States Constitution.

The religious question was much in evidence, and came dramatically to the fore in the ensuing controversy. People, clergy being the most vociferous in the matter, contended that a woman who graced the public platform defied Divine Law, which had clearly designated her appropriate sphere as well as the rules of common decency and womanly decorum. Common knowledge and scriptural insight assured these biblically-minded opponents that whatever the scope of this prescribed sphere, it most certainly did not extend to the dais.

Pulpits resounded with denunciations. Typical was a sermon by Presbyterian Jonathan F. Stearns in Newburyport, Massachusetts in July, 1837. He discoursed on the beneficial effects of Christianity on womanhood and acknowledged the proficiency of female public speakers but maintained that "the question is not in regard to ability, but to decency, to order, to christian probity . . . ."[1] Such an open breach of the traditional order constituted for him "rejecting the civilities of life, and throwing off the restraints of morality and piety," and Christians were liable to become "a fierce race of semibarbarians, before whom neither order, nor honor, nor chastity can stand."[2]

Among the first and certainly among the most outspoken and articulate women to speak against the charges of these prolific religiously-motivated critics were the Grimke sisters Angelina and Sarah. As two of the most active female abolitionists, they weathered the brunt of the attack. Consequently much of this chapter is necessarily devoted to their arguments. It is equally true that their well-reasoned and well-presented arguments remained influential throughout the history of the woman's movement. Many, in fact, are still cited today.

The first evidence we have of their interest in sexual equality comes from the pen of Angelina in her essay "Appeal to the Christian Women of the South," which appeared in *The Anti-Slavery Examiner* in September, 1836. Although the document is primarily directed toward the enlistment of southern women in anti-slavery activity and does not contain a developed doctrine advocating the rights of women per se, the article does manifest a deep concern for woman's *overt* participation in the cause. Angelina sustained her plea for the public participation of women by cataloging the activities of famed women in the Judeo-Christian tradition who, she claimed, acted responsibly and dutifully and knowingly defied convention to do the will of God. Lest this remained unconvincing, she further supported her allegations with reference to English women, who had courageously engaged in abolitionist activity, and women of the Ladies Anti-Slavery Society of Boston, who, though they were mobbed and their lives jeopardized by an infuriated crowd, held strong in their allegiance to the abolitionist cause. They, like the others, Angelina reasoned, were motivated by a deep sense of religious duty.

Such sentiments, together with their consistent public exposure on the speaker's platform, produced a formal protest from the Massachusetts Congregational clergy. In a pastoral letter from the General Association of Massachusetts (Orthodox) to "the Churches Under Their Care," dated July, 1837 and written by the Reverend Doctor D. Nehemiah Adams of Boston, their constituency was directed to pay due "attention to the dangers which at present seem to threaten the female character with wide-spread and permanent injury."[3] Arguing from the premise that women's duties were clearly formulated in the New Testament record, the letter proceeded to outline those duties, using such words as "unobstrusive and private," "mild, dependent, softening," and "promoting piety." The text of the letter as it is reprinted in *The History of Woman's Suffrage* is liberally spiced with exclamation points, no doubt supplied by editor Elizabeth Cady Stanton.

The pastoral letter also included a direct attack upon the female public reformer and carried within it a covert, but discernible threat: "But when she assumes the place and tone of man as a public reformer, our care and protection of her seem unnecessary; we put ourselves in self-defence against her; she yields the power which God has given her for her protection, and her character becomes unnatural."[4]

William Lloyd Garrison maintained that the letter was conceived with express concern for the behavior and activities of the Grimke sisters, and we have no reason to doubt him in this observation. Thus it was with the activities of the Grimkes first and foremost on their minds that the learned Massachusetts clergy affirmed that they could

> ... but regret the mistaken conduct of those who encourage females to bear an obstrusive and ostentatious part in measures of reform, and countenance any of that sex who so far forget themselves as to itinerate in the character of public lecturers and teachers. We especially deplore the intimate acquaintance and promiscuous conversation of females with regard to things which ought not to be named; by which that modesty and delicacy which is the charm of domestic life, and which constitutes the true influence of woman in society, is consumed, and the way opened, as we apprehend, for degeneracy and ruin.[5]

The letter brought a flurry of comment. From the pen of the poetess Maria Chapman the reply came in humorous rhyme entitled "The Times That Try Men's Souls." The poem, which follows in its entirety, is replete with theological insight and careful to separate Christian teaching from subsequent male abuse.

The Times That Try Men's Souls

Confusion has seized us, and all things go wrong,
    The women have leaped from "their spheres,"
And, instead of fixed stars, shoot as comets along,
    And are setting the world by the ears!
In courses erratic they're wheeling through space,
In brainless confusion and meaningless chase.

In vain do our knowing ones try to compute
    Their return to the orbit designed;
They're glanced at a moment, then onward they shoot,
    And are neither "to hold nor to bind;"
So freely they move in their chosen ellipse,
The "Lords of Creation" do fear an eclipse.

They've taken a notion to speak for themselves,
    And are wielding the tongue and the pen;
They've mounted the rostrum; the termagant elves,
    And—oh horrid!—are talking to men!
With faces unblanched in our presence they come
To harangue us, they say, in behalf of the dumb.

They insist on their right to petition and pray,
    That St. Paul, in Corinthians, has given them rules
For appearing in public; despite what those say
    Whom we've trained to instruct them in schools;
But vain such instructions, if women may scan
And quote texts of Scripture to favor their plan.

Our grandmothers' learning consisted of yore
    In spreading their generous boards;
In twisting the distaff, or mopping the floor,
    And *obeying the will of their lords*.
Now, misses may reason, and think, and debate,
Till unquestioned submission is quite out of date.

Our clergy have preached on the sin and the shame
    Of women, when out of "her sphere,"
And labored *divinely* to ruin her fame,
    And shorten this horrid career;
But for spiritual guidance no longer they look
To Fulsom, or Winslow, or learned Parson Cook.

Our wise men have tried to exorcise in vain
    The turbulent spirits abroad;
As well might we deal with the fetterless main,
    Or conquer ethereal essence with sword;
Like the devils of Milton, they rise from each blow,
With spirit unbroken, insulting the foe.

Our patriot fathers, of eloquent fame,
    Waged war against tangible forms;
Aye, *their* foes were man—and if ours were the same,
    We might speedily quiet their storms;
But, ah! their descendents enjoy not such bliss—
The assumptions of Britain were nothing like this.

Could we but array all our foes in the field,
    We'd teach these usurpers of power
That their bodily safety demands they should yield,
    And in the presence of manhood should cower;
But, alas! for our tethered and impotent state,
Chained by notions of knighthood—we can but debate.

Oh! shade of the prophet Mahomet, arise!
    Place woman again in "her sphere,"
And teach that her soul was not born for the skies,
    But to flutter a brief moment here.
This doctrine of Jesus, as preached up by Paul,
If embraced in its spirit, will ruin us all.[6]

The Quaker poet John Greenleaf Whittier also responded, but in a much more serious vein in a work entitled simply "The Pastoral Letter." In this lengthy poem he argued that such activity as that recently engaged in by the Massachusetts clergy was but another in a long series of persecutions and harrassments initiated by the church. He declared their intolerance and bigotry ultimately futile; it could never stand against the cry for freedom voiced by the women. In fact, Whittier maintained that it was offensive even to God. He concluded the work with an exalted defense of the Grimkes.

But ye, who scorn the thrilling tale
    Of Carolina's high-souled daughters,
Which echoes her the mournful wail

Of sorrow from Edisto's waters,
Close while ye may the public ear—
   With malice vex, with slander would them—
The pure and good shall throng to hear,
   And tried and manly hearts surround them.

Oh, ever may the power which led
   Their way to such a fiery trial,
And strengthened womanhood to tread
   The wine-press of such self-denial,
Be round them in an evil land,
   With wisdom and with strength from Heaven,
With Miriam's voice, and Judith's hand,
   And Deborah's song, for triumph given![7]

The Grimkes, of course, rushed to their own defense as well. Sarah's reply to the Pastoral Letter, "Province of Woman," was originally a letter written to Mary S. Parker, President of the Boston Female Anti-Slavery Society, in July, 1837 upon request of the latter and intended for publication in the *New England Spectator*.

In time, Sarah anticipated that the clerics' letter faced doom much "as the opinions of Cotton Mather and other distinquished men of his day, on the subject of witchcraft . . . ;" their condemnation no greater "than it now is that judges should have sat on the trials of witches, and solemnly condemned nineteen persons and one dog to death for witchcraft."[8] But since the Pastoral Letter had mainly questioned the Grimkes' right to lecture publicly in light of supposed biblical restriction, Sarah addressed herself primarily to this premise. She acknowledged that danger did exist as the clerics had warned, but from a source other than they supposed. According to Grimke, it was man himself who was endangered since it was he who had so completely usurped authority and conspired to rob women of their intellectual and spiritual dignity. The appeal sent to all New England clergymen calling on them to denounce from their pulpits such unmannerly and unchristian behavior as that engaged in by the Grimkes was doomed to utter failure whatever its immediate appeal according to Sarah Grimke.

The letter continued in the same spirited vein. Although she acquiesced and admitted that woman should move within the sphere alloted for her occupation by the Creator, she refused to comply with the male interpretation of its limits and protested against the false translation of scriptural passages which male translators so effectively used to perpetuate and sustain their own position. It could only be perversions of holy writ and distorted commentaries which upheld them. She was convinced, like many feminists who would follow, that such interpretations would change only when women began to enter the field of biblical research, for women scholars would produce varied and alternative interpretations, unfettered by the drive to claim and maintain superiority.

There was no doubt in Grimke's mind that men and women were created equal and that biblical regulation and sanction applied equally to both sexes. Consequently, she asserted with some vehemence that whatever was acceptable behavior on the part of men was equally acceptable when performed by women.

To behave as the Pastoral Letter admonish would, for Grimke, mean a denial of God-given responsibilities and could only end by contributing to further suppression of the female sex. Indeed, in her estimation, woman's previous compliance to the supposed biblical injunction that she should be dependent upon man had already done severe damage. Women as a result had resigned their natural rights, content to become merely man's vassal and plaything. The theory of dependence, far from enhancing woman, had turned her into a creature of vanity and hypocrisy, forcing her to use wile and subterfuge rather than reason.

Even more importantly, a doctrine of female dependence was utterly at variance with the scriptural demand. Sexual superiority, claimed Grimke, did not extend to the mental and moral faculties of human beings, and "if they (men) mean to intimate that mental or moral weakness belongs td woman more than to man, I utterly disclaim the charge; our sense of morality has been impaired by his interpretation of our duties, but no where does God say that he made any distinction between us as moral and intelligent beings . . . ."9

Sarah had expressed many of her opinions and biblical insights in earlier letters to Mary Parker. She continued the practice and eventually all letters were published in book form under the title *Letters on the Equality of the Sexes and the Condition of Woman*. The letters, written throughout the summer and fall of 1837, represent the first serious and systematic attempt to develop a biblically sound rationale for woman's rights.

In her attempt to present woman's role and purpose, she vowed to rely solely on the Bible, wading through what she felt were misconceptions and false translations of its basic truths. Boldly she proclaimed that her own judgment would prevail over that of acclaimed experts.

Like her predecessors she began her review with the Genesis account of creation. Accepting the term "man" as generic, she asserted that both male and female were created equal, in God's image, and entrusted with the task of exercising dominion over the earth.

The "fall" resulted in a fall from innocence, not equality. She did concede, however, that

> Had Adam tenderly reproved his wife, and endeavored to lead her to repentence instead of sharing in her guilt, I should be much more ready to accord to man that superiority which he claims; but as the facts stand disclosed by the sacred historian, it appears to me that to say the least, there was a much weakness exhibited by Adam as by Eve.[10]

The "curse" following Eve's confession of wrongdoing was, for Grimke, a simple prophecy. The resultant mandate for woman's submission, which reverberated throughout history to the present day, was the result of falsely translating the word "shall" in the phrase "and thy desire shall be to thy husband, and he shall rule over thee (Gen. 3.16c)." Had it been translated "will" as Hebrew allowed, it would have carried less of the aura of command and more truly a reflection of divine will. That it in any way implied subordination for women was adamantly refuted by Grimke, who discerned that the same expression was also directed to Cain, subjecting him to the desire of Abel. Ultimately, woman's subjection, like man's, was to God alone.

She willingly admitted in a later letter, dated October 20, 1837, equality of guilt in the "fall." She based her admission on Romans 5.12—"Wherefore, as by ONE MAN sin entered into the world, and death by sin, ..." When confronted with the opposition passage in I Timothy 2.14—"Adam was not deceived; but the woman being deceived, was in the transgression"—she reitterated the argument Murray had employed earlier, claiming that Adam was cognizant of his participation in Eve's transgression and thus the more culpable. Having offered this limited commentary, she left final decision as to deception or nondeception on Adam's part up to the common sense of the reader, whom she thought must finally concur with her view.

The real question, for Grimke, was never one of blame, but rather one of rights and responsibilities, which she thought never divisible by sex alone.

The doctrine, that the sex of the body presides over and

administers upon the rights and responsibilities of the moral, immoral nature, is to my mind a doctrine kindred to blasphemy, when seen in its intrinsic nature. It breaks up utterly the relations of the two natures, and reverses their functions; exalting the animal nature into a monarch, and humbling the moral into a slave; making the former a proprietor, and the latter its property.[11]

She never, like Wollestonecraft earlier, discredited the Genesis account or denied the charge that woman brought sin into the world. She simply denied that such an act on Eve's part proclaimed her a greater sinner or established her inferiority to man. Scripture afforded Grimke no evidence that God ever sought to deprive woman of equality, and she demanded that men

. . . take their feet from off our necks and permit us to stand upright on that ground which God designed us to occupy. If

he has not given us rights which have, as I conceive, been
wrested from us, we shall soon give evidence of our inferiority,
and shrink back into that obscurity, which the high soled (sic)
magnanimity of man has assigned us as our appropriate
sphere.[12]

Indeed, if God had appointed man lord over woman, Grimke
argued, it would contravene his own commandment to worship God
and worship no other gods, as well as nullify all cautions regarding
putting one's confidence in man. The Decalogue, she declared,
despite its comprehensiveness, contained no command instructing
women to obey their husbands.

The domination of woman came about from a lust for power;
woman merely served as its first victim. The "curse" was therefore
not a command, but a simple prediction of the power struggle to
follow and ultimately the triumph of the physically stronger male.
The present circumstance of women was where man had placed her,
not God. In Grimke's words, "Surely no one who contemplates, with
the eye of a Christian philosopher, the design of God in the creation of woman, can believe that she is now fulfilling that design.
The literal translation of the word "help-meet" is a helper like unto
himself; it is so rendered in the Septuagint, and manifestly signifies
a companion."[13]

New Testament passages, which will later form the core of
opponents arguments, were not overlooked by Grimke either.
Christianity, in spite of its fine sentiments, had thus far only min-
imally affected the status of women. According to Grimke, although
Christianity had protected women from severe physical mistreat-
ment in most cases, it had not noticeably elevated her position in
society.

Although she entertained grave reservations about the benefits of Christianity, it was evident to Grimke that Jesus had issued
no commands to wives to obey their husbands; and his commands,
however construed, were always addressed equally to men and
women.

According to Grimke, the dogma of female inferiority which had become engrained in Christian tradition stemmed directly from a few passages in the Pauline epistles, and she endeavored to deal with these passages by setting forth two personal assumptions before drawing any conclusions. Foremost was her assertion that the "antiquity of the opinions based on the false construction of those passages, has no weight with me: they are the opinions of interested judges, and I have no particular reverence for them, merely because they have been regarded with veneration from generation to generation."[14] Earlier she had claimed freedom from the superstitious reverence accorded the King James Version of the scriptures, insisting that its translators were not inspired.

Her second assumption averred that although Paul was a true apostle, he was nevertheless influenced by Jewish prejudices not unlike Peter's aversion to the uncleanness of the Gentiles. In short, she maintained that Paul was a product of his times and cultural background, and thus much of what he said was conditioned by the social customs of his day. This argument will surface repeatedly in later decades.

Her irreverent stance toward tradition and her exclamation of Pauline prejudice toward women afforded Grimke ample leeway for refutation of passages adverse to women. Attacking commentator Matthew Henry on his exposition of I Corinthians 11.3 and Ephesians 5.23 (two crucial passages), she declared that such commentary was rooted in male egoism and served only to inflate male superiority at the expense of women. Henry had argued that woman was God's secondhand representative and a mere reflection of the glory of man, deriving honor from man while occupying the position of subject. This idea of male superiority Grimke labelled absurd, and she wondered how any reasonable man could ever suppose it to be divinely inspired. She again accounted for such belief only by conjecturing that its origin stemmed from the male desire for supremacy, which, in turn, stemmed from his fallen state and sinful nature.

Ephesians 5.22-25, Colossians 3.18-19 and I Peter 3.2-7, passages dealing with relationships between husbands and wives, were understood by Grimke as reflective of the apostles' attempts to instruct converts who were married to unconverted mates. Her reasoning for dispensing so easily with such controversial passages via such an interpretation is absent from her letters, and we can only assume that its validity was solely grounded in her own unique insight.

In her interpretation, the admonition for husbands to love their wives was but a practical rule of conduct for those tempted to despise their wives who persistently clung to pagan superstitions and practices. Likewise, submission of wives to husbands guarded against possible haughtiness on the part of Christian wives married to unconverted husbands. Ultimately she concluded that such passages calling for submission and subjection were designed by the apostles to call for obedience to the divine principle of non-resistance to evil and did not in the least suggest that governors, masters or husbands exercise the authority they now claimed.

The New Testament pronouncements against women speaking in church also came under the scrutiny of Grimke. In a letter written to Parker in September, 1837, which later acquired the title "Ministry of Women," she assured her reader that men and women possessed equal intellectual gifts and moral responsibilities and were just as equally subject to the commands of Christ; and, thus, she inferred with little difficulty that if it was the duty of man to preach the gospel message, than it was also incumbent upon women to do the same.

Eschewing any sectarian bias by virtue of her Quakerism, she argued that woman was constrained to preach the gospel, and scripture provided abundant evidential support for a female ministry. The Old Testament prophetic ministry was never reserved solely for men, and there existed sufficient evidence in the record to affirm woman's participation in that office, e.g., Miriam, Deborah, Huldah. The fact that so few female names are mentioned in the scriptural account remained for Grimke but another testimony of man's criminal design. Those who had been included had risen above adversity and prevailing hostile circumstance and gained such esteem that they simply could not be excluded.

Grimke maintained that only the priesthood spoke of sexual exclusivism and was, of course, reserved for men alone. Even here, Grimke insisted that the exclusivism had undoubtedly been initiated and sustained intentionally by men themselves. Concurrently, she challenged the belief that the Christian ministry could be traced to the priesthood. The formal order of the priesthood had been abolished by Christ along with sacrifices. The Protestant ministry descended from the prophetic office alone.

Yet woman's ultimate vindication rested essentially upon a God issued "call," which Grimke insisted had been uttered repeatedly to heretofore unyielding women, who ". . . have not dared to open their lips, and have endured all intensity of suffering, produced by disobedience to God, rather than encounter heartless ridicule and injurious suspicions."[15]

The New Testament, too, sanctioned the public participation of women in the ministry of the church, Grimke declared. In Luke 2.37-38, it was the woman prophetess Anna who first recognized and preached the Advent of Christ. At Pentacost, women were present, filled with the Holy Spirit, and spoke in foreign languages along with male believers. The context of the Pentacost account in Acts 1 and 2 confirmed it, and Peter's recitation of Joel 2.28-32—"And it shall come to pass in the last days, saith God, I will pour out my Spirit upon all flesh: and your sons and daughters shall prophesy, and your young men shall see visions, and your old men shall dream dreams: And on my servants and on my handmaidens I will pour out in those days of my Spirit; and they shall prophesy . . . (Acts 2.17-18)"—lacked credence had it not been so.

That women were not only allowed entrance to the ministry, but actually engaged in that office within the early church was also, for Grimke, apparent in the scriptural account. Phillip's four daughters preached. Paul included Priscilla, as well as Aquila, in the phrase "fellow laborers in Christ Jesus" (Romans 16.3). In Romans 16. 1, the word translated "servant" or "deaconess" with regard to Phoebe should have been translated "minister", as it was in Ephesians 6.21 when applied to Tychicus.

Grimke began her discussion of woman's right to speak in church where many later feminists would also begin, with I Corinthians 11, where Paul instructed women in proper deportment and dress when they prayed or prophesied (preached). She relied upon the commentary of John Locke, a man who favored woman's preaching, for corroboration. Another commentator, Adam Clarke, was also consulted with equally favorable results.

When faced with the admonition for woman's silence in church in I Corinthians 14, Grimke again consulted Clarke and concluded that the general thrust of Paul's words, as understood in context, was toward eliminating confusion in the assemblies of the Corinthian church. Men spoke simultaneously and women interrupted the discourses with endless questions. Order demanded silence in such a situation. Preaching itself was not the issue at all, for

> ... he tells them, 'If they will *learn* anything, let them ask their husbands at home.' Now a person endowed with a gift in the ministry, does not ask questions in the public exercise of that gift, for the purpose of gaining information; she is instructing others.[16]

I Timothy 2, another passage cited regularly by Grimke's contemporaries and subsequent opponents of woman's rights as well, did not escape her alert eye nor her exegetical scalpel. Possibly one of the most difficult passages confronting women, Grimke attacked the passage by proposing that faulty punctuation and phrase division had led to misconception of its intent. She sustained this claim with the commentary of English biblical scholar John Gurney, who translated I Timothy 2.8-9 not "I will, therefore, that men pray everywhere, lifting up holy hands, without wrath and doubting. In like manner also, that women adorn themselves in modest apparel, ..." but rather "I will therefore that men pray everywhere, ...; likewise also the women in modest dress."[17]

The apostle Paul in all passages which supposedly conflicted with I Corinthians 11.5 was, therefore, only correcting some improprieties, not condemning female preaching as opponents indicated; the women mentioned in the questionable verses were not even engaged in that activity. Thus, Grimke concluded her study with an insistence that two alternatives remained for the Christian.

> . . . either that the apostle grossly contradicts himself on a sub-
> ject of great practical importance, and that the fulfillment of
> the prophecy of Joel was a shameful infringement of decency
> and order; or that the directions given to women, not to speak
> or teach in the congregations, had reference to some local and
> peculiar customs, which were then common in religious assem-
> blies, and which the apostle thought inconsistent with the
> purpose for which they were met together.[18]

The question of biblical literalism was also addressed by the thorough and persistent Grimke. If Paul's command for silence was to be taken literally, such a command had already been broken. Women did teach in Sunday schools and they did engage in congregational singing on grand scales, both a breach of Pauline dictate to keep silent in church. Therefore, Grimke questioned the logic of those who would argue for literal translation of Pauline material while not condemning present infringements. She reasoned that man was willing to exercise flexibility of interpretation only in those matters which best served his own interests and which did not cause trespass on his bastion of power. A female ministry, though present in the early church, would, no doubt, produce unsettling problems for the contemporary organized system of spiritual power and ecclesiastical authority, which was now vested entirely in the hands of men. As an initial step toward correcting this injustice, Grimke advised women presently devoting their resources to support male seminary students to divert their energies to financing similar educations for women.

Since the Grimke sisters were the first women to speak publicly to mixed assemblies, they were often the ones singled out by opponents for condemnation, but many other women actively involved in public lecturing against the institution of slavery were similarly harassed. Women such as Lucretia Mott, Anna Dickinson, Abby Kelley and others who joined the struggle were now called upon to justify their presence on the dais or in the pulpit. Their justifications reflect the thoughts of Sarah Grimke, and it is safe to assume they were familiar with her letters to Parker reprinted in

The New England Spectator. In a very real way, Sarah, with the aid of her sister Angelina, formulated the theological arguments which would be voiced repeatedly by anti-slavery women.

Though it is impossible to rehearse the activities of all these fearless women, it might be helpful to note but a few. One of the most active women on the abolitionist circuit was the Irish-Quaker Abby Kelley. Like the Grimkes and Lucretia Mott she was an agent of the American Anti-Slavery Society and toured New England as a public lecturer against slavery. As her public speaking drew attention, she found she, too, had to defend herself against public ridicule and clerical outcry simply because she was a female with the courage to transcend the boundaries of maidenly decorum to make her views public. She quickly warmed to the task and subsequently became fearless in denouncing ecclesiastical conservatism, while affirming woman's right to speak openly.

Another convert to the cause of women's rights who cannot be overlooked was Margaret Fuller, an influential member of New England's literary society and editor of the transcendentalist paper *The Dial.* Although Fuller never formally entered into the religion-woman's rights controversy (her early death prevented such), she did prove an outspoken advocate of the woman's cause.

Her written work reveals her to be a strong critic of orthodox religion. Yet, in her *Memoirs* one discovers a woman of great religious uncertainty. On one hand, she yearned for a religious experience and appeared haunted by Christian orthodoxy. She even lamented the fact that the admired Shelley had lacked Christian faith and insisted that had he lived twenty years longer, he would have become a "fervent Christian."[19]

On the other hand, some of her most passionate language was directed against the established church and its clergy.

> There was once a soul in the religion while the blood of its martyrs was yet fresh on the ground, but that soul was always too much encumbered with the remains of pagan habits and customs; that soul is now quite fled elsewhere and in the

splendid catafalco, watched by so many white and red-robed
snuff-taking, sly-eyed men, would they let it be opened, nothing
would be found but bones.[20]

With this understanding of her nature and interest (or lack of
interest) in religion, it is not difficult to comprehend why her best
known work "The Great Lawsuit," which was first published in
serial form in *The Dial* and later in book form under the title *Woman
in the Nineteenth Century*, reflects only a cursory interest in the
conflict developing between woman's rights and theological dogma.

Reviews of the book, however, did cite her transgression of
Christian decorum, and one can reasonably speculate that had she
survived the shipwreck in New York harbor, which also claimed the
lives of her husband and small son, she might have become one of
the most astute female minds to wrestle with religious prejudices.
Her work readily identifies her almost passionate concern with
religion; and at the time of the disasterous shipwreck which took
her life, she was returning to the United States with the express
purpose of attending the next woman's rights convention, to be
held in Syracuse, New York in September, 1852. By that time,
religion had become a convention issue, and she surely would have
been exposed to its priority and strength.

Another enlistment in the woman's cause only a year before
the Seneca Falls Convention was Lucy Stone, an 1847 graduate of
Oberlin College who had delivered her first woman's rights address
the same year from the pulpit of her brother Bowman's church in
Gardner, Massachusetts. She was to prove a courageous and learned
debater in the theology-woman's rights conflict.

The determination and stubbornness of this remarkable woman was evident at an early age and surfaced many times previous to
her formal alinement with the woman's movement. As a child, the
scriptural passages which supposedly confirmed female subjection
drove her to despair and, by her own admission, suicidal thoughts.
But anger triumphed over thoughts of suicide and, rising above
personal anguish and disappointment, she decided to go to college.
Her express purpose was to study Hebrew and Greek and thus

determine for herself whether such texts proclaiming female inferiority were correctly translated. She did go to college and studied both languages successfully, and she did determine that the troublesome passages of childhood were, indeed, mistranslated.

As a young woman, her stubbornness again asserted itself. This time in a congregational meeting. The assembly was intent on removing an abolitionist from its diaconate; and when the vote was taken, Stone voted to retain the abolitionist. At first she did not realize that as a woman she was not entitled to vote in the assembly; but even after she realized her vote was not being counted, she raised her hand for the vote another six times. Her daughter Alice Stone Blackwell recalled many years later that on her mother's deathbed she still considered "that one uncounted hand . . . a visible protest against the subjection of women in **Church** and State."[21]

When Stone assumed the role of active abolitionist and feminist, she, like the others, was subject to numerous attacks. In Washington, Connecticut, a minister likened her to Jezebel and told his congregation that she trampled underfoot God's commandment for silence in the church and came a follower of Satan disguised as an angel. The result of such attacks, her daughter claimed, was

> . . . a distrust, if not an actual antagonism, toward organized religion, which lasted with her for many years. Though her object in going to college had been to satisfy herself whether the texts quoted in defense of the subjection of women were correctly translated, in later life she attached little importance to the texts; but she always believed and maintained that the Bible, rightly interpreted, was on the side of equal rights for women.[22]

Any woman who chose to speak out on the slavery issue found that to do so meant she must first claim the right to speak publicly as a woman. To secure rights for the Black slave necessitated their coming to grips with their own basic rights; the two causes were now unavoidably conjoined. Forced repeatedly to justify their exposure on the public lecturn, the women began to develop the arguments originally shaped by the Grimkes, and they would use them vigorously and continuously throughout the coming decades to challenge all opponents, the most belligerent and the more benevolent.

Notes

[1]Jonathan F. Stearns, "Discourse on Female Influence," *Up From the Pedestal*, ed. Aileen Kraditor (Chicago: Quadrangle, 1968, p. 49. [The article, originally published in 1837, was a sermon delivered by The Rev. Stearns in First Presbyterian Church, Newburyport, Ms. on July 30.]

[2]*Ibid.*, p. 50.

[3]"Pastoral Letter of the General Association of Massachusetts (Ortho-dox) to the Churches Under Their Care," *The History of Women Suffrage*, eds. Elizabeth C. Stanton, Susan B. Anthony and Matilda J. Gage, I (New York: Fowler and Wells, 1881), p. 81. Hereafter cited *HSW*.

[4]*Ibid.*

[5]*Ibid.*, pp. 81-82.

[6]Maria Weston Chapman, "The Times that Try Men's Souls," *HSW*, I (1881), 82-83.

[7]John Greenleaf Whittier, "The Pastoral Letter," *HSW*, I (1881), 86.

[8]Sarah Grimke, "The Pastoral Letter of the General Association of Congregational Ministers of Massachusetts," *Letters on the Equality of the Sexes and the Condition of Women* (1838; rpt. New York: Burt Franklin, 1970), p. 14. Hereafter cited *ESCW*. [These letters, dating from July 11, 1837 to October 20, 1837, were originally addressed to Mary S. Parker, President of the Boston Female Anti-Slavery Society and first achieved publication in the anti-slavery paper *The New England Spectator*.]

[9]*Ibid.*, p. 18.

[10]Sarah Grimke, "The Original Equality of Woman," *ESCW* (1838), p. 6.

[11]—, "Man Equally Guilty with Woman in the Fall," *ESCW* (1838), p. 117.

[12]—, "Woman Subject Only to God," *ESCW* (1838), p. 10.

[13]—, "Social Intercourse of the Sexes," *ESCW* (1838), p. 23.

[14]—, "Relation of Husband to Wife," *ESCW* (1838), p. 91.

[15]—, "Ministry of Women," *ESCW* (1838), p. 103.

[16]*Ibid.*, p. 111.

[17]*Ibid.*, p. 113.

[18]*Ibid.*, p. 114.

[19]Ralph Waldo Emerson and others, *Memoirs of Margaret Fuller Ossoli* (Boston: Roberts Brothers, 1881), p. 166.

[20]Katherine Anthony, *Margaret Fuller: A Psychological Biography* (New York: Harcourt, Brace, 1921), p. 159.

[21]Alice Stone Blackwell, *Lucy Stone: Pioneer of Woman's Rights* (Boston: Little, Brown, 1930), p. 23.

[22]*Ibid.*, p. 59.

Chapter III

The Loyal Opposition

Opposition to woman's right to speak in public meetings of mixed audiences did not find adherents only among clergy intent upon enforcing supposed biblical dictate. Many well-known and well-intentioned women also stood aghast that some of their sex should defame theselves by speaking audaciously as public lecturers and thus subject themselves to the accompanying ridicule. Among their number stood two women who were very strong advocates of female education—Catherine Beecher and Sarah Josepha Hale, editor of the popular *Godey's Lady's Book*. Though both women argued forcefully for greater opportunities for women in fields then dominated or restricted to male employment, neither could bring herself to openly support the challenges voiced by the public debaters.

Catherine Beecher, a pioneer in expanding the field of education for women, included in her book *An Essay on Slavery and Abolition*, published in 1837, numerous references to the duties of American women as she understood those duties. Even a cursory reading of the work reveals Beecher as a strong supporter of women as homemakers and housewives despite her stance on female education. For women to enter so brazenly into public life via the speaker's lecturn was nothing less than wilful abandonment of woman's divinely appointed sphere. So convinced was she of this fact that she argued if women were to follow the lead of present feminists, the security of the American family structure was seriously endangered.

Her arguments incensed the Grimkes, and the task of defense and refutation fell to Angelina. In a direct response entitled *Letters to Catherine Beecher*, Angelina Grimke refuted point by point the arguments posed by Beecher, often in blunt, uncompromising language.

Beecher had asserted that heaven had appointed women a subordinate position and that men and women exercised different modes of power. Both claims insisted Grimke in a letter dated August 28, 1837 were biblically unfounded. Beecher's insistence that women must exercise principles consistent with peace, benevolence and generosity rather than overt intellect and physical power was ridiculed by Grimke who thought it appealing to the egotistical desires of the "fashionable belle, whose idol is herself" and not the "humble Christian, who feels that it is truth which she seeks to recommend to others, . . ."[1]

Many of Angelina's biblical arguments are similar to those of her older sister Sarah, and she recommended Sarah's letters to Beecher for a more complete statement of her *own* views on the subject. She also called upon noted biblical exegetes to substantiate her own exegesis. When referring to the question of women speaking at the Pentecost experience (she, of course, maintained they did), she concluded: "This is the plain matter of fact, as Clark and Scott, Stratton and Locke, all allow. Mine is no 'private interpretation,' no mere sectarian view."[2]

Grimke's main contention with Beecher was the latter's attitude, which Grimke declared furthered the suppression of women. Beecher's fine, but trite, traditional sentiments were appalling to Angelina Grimke. Beecher had argued that "All the generous promptins of chivalry, all the poetry of romantic gallantry, depend upon woman's retaining her place as dependent and defenceless, and making no claims, and maintaining no rights, but what are the gifts of honor, rectitude and love."[3] Such sentiment Grimke found "beneath the dignity of any woman who names the name of Christ. . . . Such a one loathes such littleness, and turns with disgust from all such silly insipidities. Her noble nature is insulted by such paltry, sickening adulation, and she will not stoop to drink the foul waters of so turpid a stream."[4]

What Beecher had suggested as proper behavior and demeanor for women Grimke found blatant foolishness and hoped such ideas would soon be withdrawn. For Grimke a woman's rights were granted her by God; they were not a gift from man as Beecher asserted. They were nothing less than a permanent endowment of her created being, existing as long as God's command still prevailed.

Grimke also scoffed at Beecher's insistence that men and women occupied appropriate offices. There could be no simple line of separation between the duties of men and women as moral beings. In fact Grimke's Quaker convictions come to the fore in response to Beecher's contention that the use of physical force and coercive power belonged only to the male; she found such combatant attitudes totally at variance with the principles of scripture.

Beecher had also insisted that a woman's place had been ascertained by legal means and she abhorred the current practice of women petitioning their grievances to Congress, a practice she thought not only unwise but indecorous.[5] Grimke's rejoinder was caustic. Jealously guarding it as the only political right then possessed by women, she likened the woman's rights issue to colonial America. Like the colonists they were taxed without representation, and like the colonists they were governed by laws which they had no part in framing. Surely they should be allowed the one avenue of remonstration open to them. She implied that Beecher lacked faith in the abilities of American women:

> Art thou afraid to trust the women of this country with discretionary power as to petitioning? Is there not sound principle and common sense enough among them, to regulate the exercise of this right? I believe they will always use it wisely. I am not afraid to trust my sisters—not I.[6]

Beecher's insistence that since men had elected legislators, they ought to be the only ones to avail themselves of the right of petition Grimke found poor logic indeed. Because women could not vote was a poor reason for depriving them of the right of petition.

Grimke continually maintained that moral duty took precedence over the demands of Congress; to reverse the priority was to obey man rather than God—a scriptural affront. Principles could never be sacrificed to power and special interests. She questioned Beecher's loyalty: "If thou canst consent to exchange the precepts of the Bible for the opinions of such a body of men as now sit on the destinies of this nation, I cannot."[7]

Defying Beecher's implication that God had given woman, his greatest gift, to man, Grimke argued that not only was such not the case, but woman "was created like him, in the image of God, and crowned with glory and honor; created only a little lower than the angels,—not, as is almost universally assumed, a little lower than man; on her brow, as well as on his, was placed the 'diadem of beauty,' and in her hand the sceptre of universal dominion."[8] Duties did not originate from a difference in sex as Beecher concluded, but from "the diversity of our relations to life, the various gifts and talents commited to our care and the different eras in which we live."[9]

Grimke did not spare the church in her rebuttal either. Woman's exclusion from the ministry and the decision-making processes of the church were nothing less than "a violation of human rights, a rank usurpation of power, a violent seizure and confiscation of what is sacredly and inalienably hers . . . ."[10] Until the church recognized this, she thought it could do nothing to accomplish a permanent reconciliation of the world. Going even further than many of her courageous colleagues, Grimke boldly affirmed, "If Ecclesiastical and Civil governments are ordained of God, then I contend that woman has just as much right to sit in solemn counsel in Conventions, Conferences, Associations, and General Assemblies, as man—just as much right to sit upon the throne of England, or the Presidential chair of the United States."[11]

The basic question for Grimke was one of human rights, not his rights versus her rights. Her participation in the abolitionist crusade had sensitized her to this issue. Whereas Beecher was want to argue social duty and appropriate behavior, Grimke spoke of moral duty stemming from the created nature of men and women as moral beings. With such an approach, sexual differences were insignificant. A dichotomous doctrine of male and female virtues was anti-christian.

> By this doctrine, man has been converted into the warrior, and clothed with sternness, and those other kindred qualities, which in common estimation belong to his character as a *man*; whilst woman has been taught to lean upon an arm of flesh, to sit as a doll arrayed in 'gold, and pearls, and costly array,' to be admired for her personal charms, and caressed and humored like a spoiled child, or converted into a mere drudge to suit the convenience of her lord and master.[12]

The result of such a bifarious doctrine was the loss of women's essential rights while granting to men a "charter for the exercise of tyranny and selfishness, pride and arrogance, lust and brutal violence."[13] Instead of woman being a full partner of man and a fulfilled being, she became an appendage and a toy—an inferior. Unless human rights were secured, woman would continue to act the buffoon and the slave and man the coarse belligerent.

The verbal feud between Beecher and the feminist movement would continue for several decades, even though she later liberalized some of her opinions. Whatever Beecher may have accomplished in fostering educational opportunities for women, she never became a full-fledged supporter of the public role of women.

Another prominent feminist/anti-feminist was Sarah Josepha Hale who occupied the unique and respected position of female editor of a nationally known, well-read woman's magazine—*Godey's Lady's Book*. The content of her editorials placed her among the more liberally-minded women of her day.

A perusal of the editorial pages of *Godey's* leads one to yet another conclusion. For although she contended for greater educational benefits for women as had Beecher and became one of the most adamant and outspoken women for medical schools for the training of women physicians, her editorials remained surprisingly mum with regard to the political and legal rights of women. The confusion of the historian abates only when confronted by the synopsis of her biblical understandings as they achieved published form in the introductory pages of her *Woman's Record, or Sketches of All Distinguished Women, From the Creation to A. D. 1854.*

Though the *Woman's Record* was not published until 1855, seven years after the Seneca Falls Convention, her views deserve mention in this chapter, if only to explain why a woman in such an advantageous and influential position should remain silent during these crucial, formative years of woman's rights.

A glance through the *Record* reveals her prejudices. While endeavoring to offer brief biographies of famous women throughout history, beginning with Eve, she included no woman's rights activists. Only the Hicksite Quaker Lucretia Mott is mentioned and, then, with a good deal of reservation.

Hale conceded that Mott possessed a persuasive speaking style, but insisted that this ability only prevented her listeners from noting fallacies readily discernible when one confronted her written work. For Hale, Mott was an infidel, totally ignorant of the true demands of scripture. She accused Mott of instructing women in ways designed to lead them to become more like men, obscuring their femininity. The idea of women occupying positions then restricted by convention to men was repugnant to Hale who, like so many of her sex, could not step beyond tradition on the issue: "What a degrading idea; as though the worth of porcelain should be estimated by its resemblance to iron! Does she (Mott) not perceive that, in estimating physical and mental ability above moral excellence, she sacrifices her own sex, who can never excel in those industrial pursuits which belong to life in this world?"[14]

Her charge that Mott was willing to sacrifice moral excellence so readily leads one to surmise that she did not fully understand Mott's intents, yet it is this "sacrifice of moral excellence" which prevents Hale from aligning with the feminists. Like many of her opponents, the Bible was the final guide and expositor of woman's rights and duties. But unlike her opponents, biblical research led her to the point of denouncing the woman's rights movement: "I have no sympathy with those who are wrangling for " 'Woman's rights;' " not with those who are foolishly urging my sex to strive for equality and competition with men."[15]

Unwilling to concede that the scriptures encouraged the abuse of women, she maintained that the time-honored directives of scripture did not depreciate woman's worth, but rather enhanced it. Such was undeniable since creation was on an ascending scale. With a simple logic she reasoned that since woman was the last work of creation, woman must reflect the epitome of human nature and occupy the position closest to the angelic. What the feminists' now proposed was for Hale a forfeiture of this position.

The Bible expounded no doctrine of equality between the sexes for Hale. In creation the sexes differed in mode of creation, material of creation and function. Women did not, maintained Hale, possess either the physical strength or the mental acuity required for participation in the task of subduing and governing the world. Her study of scripture, history and philosophy convinced Hale that "the difference between the constructive genius of man and woman is the result of an organic difference in the operations of their minds."16

Woman's knowledge was intuitive; her task, to inspire and morally instruct man. Following this notion, Hale did offer a small ray of hope for womankind, though she, like many others, did not or was unwilling to investigate all the possible implications of her insight. She insisted that Paul's admonition that woman was made "for man" did not allow men to relegate women to positions of inferiority or envision women as made solely for the satisfaction of sensual desire. Woman was not the most blameable in "the fall". Like Murray and adversary Sarah Grimke, she, too, affirmed that Adam, with his greater strength and wisdom was the most criminal. Yet the result of the "fall" was a triumph of the sensual over the moral—man would rule. Hale even countered the argument which insisted that women received the severest sentence and the greatest humiliation following the "fall". Adam, not Eve, received the brunt of God's anger; condemned to a life of hard labor, his only hope lay in the promise extended to Eve in Genesis 3.15.

Hale's aggrandized picture of women leads one to speculate about the extent of her knowledge of the American woman's true condition. Her angelic conception of women did not allow inclusion of the calloused hands and overworked, unrewarded bodies of many of her sex. With this observation, her advice as to a woman's task is tragic indeed. She informed her readers to " . . . leave the work of the world and its reward, the government thereof, to men; our task is to fit them for their office, and inspire them to perform it in righteousness."[17]

The tragedy of Sarah Josepha Hale is that a woman of her bearing and position could have done a great deal to further the status of women in the United States. Her shallow, lopsided theology and her inflated opinion of the real station of women denied the woman's movement a potential champion.

Feminine frankness and their open trampling of tradition made not only conservative women uneasy, but even male abolitionists feared that the growing concern for woman's rights among female abolitionists would overshadow their primary cause—the abolition of Black slavery in the United States. While men such as William Lloyd Garrison seemed less than troubled by this entrance of feminine abolitionists into a new area, others were not possessed of the same equanimity of mind.

Wendell Philips and Theodore Weld, although not adverse to woman's rights on principle, cautioned the women repeatedly to wait for a more auspicious occasion to air their grievances while, at the same time, urging them to concentrate on the anti-slavery struggle. For Philips and Weld, and even the poet John Greenleaf Whittier, the two causes were separate and could be treated as such. The women realized that this was impossible.

Whittier took the liberty of addressing a letter to the Grimkes in August, 1837. Claiming that their activities in and of themselves were sufficient testimony to their belief in the equality of women, he questioned the necessity of their entering the field of controversial writers on the issue. Suggesting they are abandoning the unfortunate and miserable slave for a "trifling oppression," a "paltry grievance," and a "selfish crusade," he places the blame for their divergence on the notorious Pastoral Letter, which he assured them "can do you no harm if you do not allow its splenetic and idle manifesto to divert your attention for the great and holy purpose of your souls."[18] Apologizing for his strong statement, he admonishes them "to forget everything but our duty to God and our fellow beings; to dethrone the selfish principle, and to strive to win over the hard heart of the oppressor by truth kindly spoken."[19]

Whittier was concerned about the possible damage which might accrue to the abolitionist fight. This was also the fear expressed by Amos A. Phelps, another noted abolitionist, who advised the women to confine their speaking to members of their own sex rather than impair the anti-slavery cause. The Grimkes responded to Phelps with a little advice of their own. After affirming that duty mandated their behavior, they urged Phelps to rethink his position lest he unwittingly align himself with the stance taken by the authors of the Pastoral Letter. Angelina Grimke's response to Whittier came in a letter dated August 20, 1837 and addressed to both Whittier and Theodore Weld, since she had received a similar letter from Weld.

Defending Sarah's *Letters* to *The Spectator* and her own to Catherine Beecher (Whittier's reference to entering the field of controversial writers), she asserted that neither had intially aroused the public; the Pastoral Letter was responsible for that. This clerical denunciation had paniked the clergy, who envisioned an invasion of the pulpit if women were allowed to speak openly. The panic in turn stimulated the more reactionary arguments to a even greater pitch. Angelina charged both men with overlooking this pertinent fact.

Angelina insisted that an attack upon their rights was a personal attack and needed to be dealt with or their emancipation efforts would be impossible. The issues were joined; and when Whittier and Weld questioned their timing, Angelina countered by affirming that the time to assert a right was precisely at the time that the right was being abused or denied. Not only was it the right time for the woman's issue to be broached, but an outspoken defense was essential for the benefit of the anti-slavery cause as well. She marvelled that they did not realize "the leaven which the ministers are so assidously working into the minds of the people must take effect in the process of time, and will close every church to us, if we give the community no reasons to counteract the sophistry of priest and levities."[20]

Comparing the woman's position to that of the Black slave, she denied any selfish motivation, maintaining that they were motivated only "by the full conviction that if we are to do any good in the Anti Slavery cause, our right to labor in it must be firmly established; not on the ground of Quakerism, but on the only firm bases of human rights, the Bible."[21] To surrender the right to speak in public prefaced the gradual but sure surrender of other rights; the very welfare of women was at stake.

Angelina also reasoned that women need this valuable instruction lest they gain only the one-sided view voiced by opponents. Women needed to become accomplished in stating their cause against those who would seek to discredit them by distorting scripture and the angered cries for proof. If they were not, they would be driven disgraced from abolitionism itself. Sarah's appended message to the same letter advocated proficiency to the degree that the burden of proof would be placed upon their opponents, who would then need to prove why a woman should *not* speak in public gatherings.

This letter also contained one of the Grimkes' fiercest attacks upon organized religion. Angelina interpreted the attack made by the Massachusetts clergy in words suggestive of a conspiracy. *They* (the clergy) denied women participation in any moral reform unless they first outlined the limits of woman's participation. *They* engaged in namecalling —comparing the sisters to the notorious freethinker Fanny Wright. *They* actively schemed against the sisters and shamed persons into nonattendance at their lectures. The logical outcome of this conspired effort, if left unchallenged, was a continuous retreat on the part of women. So angered was Angelina by the adversity of the clergy, that in a rare burst of iconoclasm, she argued that "the whole Church Government must come down, the clergy stand right in the way of reform, and I do not know but this stumbling block must too be removed before Slavery can be abolished, for the system is supported by them; it could not exist without the Church as it is called."[22]

A week later in a letter written to the sympathetic Henry C. Wright, a social radical and ardent supporter of the Garrisonian faction, the Grimkes revealed more of their true feelings regarding the uproar occasioned by their now growing interest in woman's rights. Although saddened by the defection of clerics from the abolitionist ranks because of their vehement stance and troubled by the anxiety expressed by stalwart abolitionists Whittier and Weld, Sarah declined to surrender her right to address any moral issue. Convinced she was not acting out of personal interest but divine command and believing she herself was not responsible for the consequences of doing God's will, she lamented "the narrow minded policy of Christians, of abolitionists, trying to keep asunder the different parts of Christianity as if it were not a beautiful and harmonious system which could not be divided."[23]

For Sarah Grimke the resolution of the tension was clear. If her embarrassment of the Abolitionist cause proved intolerable to the faint-hearted, she was prepared to remove herself or be removed from the Anti Slavery Society: "If my connection with A. S. must continue at the expense of my conscience I had far rather be thrown out of the A. S. ranks; . . . ."[24]

Expressing a concern for the mercenary aspects of organized religion, she informed Wright of her intention of writing two essays on the ministry of women. Both essays, according to Grimke, had little chance of being published. Both, however, were later published in her *Letters on the Condition of Women.*

To Wright she directed a number of theological inquiries, ostensibly to aid in the composition of the "letters". Typical of Sarah Grimke, she supplied her own answers, but looked to Wright for confirmation. Most of the questions hinged primarily on the issues of translation and/or the original Greek text's rendering of words and phrases: Were the terms "man" and "brethren" generic? Was the same Greek word used for "women" and "wives"? Was not Junia a woman? What was the correct translation of "minister" in Ephesians 6.21? How would one accurately render I Corinthians 7.12-13?

The most lengthy and most candid debate of the issue, however, occurred in an exchange of letters between Theodore Dwight Weld and the Grimkes, particularly Angelina who was soon to become Weld's wife. Several days before Whittier had addressed his

apprehensive letter to the Grimkes, Angelina had written to Weld
acknowledging the fuss which she and her sister had produced by
their public lecturing. She expressed admiration for Sarah's terse
response to the Phelps' letter, while, at the same time, acknowledging some anxiety about the possibility that the Anti Slavery Society's
Executive Committee would renounce them.

She assured Weld that she regretted the emergence of this
"new contest" prior to the resolution of the slavery question and
attributed its appearance to "a concatenation of circumstances over
which we had no control."[25] Nevertheless, she saw both the time-
liness and importance of the issue for women and American society.

Like her sister Sarah she took some of the clerical charges
as a personal insult and cause for moral outrage, noting specifically
the sermon of the Reverend Hubbard Winslow of Boston on the
divine limitations of woman's activities. And she encouraged Weld to
read Sarah's letters in *The Spectator* and offer his opinion. She herself proposed to write a response to Winslow's sermon.

The issue was a moral one for Angelina, i. e., whether or not
women would be forced to surrender moral responsibility. It was
not a question of Quaker sentiment as some had opined, but of
biblical truth and the natural rights of women. She refused to be
silent on the issue; and, noting that Mary Parker of the Boston Anti
Slavery Society had assured her that the Boston women would stand
with them even if everybody else deserted them, she asked if Weld
could not do the same.

Weld's reply arrived a few days later. Consistent with his
character, he dealt systematically with the issue. Presenting the
Grimkes with what he thought to be shocking liberality, he assured
them that from early childhood he had advocated woman's mental,
moral and spiritual equality, and he even challenged the sisters as to
whether they or he reflected the most liberal stance on the issue.

While agreeing that women should equally participate in state
and church and fully in agreement with them on the principle involved, Weld nevertheless expressed regret over the fact that they
had decided to publish their views. Like Whittier, he maintained

that their actions spoke louder than words. Their continued public speaking was a practical refutation of the inferiority of women and the arguments of opponents.

Weld found them invaluable to the abolitionist movement, and their recent incursion into the arena of woman's rights could only jeopardize their contribution to it. He also thought that as Quakers they would be less effective in the woman's rights field since such was a "Quaker doctrine" and would be treated as such by most.

Their new interest was diverting their energies from the greater work. He plead with them:

> Now can't you leave the lesser work to others who can do it better than you, and devote, consecrate your whole bodies, souls and spirits to the greater work which you can do far better and to far better purpose than any body else. Again, the abolition question is most powerfully preparative and introductory to the other question. By pushing the former with all our might we are most effectually advancing the latter.[26]

Angelina's response was the previously noted letter addressed jointly to Weld and Whittier, wherein she repeatedly attacked what she thought to be the fallacies of their logic, i. e., the issues were separable, their views were prompted by their Quakerism, they would ultimately damage the abolition movement, etc.

Weld's response arrived within the week. Since the first page of the letter is missing, his full reply is unavailable. The remainder of the letter, however, suggests that he began by once again assuring the sisters of his lifelong dedication to the principle of women's equality. Yet the extant portion of the letter reaffirms his insistence that to overtly and unapologetically push the question would only lead to a more belligerent opposition and weaken support for abolition. Only their continuous activity would assure their antagonists of their ability, not their verbiage. Ministers would be most effectively persuaded by their public success, not by doctrinal irritation.

> Now if instead of blowing a blast thro' the newspapers, sounding the onset and summoning the ministers and churches to

surrender, you had without any introductory flourish just gone right among them and lectured when and where and as yu could find opportunity and paid no attention to criticism, but pushed right on without making any ado about "attacks" and "invasions" and "opposition" and have let the barkers bark their bark out, within one year you might have practically brought over 50,000 persons of the very moral elite of New England.[27]

Once again affirming the separability of the issues, he lectured them as if he were a teacher faced with incorrigible pupils. Citing past history for example, he informed them that moral reform was always accomplished by advancing and tenaciously holding to one main principle; any digression doomed the reform. The great principle now being advanced was human rights and to digress to a derivative of that—woman's rights—as they advocated, would endanger the realization of the major reform. For corroboration of his point he cited nothing less than the Reformation and even asked (with exclamation points attached) whether or not they had read the New Testament. Such was Christ's methodology according to Weld.

Closing the epistle by claiming that in the past three years the abolition movement had significantly advanced the cause of woman's rights, he now accused them of "putting the horse before the cart," "dragging the tree by the top," and not allowing the greater issue of human rights to open the way to the lesser issue of woman's rights.

Several weeks passed before Sarah's curt response to Weld. She scoffed at Weld's personal examples of his early conviction on the matter and rather matter-of-factly informed him that she *had* read the New Testament, to her edification she supposed, and still could not agree with him. Rather than abandoning the cause of the slave, she informed Weld that the exercise of their rights as women promoted their effectiveness as moral reformers.

Acknowledging that she had not said half of what she would like to, she allowed Angelina to conclude the letter. Angelina informed Weld of Sarah's anger. Unappreciative of Weld's scolding which she considered unjust and unmerited, Angelina demanded to know what was wrong with Weld. She further accused Weld of making a monster out of a molehill and resolutely proclaimed that she remained unconvinced by his arguments.

Weld did not reply immediately. The last letter in the series devoted to this issue is dated October 10, 1837. In it Weld concluded the previous two-month long discussion by insisting that any continued debate between them on the subject was unprofitable, particularly via the mails. He claimed that he was being misunderstood, both his statements and their implications. With that the matter is abruptly dropped from his correspondence with the sisters. Neither of the parties in the debate had altered their opinions.

Lest the reader suppose that most prominent male abolitionists were reticent on the woman question, it must be reiterated that the Garrisonian faction of the movement remained openly in support of the feminists. Indeed Garrison himself was to become one of the most vociferous advocates of the woman's cause.

Not all clerics of the day were antagonistic to woman speakers, or even woman preachers, either. There were always exceptions, and one such exception was Almond Davis. In the introduction to his book *The Female Preacher, or Memoir of Salome Lincoln*, published in 1843, Davis presented a superb argument for the right of women to participate in the pulpit ministry. Maintaining that many things rejected by the world are approved by God and that God's ways are often not man's ways, he discredited biblical texts like I Corinthians 14 which demands woman's silence as oppressive and prompted solely by the chaotic conditions then present in the Corinthian assembly. Instead, he quoted I Corinthians 11.5 as supportive of woman ministers and insisted that women did exercise a preaching function in the early church, refering to the women involved in the pentecost experience, Phillip's four daughters, Priscilla expounding the gospel to Apollos, the Samaritan woman at the well, and Mary Magdalene's role the first Easter morning.

For Davis, denying women access to the pulpit presuposed a sacredness granted the pulpit which he could not condone.

> ... I have yet to learn, that the pulpit is a more sacred place,
> than any other portion of the house. And if it is right for wo-
> man to speak in public conference, it is right for her to quote
> passages of scripture, and if right to quote passages of scrip-
> ture, it is also right to take a passage as the foundation of re-
> marks; and as the desk is not the sanctum sanctorum of God's
> house, it is equally right to enter that—with a text selected
> from the word of God.[28]

For every Almond Davis, Henry Wright and William Lloyd
Garrison there was an Amos Phelps, John Greenleaf Whittier and
Catherine Beecher. Thus, not only were the early feminists beset
by overt anger and public derision, they were also crippled by the
hesitance, reservation and narrowmindedness of their supposed
closest compatriots. It is a credit to the moral and mental stamina
of these early champions that they were not easily dissuaded from
either their convictions or their activities. Later Weld, Phillips and
other noted male abolitionists would come to appreciate their
position.

Notes

[1]Angelina Grimke, "The Sphere of Woman and Man as Moral Beings
the Same," *Letters to Catherine Beecher, in Reply to an Essay on Slavery and
Abolition, Addressed to A. E. Grimke* (1838; rpt. New York: Arno, 1969),
p. 105. Hereafter cited *LCB*. [The reader is referred to Catherine Beecher's
*An Essay on Slavery and Abolition with Reference to the Duty of American
Females* (Philadelphia: Henry Perkins, 1837.]

[2]*Ibid.*, p. 106.

[3]*Ibid.*, p. 107.

[4]*Ibid.*

[5]*Ibid.*, p. 110.

6*Ibid.*, p. 112.

7*Ibid.*, p. 110.

8Angelina Grimke, "Human Rights Not Founded on Sex," *LCB* (1838), pp. 116-17.

9*Ibid.*, p. 115.

10*Ibid.*, p. 119.

11*Ibid.*

12*Ibid.*, pp. 115-16.

13*Ibid.*, p. 116.

14Sarah Josepha Hale, *Women's Record, or Sketches of all Distinguished Women, From the Creation to A. D. 1854.* (1855; rpt. New York; Source Book, 1970), p. 753.

15*Ibid.*, p. xxxvii.

16*Ibid.*, p. xlvi.

17*Ibid.*, p. xlv.

18John Greenleaf Whittier Letter to Grimkes, August 14, 1837, *The Letters of Theodore Wild, Angelina Grimke Weld and Sarah Grimke*, eds. Gilbert H. Barnes and Dwight L. Dumond (New York: Appleton, Century, Crofts, 1934), I, 424. Hereafter cited *Weld-Grimke Letters*.

19*Ibid.*

20Angelina Grimke letter to Theodore Weld and John Greenleaf Whittiers, August 20, 1837, *Weld-Grimke Letters*, I (1934), p. 428.

21*Ibid.*, p. 429.

22*Ibid.*, p. 431.

[23]Grimkes' letter to Henry C. Wright, August 27, 1937, *Weld-Grimke Letters*, I (1934), p. 437.

[24]*Ibid.*

[25]Angelina Grimke letter to Theodore Weld, August 12, 1937, *Weld-Grimke Letters*, I (1934), 415.

[26]Theodore Weld letter to Grimkes, August 15, 1837, *Weld-Grimke Letters*, I (1934), 426.

[27]Theodore Weld letter to Grimkes, August 26, 1837, *Weld-Grimke Letters*, I (1934), 433.

[28]Almond Davis, *The Female Preacher or Memoir of Salome Lincoln* (1834; rpt. New York: Arno, 1972), p. 13.

Chapter IV

Seneca Falls

The impetus for organization of a formal woman's rights movement climaxed eight years before the actual convening of the now historic woman's convention in Seneca Falls, New York. The occasion was the World Anti-Slavery Convention held in London in June, 1840. The convention opened with a heated debate when an attempt was made to seat duly elected female delegates from the American Anti-Slavery Society.

The issue of the direct participation of women in the proceedings of anti-slavery societies in the United States had been a spirited one for several years. It had eventually led to abolitionist rivalry and ultimately schism. The irrepressible Garrison accounted for a good deal of the furor which enveloped the issue.

As early as December 15, 1837 Garrison had informed the readers of *The Liberator* of his support of universal emancipation, which he avowed called for the redemption of both women and men from the bonds of servitude. He proposed to "go for the RIGHTS OF WOMEN to their utmost extent."

Such sentiment produced further unrest in the abolitionist ranks, which were already tried by Garrison and his more radical notions. The issue was to reach a head in May, 1838 at the annual meeting of the New England Anti Slavery Convention. Oliver Johnson, a loyal Garrisonian, moved that women be received into the organization on equal terms. The motion carried, prompting several in the minority to withdraw and precipitating the resignation of the Reverend Amos A. Phelps.

The following September provided another victory for women as the delegates to the Peace Convention, called by Garrison, not only received them as members but admitted them to convention committees. The action was not without protest, however. When the Quaker Abby Kelley was appointed to the business committee, several men asked that their names be removed from the convention lists and promptly withdrew.

The battle had just begun. In January, 1839 when the Massachusetts Anti Slavery Society met, the Reverend Charles T. Torrey, a dissenter at the earlier New England Convention, led a small faction in an attempt to deprive women of the right to participate. His proposal was defeated, and once again Amos Phelps resigned as recording secretary and member of the society's board of managers.

The stage was set for schism, and it occurred in May of the same year at the New England Anti Slavery Convention, which a year earlier had accepted women as equal members. Phelps offered a resolution which would allow only male participation, arguing primarily precedent. Wendell Phillips presented a counter-resolution calling for the participation of both men and women. Once again the anti-feminist abolitionists were defeated and withdrew to form the Massachusetts Abolitionist Society. Soon other local societies split over the same issue.

Local schisms prefaced a schism of even greater magnitude on the national level. At the American Anti Slavery Society's annual convention in 1839 when Nathaniel Clover moved that the role of delegates be restricted to men only, Ellis Gray Loring, a Garrison supporter, amended the resolution to admit all persons who were recognized delegates from auxilliary societies or members of the American Anti Slavery Society.The Clover resolution was soundly defeated while the Loring amendment won the support of the convention. Once again a verbal protest was presented, written by James G. Birney and representing the position of 123 delegates.

The formal break finally occurred at the next annual convention of the society, meeting in New York City in May, 1840. Garrison, fearing that opponents would wrest power by outnumbering his supporters, encouraged New England loyalists to attend the convention by hiring the steamboat Massachusetts to transport them to New York.

Upon the absence of Chairman Arthur Tappen, the chair was assumed by Francis Jackson, one of the vice presidents, who immediately appointed Garrison and ten others, including Abby Kelley to the Business Committee. When he announced that her appointment was confirmed viva voca, a division was called for. When the vote was tallied, it was found that the Kelley appointment was sustained by a vote of 557 to 451.

Angry opponents, led by Lewis Tappen, immediately withdrew to form the American and Foreign Anti Slavery Society. Throughout its thirteen year existence it would allow for separate women's societies represented at the annual conventions by male delegates. The rationale for its formation included the charges that the American Anti-Slavery Society had abandoned its primary purpose and, contrary to the directives of the Society's constitution and the usages of civilized society, introduced a practice which would only prove detrimental to the abolitionist movement. This on the eve of the World Anti Slavery Convention to be held in London a month later.

Although they had not specifically denoted that delegates were to be male in their first invitation to abolitionists, the Executive Committee of the World Convention, having learned that the Boston abolitionists had appointed women delegates, issued a second call which specified that delegates be "gentlemen". Nevertheless, when delegates from the American Anti Slavery Society arrived in London, their number included several women—Sarah Pugh, Lucretia Mott, Ann Phillips, Maria Chapman, Harriet Martineau and Elizabeth Cady Stanton.

The London Committee was aghast; and when Wendell Phillips fomally presented the credentials of the women delegates to the committee, they refused to seat them. Phillips then chose to present the issue to the full convention. Instructed by his wife not to "shilly-shally" on the issue, he voiced an eloquent plea on the women's behalf, but to no avail. The debate was fierce, and clerical opposition was undeniably present and extremely vocal. The women were ordered to sit in a curtained balcony, while below them the male delegates decided their fate.

> Learned Doctors of Divinity raced about the convention hall, Bibles in hand, quoting words of Scripture and waving their fists beneath the noses of disputing brethren who did not know woman's place. Burnet argued woman's subjection was divinely decreed when Eve was created, and he was willing to show all comers the exact passage. Exasperated George Bradburn again sprang to his feet. "Prove to me, gentlemen," he cried with tremendous emphasis, "that your Bible sanctions the slavery of woman—the complete subjugation of one-half of the race to the other—and I should feel that the best work I could do for humanity would be to make a grand bonfire of every Bible in the Universe.[1]

Despite the aid of skillful orators of the caliber of Bradburn and Phillips, the women were denied admission and forced to remain in the gallery as interested spectators. Even a protest, drawn up by Professor Adam of Harvard and signed by several American delegates, was tabled and refused inclusion in the Convention proceedings.

When Garrison arrived, late because he decided to remain at the New York convention until its conclusion, he was angered and refused to participate in the assembly. As a silent protest he sat with the shunted women delegates in the gallery.

Numerous attempts were made to encourage him to join the proceedings on the convention floor. When his name was mentioned, the delegates rose in mass, faced the gallery and applauded wildly. A resolution was passed expressing the unanimous desire of the convention for his participation. The London Committee even sent him a special invitation. None of the attempts moved Garrison, and the convention was forced to continue minus the world's leading abolitionist, a fact duly noted by the local press.

If the attitude and action of the convention proved an insult and affront to women, the occasion of the convention itself furthered the interests of woman's rights by bringing together for the first time Mott, the stately Hicksite Quaker Lucretia Mott, now 47 years old, and the young, energetic and recently married Elizabeth Cady Stanton.

The two women spent many hours together, discussing not only abolition, but, in light of recent events, the subject of women's rights. Stanton, not yet involved in the issue of woman's equality, was greatly impressed with Mott, whom she later claimed gave her a new sense of freedom and dignity and opened up a whole new world of thought for her. She also heard Mott preach in a Unitarian church in London. To hear a woman address an assembly was a new experience for Stanton, and she was to write of the event later: "When at last I saw a woman rise up in the pulpit and preach as earnestly and impressively as Mrs. Mott always does, it seemed to me like the realization of an oft-repeated happy dream."[2]

Their friendship cemented by their shared concerns, both women vowed to organize a woman's rights convention when they returned to the United States. It was a dream which would have to wait eight years for realization, as Mott, beset with illness and family responsibilities, and Stanton, occupied with beginning a family and the demands accompanying her husband's legal studies and new law practice in Boston, could find little time to devote to such an undertaking.

In 1847 the Stantons moved to Seneca Falls, New York. Elizabeth, now the mother of three (four more children would follow) found life narrowed to domestic routine, far less intellectually and socially stimulating than Boston had been. Her resentment built.

It was during this time of personal discontent that a letter arrived from Lucretia Mott inviting her to tea at the nearby home of Mrs. Jane Hunt in Waterloo. It was predictable that the women— Mott, Stanton, Hunt, Martha C. Wright and Mary Ann McClintock— would turn the conversation to the issue of women's rights. They agreed to call a woman's rights convention to be held at Wesleyan Chapel in Seneca Falls the following week, and the following announcement was sent to the *Seneca County Courier*:

WOMAN'S RIGHTS CONVENTION—a convention to discuss
the social, civil and religious rights of woman will be held in
the Wesleyan Chapel, Seneca Falls, N. Y., on Wednesday and
Thursday, the 19th and 20th of July current; commencing at
10 a.m.

The women had few plans that afternoon about the conduct
of the meeting. Only Lucretia Mott was mentioned as a speaker, and
they had agreed only that the first day would be open only to
women, the second open to the general public.

The next day, however, they met at the McClintock home and
drew up an agenda for the convention, a Declaration of Sentiments
patterned after the Declaration of Independence and a set of resolutions which would clearly present their demands. The final draft
was the responsibility of Stanton, who took the initiative in drawing
up the final resolutions. Her inclusion of the right of elective franchise for women angered her husband who refused to attend the
convention because of it. Even Lucretia Mott asked that Stanton
withdraw the demand, but Stanton would not relent and it remained
in the list of resolutions to be adopted by the convention.

On July 19, 1848 what the planners thought would be but a
handful of people turned out to be a crowd of three hundred persons, forty of them men including the Black orator Frederick Douglass, the esteemed Samuel D. Tilman and the ever-sympathetic husband of Lucretia Mott.

Although it was a woman's convention, no woman of the day
had ever chaired an open meeting (contrary to earlier plans men were
allowed to be present at both sessions). The chair was assumed by
James Mott.

Few women present knew the immensity or complexity of
the task which lay before them. If they had, they might have realized at the same time how ill-prepared they were that day to meet
it. Yet, if on July 19, 1848, women possessed few of the technical
skills required for leadership, they did not lack commitment to
sound democratic principles nor sensitivity to the injustices suffered
by their sex.

The meeting opened with Lucretia Mott explaining the purpose of the convention. She was followed by Stanton who read the Declaration of Sentiments and delivered her first public address, an event not without trepidation. After some discussion, minor changes were made in the Declaration.

On the second day the assembly voted on the Declaration and the resolutions. All passed with no opposition, until the ninth or suffrage resolution was presented. Many argued that to pass such a measure at this time would doom the movement before it got started. Nevertheless, Stanton with the aid of Frederick Douglass, who, like Stanton, felt it was a necessary right if true equality was to be secured, succeeded in having the resolution accepted. By the end of the convention, over 100 men and women had affixed their names to the Declaration and Resolutions, and Stanton pronounced the convention a success.

The participants at Seneca Falls were well aware that religious prejudice was one of the root issues attending their struggle, and deliberations on the religious issue were very much in evidence as the women present sought to set down concerns and formulate grievances. Indeed, the initial announcement of the meeting had expressly informed its readers that the intent of the convention was to discuss not only the social and civil conditions of women, but the religious condition as well.

Therefore, when convention participants proposed to construct a formal declaration encompassing their goals and outlining their complaints, the religious dimension was included. The Declaration of Sentiments contained among its listed grievances an attack upon religious attitudes which, its authors maintained, enforced woman's present degraded status and subordinate position. It further insisted that man was guilty of propounding a double standard of morality because of these attitudes which resulted in an intolerance of certain behaviors of women while ignoring similar behavior among members of their own sex.

Not only had man unilaterally judged female behavior, the document claimed, but he had "usurped the perogative of Jehovah himself" by "claiming it as his right to assign for her a sphere of action, when that belongs to her conscience and to her God."[3] The outcome of such pomposity on the part of man had destroyed woman's self-confidence and self-respect. It had also succeeded in undermining her will, for woman was now reasonably content in her docility, apathy and dependence upon man.

The Declaration also revealed a sensitivity to the question of woman's participation in the working of the church, noting as a grievance man's "claiming Apostolic authority for her exclusion from the ministry, and, with some exceptions, from any public participation in the affairs of the Church."[4] The Sentiments concluded with a proposal that any active campaign include attempts to enlist support for their ideas in both press and pulpit.

If the Declaration of Sentiments in its adopted form reflected the convention's animosity toward contemporary religious attitudes, the resolutions passed in convention were even more pointed. Of the twelve resolutions drawn up and accepted by the convention, five were expressly directed toward the religion-woman's rights conflict, while the remaining seven contained a noticeable undercurrent of religious belief and concern. Religious ideology was the single, most pervasive concern.

The convention, in resolution form, affirmed woman's inherent equality with man and contended that she be recognized and treated accordingly. The women reasoned that if man chose to accord women moral superiority, and many did, then logic demanded that he also encourage women to actively engage in the speaking and teaching ministry of the church where it would prove beneficial.

Another resolution argued for the abandonment of the double standard approach to morality even more forcefully than the earlier mention in the Declaration. Still another admonished women to awaken from their lethargy, a lethargy which the women insisted had been fostered by distorted traditions and the misappropriation of biblical texts. At the end of the first day of deliberations, the convention issued what might be termed a catch-all resolution.

Grounded firmly in the belief that woman was man's created equal, it argued that since woman was

> ... invested by the Creator with the same capacities, and the same consciousness of responsibility for their exercise, it is demonstrably the right and duty of woman, equallly with man, to promote every righteous cause, by every righteous means; and especially in regard to the great subjects of morals and religion, it is self-evidently her right to participate with her brother in teaching them, both private and in public, by writing and by speaking, by any instrumentalities proper to be used, and in any assemblies proper to be held; and this being a self-evident truth, growing out of the divinely implanted principles of human nature, any custom, or authority adverse to it, whether modern or wearing the hoary sanction of antiquity, is to be regarded as a self-evident falsehood, and at war with mankind.[5]

The resolution was comprehensive in design and undeniably directed toward opponents who argued biblically enforced traditionalism. However, the resolution was not comprehensive enough for Lucretia Mott, and the evening session of the final day brought still another resolution, drafted by Mott. Lest prior resolutions be lacking in candor or their statements too weak or too general to reveal woman's serious commitment to their cause, the Mott resolution informed the convention that success depended upon devotion to and effort on behalf of securing equality for women in all areas of social existence, even to "overthrowing the monopoly of the pulpit."[6]

For an assembly called on such short notice it accomplished a great deal, particularly in setting forth the guideline and directives of a woman's movement. Stanton's insistence that the convention was a success was merited, but few were prepared for what was to follow. What they had understood to be a small parochial meeting gained national attention, and venom poured forth from the press and the nation's pulpits. Many convention attendees were both surprised and perplexed by the infuriated criticism of their efforts at Seneca Falls. A few of the timid and faint-hearted asked that their names be removed from the Declaration of Sentiments. Even

Stanton admitted some fear as editors labelled them Amazons and love-starved spinsters engaged in a petticoat rebellion intent upon demoralizing women and destroying the American family.

As far away as New York City *The Herald* printed the full text of the Declaration, hoping that by doing so it would discredit the women. Stanton was elated; they could have hoped for no better means of disseminating their views.

Greeley's *New York Tribune*, as was to be the case in succeeding years, attempted some objectivity. Though personally adverse to the women's demands, he nevertheless recognized it as a natural right. He would later open up the columns of the *Tribune* to Stanton and other feminist activists.

What the women suspected would be a quiet beginning had produced a verbal earthquake. Those women who remained undaunted by the derision agreed to call another meeting two weeks later at the Unitarian Church in Rochester. The women's movement had officially begun.

Notes

[1]Lloyd C. M. Hare. *The Greatest American Woman: Lucretia Mott* (New York: Negro Universities, 1937), pp. 132-33.

[2]*Eminent Women of the Age: Being Narratives of the Lives and Deeds of the Most Prominent Women of the Present Generation*, eds. James Parton and others (Hartford: S. M. Betts, 1869), p. 372.

[3]*Proceedings of the Woman's Rights Conventions Held At Seneca Falls and Rochester, N. Y., July and August, 1848*, (1870; rpt. New York: Arno, 1969), p. 7.

[4]*Ibid.*, pp. 6-7.

[5]*Ibid.*, pp. 4-5.

[6]*Ibid.*, p. 9.

Chapter V

Be It Resolved . . . .

When the women met for a second convention in Rochester, New York on August 2, 1848 to consider the rights of women, "politically, religiously and industrially,"[1] significant organizational changes had occurred. The group of women who had planned the meeting determined that, unlike the Seneca Falls meeting, this convention would be presided over by women and accordingly proposed the Quaker Abigail Bush for President, Laura Murray for Vice President and Elizabeth McClintock, Sarah Hallowell and Catherine A. F. Stebbins as secretaries. McClintock immediately declined the office on the ground that the convention was ill-prepared for female officers. Even Stanton and Mott refused to participate for the same reason, until the competence of Ms. Bush reversed their objection. From that day forward the women conducted their conventions without male assistance.

The Rochester convention was primarily a reiteration of the Seneca Falls assembly. The Seneca Falls Declaration with its attached resolutions was reread and, after considerable discussion and debate, approved. The suffrage amendment secured an even greater margin of victory. New resolutions were also introduced, and once again religious prejudices were addressed. In resolution form the women deplored the attitude of apathy and indifference evidenced on the part of many women and blamed it for her "inferior position in social, religious, and political life."[2] They also resolved that it was the "duty of woman, whatever her complexion, to assume, as soon as possible, her true position of equality in the social circle, the church, and the state."[3]

Once again clerical opposition was very vocal following the

convention proceedings. Elizabeth Stanton's plea that disagreements be voiced in the convention hall and not later from the pulpit when convention members had little chance of rebuttal did nothing to stem the tide of ecclesiastical diatribe. The Reverend Byron Sunderland of nearby Syracuse, later a chaplain of the United States Senate, preached a derogatory sermon, taking for his text, "The woman shall not wear that which pertaineth unto man; neither shall a man put on a woman's garment; for all that do so are an abomination to the Lord thy God" (Deut. 22.5). He reprimanded the women and accused them of seeking to topple Christianity itself. Their assertion that Christianity was wrong in its heretofore expressed interpretations was a challenge so grave that it might eventually throw the whole of Christendom back into another dark ages. To admit that the Bible might be wrong in regard to the status accorded women opened a Pandora's box for Sunderland. Was it not possible, he argued, for religious skeptics and infidels to now question whether it was equally wrong in any matter they so chose to scrutinize and reject? Sunderland further maintained that to deny the efficacy of the Bible was to deny Christ himself, and therefore "the believer in woman's rights, like the Abolitionist, was anti-Christ and the Devil's agent. Lucretia (Mott) and her associates were vicious women!"[4]

Although opponents like Sunderland reacted to the full deliberations of the convention, it was often the resolutions passed in convention which comprised the most important elements in convention proceedings, as the women developed the convention resolution into an effective and precise statement of their demands. Indeed, the passage of resolutions more than anything else served to infuriate their oppositon, producing venomous denunciations in the press and equally virulent tirades from the nation's pulpits. Unfortunately, at times they also served to foster internal tension and debate.

In Worcester, Massachusetts in October of 1850, women began the practice of calling annual national women's conventions, a practice that would continue until the outbreak of the Civil War when women's concerns would be somewhat altered. The only exception to the above practice was the year 1857. Like the earlier conventions, the national conventions continued to issue resolutions with regularity; and, just as often, to defend them against the abusive reactions of anti-feminists.

By the time the third national woman's rights convention met in Syracuse, New York, September, 1852, American feminists were both adamant and eloquent in their stance against ecclesiastical suppression and the vehemence which greeted them from America's pulpits.

Letters poured into the Convention to be read before the entire body of delegates. Elizabeth Cady Santon wrote, and her letter was read by a young woman attending a woman's rights convention for the first time—Susan B. Anthony. "In her present ignorance, woman's religion, instead of making her noble and free, by the wrong application of great principles of right and justice, has made her bondage but more certain and lasting, her degradation more helpless and complete,"[5] warned Stanton. The warning, in rudimentary form here, was to be carefully developed by Stanton in subsequent years as she came to view the church as more and more a barrier to the success of woman's rights. The notion would also later alienate her from many women in the movement.

The Reverend A. D. Mayo also wrote to assure the convention that he was an ardent supporter of the principle of female equality. His conviction was based upon scripture, and his letter informed the women that he entertained the belief in sexual equality not simply because he believed in woman's rights per se, but because he adhered to the Chritstian religion, a religion which he knew recognized "neither male nor female" in its claim upon an individual's conscience.

This convention, like its predessors, produced great reaction in the press, both locally and as far away as New York City. The immediate stimulus was a resolution proposed by the Reverend Antoinette Brown, a Congregationalist minister and graduate of Oberlin College. Her resolution requested that the convention, en masse, acknowledge that "the Bible recognizes the rights, privileges and duties of woman as a public teacher, as in every way equal with those of man; that it enjoins upon her no subjection that is not enjoined upon him; and that it truly and practically recognizes neither male nor female in Christ Jesus."[6] In and of itself the resolution was not radical in make-up and reflected little beyond what had previously been articulated in former convention deliberations. Its straight-forwardness was welcomed by some, while others felt it represented a step too premature and too dangerous for the convention to endorse. Despite the articulated hesitation of a few of the convention members, the resolution might have passed had it not challenged by the religious skeptic Ernestine Rose.

After a good deal of debate had passed on the resolution, Rose, a Polish immigrant and severe critic of religion, took the floor to proclaim that Brown's interpretation of scripture evidenced in the resolution was solely that of her own construction and thus no better nor worse than any other interpretation. Since this was the case, she declared, it could not be construed as reflective of the opinions of all convention delegates and, thus, did not merit adoption by the convention as the official and formal doctrine of the convention. Rose, of course, personally rejected both the biblical interpretations of anti-feminists and fellow woman's rights advocates, preferring to argue the feminist issue solely on a platform of human rights and freedom, which she in turn based on the fundamental laws of humanity. For that, she stated, "we require no written authority from Moses or Paul, because those laws and our claim are prior even to these two great men."[7]

Rose's challenge was convincing and the Brown resolution was defeated, but this fact did not stay the press from violent denunciation and ridicule. *The Syracuse Star* labelled the convention the "Tomfoolery Convention" and described its participants as "poor creatures who take part in the silly rant of " 'brawling women' " and Aunt Nancy men [who] are most of them " 'ismizers' " of the rankest stamp, Abolitionists of the most frantic and contemptible kind and Christian sympathizers with such heretics as William Lloyd Garrison, Parker Pillsbury, C. C. Burleigh and Stephen Foster, . . . all woman's righters and preachers of such damnable doctrines and accursed heresies as would make demons of the pit shudder to hear."[8] The newspaper closed its account with a selection of biblical passages for the consideration and enlightenment of convention 'heretics.'

The New York Herald, in an editorial of September 12, 1852, spared no abuse either as it called the entire convention a farce. Its editorial informed readers that the Christian code, as revealed in the Bible, had been voted down by the ladies at the Syracuse convention, and the laws of nature erected in its place. A biased editorial it was, and one wonders what its writer might have discoursed upon had the Brown resolution found favor with the convention attendees. No doubt the women would have fared equally as well!

Months after the convention had adjourned, the pulpit and press continued to condemn the proceedings of the assembly. The Reverend Sunderland preached yet another sermon of condemnation, this time refering to the gathering as the "Bloomer Convention" in reference to the new style of dress some women in the movement had lately adopted. His fellow cleric at Syracuse's St. Paul's Episcopal Church, The Reverend Ashley, also directed an invective against the principle of woman's equality. These enraged ecclesiastics did not limit themselves to verbal attack from the pulpit alone. Ashley's sermon was printed in pamphlet form and circulated throughout the state, while others published their derogations in the always receptive *Syracuse Star*.

As in previous times, the women were hindered in replying to the accusations. Their attempts to have articles published in rebuttal were stonily accepted by editors, then ignored and never printed.

The fury of press and pulpit did not intimidate the women, however; nor did it stop them from calling future national conventions. Consequently, it did not restrain those conventions from issuing additional resolutions bent on challenging religious beliefs condemning of woman's equality. Some later resolutions, one might reasonably opine, were intentionally composed to incite opposition.

Two years after Syracuse, the women held their annual national convention in Philadelphia. The presence of the always incendiary Garrison made it a memorable event in the annals of the woman's movement.

At the close of a debate on the biblical position of women,

Garrison rose to offer two resolutions. Both would be unanimously adopted despite their inflammatory rhetoric. The first, although it noted exceptions, declared "that the most determined opposition it (the woman's movement) encounters is from the clergy generally, whose teachings of the Bible are intensely inimical to the equality of woman and man."[9] The second resolution continued where the first left off and was aimed squarely at the Bible itself. No book, whatever its teaching, claimed priority over the rights of human beings, whatever their race or sex, declared Garrison. Garrison suggested that this type of deification of the Bible lay behind much of the anti-feminist animosity.

With the passage of these Garrisonian resolutions in 1854, the woman's rights movement had formally pitted itself against established orthodoxy and centuries of ecclesiastical traditionalism. Yet the use of resolutions in the woman's rights-religion controversy continued. It might even be said that the resolution was vital to the ongoing ideological confrontation. As late as 1878, the woman's movement was still in the midst of defining its position vis a vis the church and theological dogma with the use of convention resolutions. However, by this time the language used had become both explicit and uncompromising to an extreme degree.

In the National Woman's Suffrage Association's annual meeting in Rochester, New York, July 19, 1878, Matilda Joselyn Gage introduced ten resolutions—three were directed at the church itself. The first maintained that the "lessons of self-sacrifice and obedience taught woman by the Christian Church have been fatal, not only to her own vital interests, but through her, to those of race." Another admonished women to claim the Reformation principle of individual conscience and thus be guided in scriptural interpretation by reason, not simply by what the ecclesiastical structure pronounced as authoritative. The third resolution, like the first and reminiscent of earlier convention resolutions, contended that religious teachings had concentrated to such an extent on cajoling women about the rewards of a future existence that women now ignored present responsibilities and thus "she (woman) and the children she has trained have been so completely subjugated by priestcraft and superstition."[11]

The Gage resolutions provoked clerics throughout New York State. One of the more vocal and vehement in response was The Reverend A. H. Strong, president of the Baptist Theological Seminary in Rochester. In a sermon he spoke of the many benefits Christianity had procured for the female sex, but continued to uphold the theory of common law, which insisted that husband and wife were one in the eyes of the law—that "one" being the husband. A woman who allowed herself to be convinced of anything as absurd as the right to vote, he warned his congregation, jeopardized her dignity and teetered on the brink of disgrace· and wickedness."[12]

The feminist paper *The National Citizen* countered by disclaiming Strong's views, which, it asserted, were most assuredly founded upon a gross misunderstanding of scripture and church history. Had not theology and the church, in their penchant for punishing through torture and persecution those who dissented from their cherished opinions, claimed among their victims a vast number of women? Strong's views were designed, according to *The Citizen*, to cripple woman's conscience and self-will in a deliberate attempt to keep her in a state of slavery.

Two years later, religion still claimed a position of priority in convention deliberations. When the Twelfth Annual Convention of the National Woman's Suffrage Association met in Lincoln Hall, Washington, D. C., January 21-22, 1880, a resolution of major importance was offered for convention approval. Introduced by Sara Andrews Spencer, it soundly condemned the masculine monopoly of the pulpit.

> Resolved, That the assumption of the clergy, that woman has no right to participate in the ministry and offices of the church is unauthorized theocratic tyranny, placing a masculine mediator between woman and her God, which finds no authority in reason, and should be resisted by all women as an odious form of religious persecution.[13]

Still the women had not finished with the practice of hurling resolutions at the church and its minions, or so it seemed in 1885, when religion again played a prominent role in the composition of convention resolutions. Unlike previous conventions however, the resolutions did not fare as well and were ultimately tabled; the climate had changed somewhat.

Written by Clara Bewick Colby of Nebraska, they were read to the convention body by Elizabeth C. Stanton.

> WHEREAS, The dogmas incorporated in the religious creeds derived from Judaism, teaching that woman was an afterthought in creation, her sex a misfortune, marriage a condition of subordination, and maternity a curse, are contrary to the law of God as revealed in nature and the precepts of Christ; and, WHEREAS, These dogmas are an insidious poison, sapping the vitality of our civilization, blighting woman and palsaying humanity; therefore, Resolved, That we denounce these dogmas wherever they are enunciated, and we will withdraw our personal support from any organization so holding and teaching; and,
> Resolved, That we call upon the Christian ministry, as leaders of thought, to teach and enforce the fundamental idea of creation that man was made in the image of God, male and female, and given equal dominion over the earth, but none over each other. And further we invite their co-operation in securing the recognition of the cardinal point of our creed, that in true religion there is neither male nor female, neither bond nor free, but all are one.[14]

Although the resolutions were rather terse statements of conviction, they were, at the same time, little more than restatements of earlier convention pronouncements. The language may have been sharper, or blunter, but there were no surprising innovations of thought. Yet, unlike earlier resolutions, they produced discussion of such magnitude that debate carried into the following day.

Friends were pitted against friends. Stanton, speaking in favor of adoption, asserted that women must now *demand* equal rights within the church structure, which, she insisted, women had previously possessed in the first three centuries of the church's existence. Susan B. Anthony, an old cohort of Stanton's, alined with resolution opponents and thus against her longtime friend. Anthony, admitting her old Garrisonian bias, denied that the question of human rights could be settled on the basis of biblical interpretation, for no two exegesis were alike. In this she also echoed the words of Ernestine Rose at the 1852 convention. One of the woman's goals, she conceded, was unquestionably equality in the church, but a discussion designed to elicit responsibility for perpetuated dogmas could not possibly serve the interests of the movement. "Let those who wish go back into the history of the past (sic), but I beg it shall not be done on our platform,"[15] requested Anthony.

Others clustered about the Anthony faction. Some defended the Bible; others, the church. The most convincing argument proved to be the one advanced by Harriette R. Shattuck of Massachusetts, who stated that the church was becoming more and more receptive to the issue of woman's rights and to antagonize them now would be foolhardy. It was an argument which would play an increasingly decisive role in future controversies.

Despite the able arguments of Colby in defense of her resolutions and those of Pennsylvanian Edward M. Davis, the opponents were clearly the majority. Even Davis' insistence that the movement take a definitive stand on the subject since not one religious body had ventured to do so seemed to fall on deaf ears.

In a last desperate attempt to reclaim defectors, Stanton spoke with great conviction, averring that religion, wherever it was found and in whatever form it appeared, proved to be the most important factor in woman's degradation. How were women to shed the shackles which had chained them for centuries if they were now unwilling to attack the issue at its source, she asked. Cataloguing the offenses perpetrated by the church against womanhood, she concluded, "We want to help roll off from the soul of woman the terrible superstitions that have so long repressed and crushed her."[16] That she thought the disputed resolutions a step in the right direction was understandable, but even this eloquent plea was futile. Opponents tabled the resolutions.

At this point, the matter might have utterly vanished from the floor of future national conventions had Stanton been a woman possessed of a less stuborn nature. For another ten years she would press the matter, refusing to allow conventions to ignore it.

When the annual convention met the following year, again in Washington, D. C. as had become the practice of the National Woman's Suffrage Association now distinct from its sister organization the American Woman Suffrage Association, Stanton proposed yet another resolution, this time via letter. Read in the first executive session, the resolution specifically recommended in very strong language that the "question of woman suffrage should now be carried into the churches and church conventions for their approval, and that more enlightened teaching from the pulpit in regard to women should be insisted upon."[17]

Helen M. Gougar, a member of the committee from Indiana, moved immediately that the resolution be tabled and not brought before the convention. She cited the debate of 1885 as having "done more to cripple my work and that of other suffragists than anything which has happened in the whole history of the woman suffrage movement."[18] She insisted that the Association was for suffrage and not to discuss religious dogma. To engage in the latter could only be interpreted as overt antagonism of factions which the women now hoped to convert to the cause of woman's rights.

Opinion in the committee divided, and argument ensued. Some asserted that the church could no longer be regarded as an enemy although they were willing to concede that such might have been the case during Stanton's early days in the movement. They now insisted it was growing ever more cooperative and reflected a less hostile attitude toward the movement. Another executive argued that the resolution should be amended in such a way as to antagonize and alarm no one. Still another deplored "this fling at masculine interpretation of the Scripture."[19]

Stanton was not without supporters either. Clara Colby and Edward Davis, proponents of the defeated resolutions of the preceding year, rallied to her side. Convinced of the merit of Stanton's proposal, Colby maintained that Stanton was demanding nothing more in her resolution than earlier feminists had demanded of the movement in its confrontations with the state. The only noticeable difference in Colby's mind was that Stanton had now substituted the church in place of the state. Davis, fully resolved to Stanton's

observation that the church presented the most formidable barrior
to woman's progress, assured dissenters that Stanton's resolution not
only deserved their undivided attention, but constituted the most
important issue then facing the convention.

Failing to achieve a consensus or to table the proposal, the
Executive Committee, upon a motion by Anthony, decided to refer
the entire matter to the whole convention. Surprisingly, when the
final vote was taken in the convention, the Stanton resolution passed with a vote of 32 to 24. Opponents maintained that it carried
only because the convention was not properly constituted as a dele-
gate body, and they hastened to correct the oversight. Before the
convention had adjourned, it had reorganized with only accredited
delegates entitled to vote.

I think it only fair to mention that Stanton's insistence that
women take their cause directly to the ecclesia was not an extraordinary demand in light of the movement's history. Seneca Falls
had demanded just that, and repeated attempts had been made to
actively enlist clerical support for woman's rights throughout the
history of woman's rights activities. Most overtures had failed dis-
mally. However, Harriet Robinson in her book *Massachusetts in the
Woman Suffrage Movement* records one story of success, or partial
success. It occurred in 1880 or five years prior to the Colby-Stanton
resolutions in 1885. It merits attention here because, unlike previous futile efforts, it foreshadowed a new spirit abroad in orthodoxy—the same spirit later acknowledged by Stanton's opponents.

The Massachusetts Woman's Suffrage Association issued a
memorial to the Methodist, Baptist and Unitarian churches of Boston, asking responsible clergymen to bring the question of woman
suffrage before their respective congregations. Only the Methodists
responded, including the then President of Boston University who
took the affirmative. In the Association's annual minutes the following year, six of twenty-four speakers (fully one-fourth) were Methodist clergymen. Clerics from other orthodox churches were to
follow in significant numbers. There was definitely a new spirit of
liberalism evidenced in the churches.

The movement had, of course, never lacked support from Universalists, Unitarians, Transcendentalists, Quakers and Free Religionists, but the main branches of Christendom had contributed only a handful of courageous individuals during the early decades of the movement. Now, it appeared that after thirty years of organized struggle the women's movement had finally secured a powerful ally.

Courageous individuals had given way to formal, corporate action. In 1874 the annual conference of Michigan's Methodist State Association, under the promptings of Bishop Gilbert Haven, had petitioned Michigan's state legislature to admit women of the state to elective franchise. The same year the annual conference of the Methodist Episcopal Church in Des Moines, Iowa, again prodded by Bishop Haven, passed several resolutions in favor of woman suffrage. Iowa's Universalist Association followed, resolving in its state convention that women were entitled to all social, religious and political rights then accorded to the male sex.

Many denominations also took steps to liberalize restrictions upon woman members. The Episcopal Church, at a Diocesan Convention in Davenport, Iowa, voted to remove the word "male" from the canon and therefore allow women to vote for vestrymen. A small step, perhaps, but a significant one for that body in 1881. In 1882, the Ministerial Association of Des Moines even went as far as to pledge in resolution form not only their personal support of woman's suffrage, but also to further its cause from their pulpits. Such activities understandably tended to mitigate Stanton's charge that the church loomed before the movement as the last great obstacle to woman's progress.

Stanton, however, refused to yield, this even though she herself was often welcomed in pulpits throughout the nation by enthusiastic parishioners and often had her sermons reprinted in local newspapers. Why she remained so unrelenting in her stance and nearly obsessed with the belief that the church constituted the single greatest barrier to the realization of woman's full equality is difficult to understand. However, one explanation may lie in her impatience and her unwillingness to abdicate a fight until the battle had been *fully* won. Yet another reason may be her early confrontations with religion and the religious establishment. She writes of an extremely telling incident which occurred when she was a young woman attending the Emma Willard Female Seminary in Troy, New York and had the opportunity to hear the great revivalist preacher Charles G. Finney:

> I can see him now, his great eyes rolling around the congregation, and his arms flying in the air like a windmill. One evening he described Hell and the Devil so vividly, that the picture glowed before my eyes in the dark for months afterwards. On another occasion, when describing the damned as wandering in the Inferno, and inquiring their way through avenues, he suddenly pointed with his finger, exclaiming "There! do you not see them?" and I actually jumped up in the church and looked around,—his description had been such a reality.[20]

Finney's preaching so terrified her that she left Willard's Seminary and returned home, plagued by nightmares which drove her repeatedly to her parents' bedroom for consolation and assurance "lest I should be cast into hell before morning."[21]

Though some, like Theodore Tilton, maintained that Stanton never lost her childhood faith in God, Stanton herself maintained otherwise and once wrote that she was "never happy in that gloomy faith which dooms to eternal misery the greater part of the human family. It was no comfort to me to be saved with a chosen few, while the multitude, and those too who had suffered most on earth, were to have no part in heaven."[22]

Whatever might have been the cause of Stanton's mounting attack on organized religion, it now stemmed from a firmly entrenched conviction. So deeply committed to the appraisal was Stanton that when the now reunited National-American Woman's Suffrage Convention met in Washington in 1891, her mailed address from England once again broached the subject. Her annual address, now customary at the insistence of President Susan B. Anthony, was entitled "The Degradation of Disfranchisement" and reaffirmed her former belief that scripture and church canon were true villains. Both were in need of extensive revision. The argument from divine authority needed to be devastated, Stanton declared, though to do so "would compel an entire change in church canons, discipline, authority, and many doctrines of the Christian faith."[23] Stanton was never one to do anything halfway!

Unlike former conventions, the address produced little comment; the silence itself telling. The younger women did not welcome her caustic messages, and even Anthony had repeatedly cautioned her old friend to stick more closely to the issue of woman suffrage. Stanton, it must be noted, had always argued for a broadening of convention interests.

The final rebuff to Stanton, however, was to come five years later after the publication of her *Woman's Bible*. Although the work was primarily a result of her own efforts, with minor contributions from other feminists and her daughter Harriet Stanton Blatch, the National Association felt her position as honorary president might link the production to the Association in the public mind. If this did occur, they reasoned that it would do irreparable damage to suffrage efforts, alienating many women whom they sought to enlist in the movement. Thus a committee resolution was introduced in an attempt to segregate Mrs. Stanton's book from the Association: "This association is non-sectarian, being composed of persons of all shades of religious opinion, and has no official connection with the so-called " 'Woman's Bible' " or any theological publication."[24]

The resolution created a long, often intense, debate on the convention floor. Among those supporting the measure were some of the most distinguished figures in the ranks of the woman's rights movement—Henry B. Blackwell and his daughter Alice Stone Blackwell, Carrie Chapman Catt and The Reverend Anna Howard Shaw. Those arguing against the resolution included Clara B. Colby, editor of the *Woman's Tribune* and a tried and true Stanton champion, and Susan B. Anthony, a friend and co-worker of Stanton's for over 45 years. Anthony's lengthy defense of Stanton and her forthright condemnation of the resolution deserves extensive consideration.

Individual opinion had been an integral part of the movement in spite of earlier accusations that this or that had harmed the cause,

Anthony argued with conviction and emotion. She cited the Ernestine Rose statement of forty years earlier which had rejected plenary inspiration of the scripture as an example and reminded advocates of the present resolution that Rose had not been banished from feminist ranks because of her less-than-popular stance. She also had not been censured, as they proposed now to do to Stanton. It might be noted that one of Rose's strong supporters at the time had been none other than Anthony herself.

Anthony also took the occasion to mention others who had previously disagreed with Stanton on substantial issues but had never taken such radical steps as those presently proposed by the convention. Lucretia Mott had alined against inclusion of Stanton's resolution to insert the demand for franchise in the Seneca Falls Declaration, but she had never thought to introduce a resolution in opposition. And again in 1860, when Stanton had argued before the New York State Legislature that drunkeness should be considered as adequate grounds for divorce, fellow feminists, who insisted that she had doomed the cause of women's rights, had never introduced a vote of censure. Later, of course, Stanton's action was widely accepted. With some emotion Anthony proclaimed, "I distrust those people who know so well what God wants them to do, because I notice it always coincides with their own desires."[25]

What they were actually doing, according to Anthony, was narrowing the field for those who might possibly involve themselves in the cause. She adeptly turned opponents' arguments against them, claiming that not only did a Christain have "neither more nor less rights in our association than the atheist,"[26] but proponents' insistence that orthodoxy would be offended was intolerant rather than tolerant as they maintained. Orthodox members of the woman's rights movement had often conducted themselves in ways Anthony herself had thought harmful to the cause, but she herself had not introduced a resolution of censure condemning that behavior and for the same reason that she could not now censure Stanton.

The issue was not theological belief for Anthony, but freedom of expression. She warned convention attendees that there was an inherent danger in what they proposed for they would establish a

precedent without limits being defined. If Stanton were censured this
year, what would keep herself or one of them from being subjected
to a similar fate next year.

Her remarks concluded with an unabashed personal defense
of Stanton, whom she doubted was fully appreciated by some of
the younger convention members.

> I pray you vote for religious liberty, without censure upon a
> woman who is without a peer in intellectual and statesman-
> like ability; one who has stood for half a century the acknow-
> ledged leader of progressive thought and demand in regard to
> all matters pertaining to the absolute freedom of women.[27]

The convention, now more fearful of alienating Christian
orthodoxy and the press than alienating one old woman voted 53
to 41 in favor of censure. Anthony was disappointed though she
understood the reasons behind the vote. Although she had argued
admirably in Stanton's defense and in defense of religious liberty,
she had also sensed a growing chasm developing between herself and
Stanton. In an earlier letter to Clara Colby, who had praised the
Woman's Bible in her *Woman's Tribune*, Anthony admitted that she
was not proud of Stanton's latest effort; even its spirit was short-
sighted according to Anthony. She rued the fact that Stanton had
changed, was now "flippant and superficial," and regarded her
(Anthony's) "judgment worth nothing more than that of any other
narrow-souled body . . . ."[28] Without denying Stanton's growing
animosity to religion, one suspects that the movement had changed
much more than the convictions of Stanton.

When the convention verdict swung against Stanton, Anthony
hurried to New York to meet with her. Stanton, noticeably indignant at the rebuff, advised that they both resign and repudiate the
entire organization they had worked so many years to build. This
was a much too drastic step for Anthony, though she later severely
reprimanded the younger women who had pushed the resolution
through the convention and requested Stanton's presence at the next
convention in hopes of reversing the decision. It was never reversed.

Though she never went on record as an advocate of the *Woman's Bible*, Anthony came close to defending it on several occasions. Once in reply to a reporter's question, she responded, "I think women have just as good a right to interpret and twist the Bible to their own advantage as men have always twisted and turned it to theirs."[29]

The convention resolution had been used by the women for decades as an excellent means for summarizing their grievances and placing them before the public mind. It had also proven to be an equally effective weapon with which to repeatedly challenge the narrow-minded traditionalism of opponents. It is ironical that it should ultimately be used against Stanton, the woman who drafted the first convention resolution fifty years earlier in Seneca Falls.

Notes

[1]*Proceedings of the Woman's Rights Conventions Held at Seneca Falls and Rochester, N. Y., July and August, 1848*, (1870; rpt. New York: Arno, 1969), title page.

[2]*Ibid.*, p. 15.

[3]*Ibid.*

[4]Lloyd C. M. Hare, *The Greatest American Woman: Lucretia Mott* (New York: Negro Universities, 1937), I, p. 203.

[5]Ida Husted Harper, *The Life and Work of Susan B. Anthony* (1898; rpt. New York: Arno, 1969), I, 77.

[6]*Ibid.*, pp. 76-77.

[7]*Ibid.*, p. 77.

[8]*Ibid.*, pp. 77-78.

[9]William Lloyd Garrison address to National Woman's Suffrage Association Convention in 1854, *HWS*, I (1881), 383.

[10]Resolution introduced by M. J. Gage at N. W. S. A. Convention in Rochester in 1878, *HWS*, eds. E. C. Stanton, Susan B. Anthony and M. J. Gage, III (New York: Susan B. Anthony, 1886), 124.

[11]*Ibid.*

[12]A. H. Strong response to Gage resolutions at N. W. S. A. Convention, 1878, *HWS*, III (1886), 125-26.

[13]Resolution introduced by Sara A. Spencer at N. W. S. A. Convention in Washington, D. C., 1880, *HWS*, III (1886), 152.

[14]Clara B. Colby resolutions introduced by E. C. Stanton at N. W. S. A. Convention, 1885, *HWS*, eds. S. Anthony and I. H. Harper, IV (New York: Susan B. Anthony, 1902), 58-59.

[15]Susan B. Anthony address at N. W. S. A. Convention, 1885, *HWS*, IV (1902), 59.

[16]*Ibid.*, p. 61.

[17]Resolution of E. C. Stanton to N. W. S. A. Convention in Washington, D. C., 1886, *HWS*, IV (1902), 75.

[18]Helen M. Gougar response to E. C. Stanton resolution 1886, *HWS*, IV (1901), 75.

[19]Harriette Shattuck comment on E. C. Stanton resolution, 1886, *HWS*, IV (1902), 76.

[20]*Eminent Women of the Age*, eds. James Parton and others (Hartford: S. M. Betts, 1869), p. 342.

[21]*Ibid.*

[22]*Ibid.*, pp. 342-43.

[23]E. C. Stanton address to N-A. W. S. A. Convention in Washington, D. C., 1891, *HWS*, IV (1902), 177.

[24]Resolution introduced in N-A. W. S. A. Convention, 1896, in response to Stanton's Woman's Bible, *HWS*, IV (1902), 263.

[25]S. B. Anthony defense of Stanton at 1896 Convention, *HWS*, IV (1902), 263.

[26]*Ibid.*

[27]*Ibid.*, p. 264.

[28]Alma Lutz, *Susan B. Anthony: Rebel Crusader and Humanitarian* (Boston: Beacon Press, 1959), p. 279.

[29]*Ibid.*, p. 280.

Chapter VI

The Convention as Religious Forum

The convention resolution was not the only vehicle for the expression of religious convictions in national assemblies. Letters to convention bodies, if accumulated, would read like a Who's Who among woman's rights advocates. Speeches also abounded, and debates were not infrequent. The latter usually arose in response to a challenge from the floor of the convention.

While it is not possible, nor the intent of the author, to record every religious argument voiced in convention, a number deserve mention, if not for the arguments cited, for the personages who engaged in them. They exemplify the movement's attempts to confront more directly what would become the most forceful argument against the woman's struggle—woman's alleged trespass of divine imperative.

Seneca Falls passed with no major challenges voiced in the convention. Apart from some disagreement on the proposed demand for elective franchise, the assembled, who came because of curiosity or conviction, manifested a surprising consensus on issues. This would not be the case in future conventions.

Less than a month later at Syracuse opposition was present and vocal. After the Declaration of Sentiments was read, Stanton invited opponents to voice their objections rather than save them for later denunciation in the pulpit. A Mr. Colton from Connecticut acceded to Stanton's request and delivered a disquisition about woman's proper sphere which he insisted was the home, not the political arena and definitely not the pulpit.

Lucretia Mott, often the first to reply to such attacks, accused

Colton, and fellow women also, of listening too much to clerical directive rather than fully appreciating the Bible, which she maintained did not prohibit a woman from serving as a religious instructor if she so chose. She thought it wise for Colton to consult his Bible again before pursuing his argument.

A number of other challenges were addressed to the franchise demand. William Bloss, maintaining that there were natural dissimilarities in the dispositions of the sexes, doubted if women would desire to exercise the right even if it were granted them. And Milo Codding claimed that women could vote effectively enough through the balloting of father, brothers or husband.

The arguments were met by Frederick Douglass and a young woman named Rebecca M. Sandford. Douglass maintained that rights rested on the capacity of individuals, not sexual differences, and declared that he would never claim a right which he was not willing to grant women as well. The question of the franchise was not one of whether woman would use the right or not, but whether men had the right to withhold it from her. Sandford, with her husband standing silently nearby, ridiculed the assertion that women were incapable of responsibly exercising the franchise. Instead, she declared that it would redeem woman's pawned integrity and thus turn her from frivolous pursuits and fickle behavior to more responsible activities. Claiming that women had "an equality of exertion, and a right to use all the sources of erudition within the reach of man, to build unto herself a name for her talents, energy and integrity," she insisted: "We do not positively say that our intellect is as capable as man's to assume, and at once to hold, these rights, or that our hearts are as willing to enter into his actions; for if we did not believe it, we would not contend for them, and if men did not believe it, they would not withhold them with a smothered silence."[1]

The last session of the convention produced yet another argument on the floor of the convention when a Mr. Sulley averred that granting equality to women would do extensive damage to the family, setting husband against wife. He enjoined the Pauline stricture calling for a woman's obedience to her husband. He was joined in his argument by a Mr. Pickard who felt that the demands expressed by the women would produce an impossible situation with regard to such things as property rights, which the biblical unity of the married pair now recognized in the legal structure avoided.

Both Mott and Stanton rose to the defense. Stanton maintained that the gospel rightly understood spoke of a oneness of equality and that property could and should be jointly held. There was no reason marriage should prove a degradation for women. Mott once again insisted that the Bible did not condemn feminist activity, but rather sustained it. Paul gave directions for woman's appearance when speaking publicly. Honorable women like Phoebe, Priscilla, Tryphena, Triphosa and the four daughters of Philip had engaged in public address and religious instruction. Opponents of woman's rights were essentially illogical, she concluded, for while imposing Pauline commands silencing woman's speaking, they neglected Paul's advice to abstain from marriage. Why, she asked, were men so anxious to follow Paul as a guide to all social problems which concerned women and to reject his council when it referred to them.

Another debate of some magnitude arose at the Second Annual Woman's Rights Convention in Worcester, Massachusetts in October, 1851. This time the women found an able defender in Wendell Phillips. Despite occasional interruptions by hissing from the audience, Phillips spoke at great length in support of the woman's cause.

Charging that the woman's movment stood in the historical mainstream of reform and against the organized selfishness of human nature, he likened the charge that women were unfit for assumption of the rights they demanded to the papacy charge in the Reformation that the masses were unfit to read the Bible for themselves. Like Luther he demanded they should be allowed to try.

> Throw open the doors of Congress, throw open those court houses, throw wide open the doors of your colleges, and give to the sisters of the Motts and the Somervilles the same opportunities for culture that men have, and let the result prove what their capacity and intellect really are. When, I say, woman

has enjoyed, for as many centuries as we have, the aid of books, the discipline of life, and the stimulus of fame, it will be time to begin the discussion of these questions,—"What is the intellect of woman? Is it equal to that of man?" Till then, all such discussion is mere beating of the air.[2]

According to Phillips the true sphere of woman was not some predetermined divine appointment, but the result of the exercise of talents and capacities of each individual woman. They were not physiologically inferior; it was the distorted notions held by men and women which had made one-half of the sex invalids. If they were allowed to exercise their abilities unrestricted, he procalimed that nine hundred and ninety-nine women out of a thousand would abandon supercilious daintiness.

Two years later at the annual convention held in Cleveland another floor debate interrupted the deliberations of the convention. A succinct defense of woman's rights was presented by no less a debater than the indomitable Lucretia Mott.

The stage was set for the confrontation when the convention attempted to set forth practical measures for the dissemination of its beliefs—a procedure recommended by the renowned Unitarian minister William Henry Channing in a letter addressed to the convention. His letter, read to the assembled convention by Antoinette Brown, presented a comprehensive list of concerns which he thought worthy of inclusion in a circular outlining woman's rights. The ninth right listed contended that women, "As members of Christian churches and congregations, heirs of Heaven and children of God, [ought] . . . to preach the truth, to administer the rites of baptism, communion, and marriage, to dispense charities, and in every way to quicken and refine the religious life of individuals in society."[3]

Such a blatant demand for what amounted to the travesty of established custom led to a lively, protracted debate and, eventually, brought a number of anti-feminists to their feet to warn the woman's righters that such a stance might lead them to embrace atheism, as they would be thrown ill-prepared into the rough waters of the outside world.

Mott labelled their argument a "man of straw" and demanded to know by what right orthodoxy designated those who entertained diverse opinions infidel. She answered her own question—inference! After affirming her adherence to the Bible and its truth, as she had many times earlier, she professed no love of biblical errors. The Bible could be abused, used irrationally to infer and corroborate many things, but, she claimed, it was also a book which could withstand any intelligent examination. In a sarcastic slap at convention critics she charged, "It is a far less dangerous assertion to say that God is unchangeable, than that man is infallible."[4] To Mott's mind their criticism rested not on the truths of scripture, but on the distortions devised and perpetuated by male translators.

A year later when the annual convention was held in Philadelphia a similar debate broke out on the floor of the convention. Once again Lucretia Mott supplied the defense, with some able assistance from Tracy Cutler, Thomas W. Higginson and the explosive William Lloyd Garrison.

The debate began when The Reverend Henry Grew of Philadelphia, father of feminist Mary Grew, took the platform and announced his disagreement with convention sentiments. Quoting passage after passage of scripture, he sought to convince convention members that the Bible consistently and quite plainly taught woman's subjection to man and man's right to exercise power and authority over women.

Cutler's response was lengthy and managed to employ all of Grew's quoted texts to sustain the opposite viewpoint. Woman must read and interpret scripture for herself, admonished Cutler,

> . . . for too long have we learned God's will from the lips of man and closed our eyes on the great book of nature, and the safer teaching of our own souls. It is a pity that those who would recommend the Bible as the revealed will of the all-wise and benevolent Creator, should uniformly quote it on the side of tyranny and oppression. I think we owe it to our religion and ourselves to wrest it from such hands, and proclaim the beautiful spirit breathed through all its commands and precepts,

instead of dwelling so much on isolated texts that have no
application to our day and generation.[5]

Mott, the next feminist to take the floor, agreed that priestcraft, not Christianity itself, had subjected women. "The veneration
of man has been misdirected, the pulpit has been prostituted, the
Bible has been ill-used,"[6] she declared. Reiterating yet again her
statement of the previous year, she insisted that the Bible was a
much maligned book used repeatedly to corroborate existent evils
and abuses, rather than used as it should be to uphold its embodied
truths. It did not order the silence of women; this Pauline instruction in I Corinthians 14 was solely given to maintain order in the
local Corinthian church. Paul had clearly consented to women
preaching (I Cor. 11.5), and the scripture attested to woman's
assumption of that role (Rom. 16.1, Acts 2, etc.). According to
Mott, only law and public opinion provided fuel for Grew's argument, not biblical pronouncement.

Undaunted by the stringent reprimands, Grew rose again.
This time he condemned the belief that the Christ event had altered
woman's subjection to man (a view held by some and articulated by
Hannah Crocker as early as 1818). Unless women were prepared to
discredit the entire Bible from beginning to end, Grew declared,
they would have to acquiesce and admit that it taught their subjection.

At this point, Higginson entered the debate. He related a story
of a Methodist clergyman who grew despondent after hearing a
Quaker woman speak in meeting. Only when his sixteen year old
daughter pointed out to the distraught cleric in the Greek New
Testament that Philip's four daughters preached did the man's depression lift. Higginson then cautioned Grew to be careful how he
used scripture, for if he did not use it rightly or with reference to its
inherent truths, all arguments build upon it were indefensible.

Still Grew refused to back down in the debate, and it might
have continued had not Garrison blustered into the controversy.
Arguing that biblical opinions regarding woman's rights were of
little concern to the majority of woman's righters, he asserted that

the laws of nature took precedence over whatever texts or books might say. He did recognize the esteem in which the scriptures were held by most Americans though he lamented that such a fact prevented so many from joining the struggle for woman's equality. Since removal of biblical debate from convention proceedings would benefit the movement in his estimation, he question the merits of continuing to bring scripture into the present discussion. He concluded his remarks with what can only be construed as a tirade against the Bible itself:

> Why go to the Bible? What question was ever settled by the Bible? What question of theology or any other department? None that I ever heard of! With this same version of the Bible, and the same ability to read it, we find that it has filled all Christendom with theological confusion. All are Ishmaelites; each man's hand against his neighbor. The human mind is greater than any book, The mind sits in judgment on every book. If there be truth in the book, we take it; if error, we discard it. Why refer this to the Bible? In this country, the Bible has been used to support slavery and capital punishment; while in the old countries, it has been quoted to sustain all manner of tyranny and persecution. All reforms are anti-Bible. We must look at all things rationally. We find women endowed with certain capacities, and it is of no importance if any book denies her such capacities. Would Mr. Grew say that woman can not preach, in the face of such a preacher as LUCRETIA MOTT?[7]

Garrison's remarks were incisive, and deliberately sharp. But he was not the one to deliver the crowning blow to Grew's challenge; that was to come from Grew's own daughter Mary. Rising to discredit her father's charges, she revealed that his stance was hypocritical since he himself did not believe in plenary inspiration. At that point, Mott again rose not only to support the statements of Mary Grew, but to demand to know why Grew had married a second time when such was antithetical to Paul's instruction on marriage. There is no record that Grew replied to either his daughter's assertion or to Mott's question.

The debate itself closed with a general attack upon the clergy, who, according to feminist Emma R. Cole, preached not Christianity, but woman's degradation. If they were correct, which Cole sincerely doubted, and Christ came into the world to proclaim such principles as had been voiced in the convention, then, Cole insisted, Christianity had little to commend itself to American womanhood.

The New York Convention, November 25-26, 1856, provided the setting for another heated debate. On this occasion, the antagonist was a young theology student from Virginia whose name is not recorded. Despite pleas that the student come forward and occupy the lecturn so that all could hear him, he demurred, and much of the debate was lost in the general din of the convention. The general thrust of his argument, however, was grounded in a demand to know whether woman's rights were founded upon nature or revelation.

The student remained dissatisfied when Thomas Higginson replied that both terms involved metaphysical definition and that, since convention members embraced all creeds and no creed, he could not presume to answer for the entire group. The student saw this as a tactic bent upon evading the issue and accused Higginson of contradiction, voicing his own conviction that woman's rights rested on neither nature nor revelation. If they were based on nature, he reasoned, they must be proved universally valid. If, on the other hand, they were founded on revelation, they must necessarily be consistent with the dictates of revelation as evidenced in scripture. The student doubted that woman could substantiate either claim and proceeded to sustain his point with biblical references and his own observation that woman's physical make-up fitted her for motherhood and housewifery rather than the roles of minister, public lecturer or lawyer.

Higginson attempted another response. Gently reprimanding the student for obvious personal attacks, he reaffirmed his individually held belief that woman's rights rested upon the argument from nature and apologized for knowing no simpler or more direct way of conveying that conviction to the persistent student. He also discredited the student's assertion that an argument from nature need contain universal recognition to be valid.

. . . there were a good many races who did not know that two and two make four. According to the gentleman's idea of natural laws, therefore, it was not natural that two and two should make four. But it had always been a question among metaphysicians, which was really the most natural condition of man—the savage or the civilized state? His own opinion was that the state of highest cultivation was the most natural state of man. He tried to develop his own nature in that way, and one of the consequences of that development was the conviction that two and two made four; while another was the conviction that his wife had as much right to determine her sphere in life for herself as he had for himself. And having come to that conviction, he should endeavor to carry it out, and he hoped by the time the young gentleman came to have a wife, he would be converted to that principle.[8]

Lucy Stone, never one to shirk an argument, also rose to voice her views in response to the young Virginian. Claiming that for herself both revelation and nature formed the basis for her demand for equality, she quoted scripture and historical precedent to sustain her position. The student, whether convinced or unconvinced, appears not to have responded.

As can be seen, an impressive number of men supported the cause of woman's equality and readily contributed their eloquence in conventions to support woman's right to speak publicly and, indeed, participate as an equal in the social and political arena, as well as assume the duties of the pulpit ministry. Many of their names are lost to history, but others, like those names mentioned above, belonged to men of great stature and respected both locally and nationally.

Worthy of special mention is the Congregationalist Henry Ward Beecher, a cleric who never hesitated to vocalize his support for the women. His address to the National Convention held in New York City in 1866 is one of the most forceful arguments for woman's political rights ever presented in a convention. Another champion was the outspoken Parker Pillsbury. An able debater, he was a frequent contributor at suffrage meetings and a prominent voice in the American Equal Rights Association. So, too, was Theodore Parker, who once opened a suffrage meeting with a prayer addressing God as "Our Father and Our Mother."

In the American Woman's Suffrage Association, the more conservative sister organization to the National Woman's Suffrage Association from 1869 to their reunion in 1891, James Freeman Clarke and Henry B. Blackwell played leading roles, providing brilliant testimony to the validity of the women's demands.

By the 1870s, many leading clerics had openly declared their allegiance to the woman's suffrage platform. Notables included Methodist Bishop Gilbert Haven, who had been a woman's rights supported for over thirty years before he publicly uttered the memorable conviction that he would not be fully satisfied until a Black woman should become President of the United States. His fellow bishop Matthew Simpson was equally committed to the cause, delivering a moving address to the National Woman Suffrage Convention in Washington, D. C., March, 1884. Still another ardent supporter was the Universalist Alexander Kent. He, like Haven, Simpson and others, denounced the misinterpretation of scripture which now continued the mistaken belief that man ruled as woman's master. Such a belief, he argued at the National Woman Suffrage Convention of January, 1889 was founded on brute force alone, not rooted in scripture.

The above-mentioned constitute but a small fraction of the many men whose untiring efforts and uncompromised arguments helped pave the way for the securing of woman's rights in the United States. Their contribution cannot be ignored; yet some of the most interesting confrontations were those in which women opposed women. Though much of the rhetoric used by both sides is reminiscent of male arguments, they also evidence a less objective, more intimate appraisal of the issue.

One of the most important female-female confrontations occurred at the American Woman Suffrage Convention in New York City, May 11-12, 1870. Although male defenders were numerous, female protagonists were also much in evidence. One after another they rose to affirm their hopes for woman's equality and to justify woman's demand for possession of the ballot.

Among them was young Grace Greenwood (Sarah J. Lippincott), Washington correspondent for the *New York Tribune*. Vowing to uphold the legislative interests of women in her news coverage, she deplored the ecclesiastical restrictions placed upon women by the church. Had not a woman a greater share in Christ, she asked, for was it not woman who gave him his humanity. With a goodly amount of sarcasm, she stated that woman's only Christian duty appeared to be praying for husbands and sons—not that she (woman) did not have a good deal to pray for here! In Greenwood's mind, there was no doubt as to woman's freedom and she urged "that many of our earnest, eloquent, high-minded religious women should make for the pulpit."9

Other women echoed her sentiments, and it seemed as if the convention would pass without any major incidents. Then Catherine Beecher, a longtime opponent of the woman's crusade, made an appearance. Aged but still committed to an anti-suffrage platform, she declined to read her own paper on a public platform, feeling it indecorous for a woman to do so. Upon her request, therefore, it was read to the convention by the Association's secretary Henry Blackwell.

Her views had softened through the years since her earlier disagreements with the Grimkes' beliefs and behavior. No longer did she condemn woman's speaking in public, woman's preaching, woman's earning an independent living, woman's organization to correct injustices or the basic principle of woman's equality with man. Although woman was not represented among Christ's disciples nor the clergy in the early church, they were not forbidden such a profession, she conceded. Their weakness, she now reasoned, accorded them a station of superiority, never one of inferiority.

Her statements seemed to reveal a major triumph for feminists—a longtime opponent had now conceded her errors. Yet any celebration would have been premature, for Beecher was still critical of the movement. She decried the movement's methodology, which she termed anti-male. She herself laid the blame for much of the injustices and sufferings endured by women upon women themselves. Her idealized picture of the American male reasserted itself once again as she claimed that all conscientious males desired only that which was best for the female sex and would grant petitions to that effect when asked properly. Properly for Beecher did not include use of the ballot box.

Her own limited experience had convinced her that men found it difficult to deny a woman's sincere request. "It is because we do not ask, or " 'because we ask amiss,' " that we do not receive all we need both from God and man," she claimed.[10] On this premise, she disqualified woman's need for the elective franchise, for men would redress any grievance women might have if asked to do so. Her former abhorrence of petitions had abated and was now replaced by a genuine belief that petitions could be utilized effectively to present woman's wrongs to appropriate legislative and judicial bodies. This right made the ballot in women's hands totally unnecessary.

She also spoke for anti-suffragist women, maintaining that retention of the ballot in male hands saved them from undue oppression. She argued that already women had more than they could do well in all that appropriately belonged to woman's sphere and to add the civil and political duties of men, which the feminists now sought, would be both unjust and oppressive. Suffrage would only minimize woman's domestic duties and characterize such duties as unimportant and disgraceful.

Her remarks did not go unchallenged. The first respondent was Mrs. H. M. Tracy Cutler of Ohio. Cutler attacked Beecher's argument at its weakest points—her romanticized concept of the American male and her failure to distinguish between right and privilege. Beecher's father and brothers were hardly representative of the average American male, scoffed Cutler. If they were, Cutler charged, laws themselves would be unnecessary. Beecher's limited perspective insured that any argument built upon it must prove faulty. Secondly, Cutler clarified the difference between right and privilege which she thought Beecher had failed to recognize. Rights, unlike privileges, were inherent, not gifts to be extended or withheld by man; rights were not given, but a natural endowment. They did not ask for rights, they sought to have them recognized.

The Beecher statement drew other rebuttals and rejoinders from the assembled feminists. The Reverend Phebe A. Hanaford insisted that woman suffrage was a sacred duty. Mary F. Davis of New Jersey demanded to know, "Do you, . . . own your own person, according to the law of God, or do you not?"[11] Still another feminist asserted somewhat angrily, "Women are not asking for bonbons in this matter. They are demanding that which belongs to them. They are not children, nor idiots, and they ought to have the same right of action as is accorded to sane men."[12]

Probably the most eloquent response came from Julia Ward Howe, author of the "Battle Hymn of the Republic." America's goal was to build a Christian state, an impossibility in her understanding as long as woman was restrained by man from exercising her God-given equality. Christianity demanded woman's recognition as an equal, argued Howe. This, even though the Eden myth persisted in changed form—man having eaten of the tree of knowledge, now hoarded all the fruit for himself and woman was forced to curb both her own and her daughter's intellect and individuality. To continue a society inclusive of this male oppression jeopardized America's purpose and posterity.

These arguments persisted; other women in future conventions claimed them as their own and continued to voice the argument that birth, nothing else, conferred suffrage rights, not state and national legislatures. Rights were a divine inheritance; man could neither confer nor take them away.

Not all feminists were in accord however. Disagreements arose within the movement, often setting feminist against feminist. An example of this heterodoxy of belief is seen in the thought of Francis E. Abbot, who challenged any attempt to justify woman's equality with reference to the Bible. In this, he echoed women like Ernestine Rose and men like Garrison. A believer in free religion and editor of the Free Religious Association's *Index*, Abbot charged that

> . . . every woman suffragist who upholds Christianity, tears down with one hand what she seeks to build up with the other —that the Bible sanctions the slavery principle itself, and applies it to woman as the divinely ordained subordinate of man—and that by making herself the great support and mainstay of

instituted Christianity, rivets the chain of superstition on her own soul and on man's soul by keeping her in subjection to himself. If Christianity and the Bible are true, woman is man's servant, and ought to be.[13]

For Abbot, the woman's movement was fundamentally anti-Christian and incapable of reconciliation with scripture. However, his position was held by a radical minority within the movement and never gained wide acceptance among the women.

It might be said that convention confrontations expose two distinct things. First and foremost was the feminists' attempts to articulate a reasoned response to the biblically charged arguments which surfaced in convention proceedings. Secondly, such debates also revealed the competing ideologies which contributed to internal dissention. The all-important principle of woman's equality was often all that held them together. Feminist commitment to this principle together with their tolerance of disparate views must certainly be credited.

Notes

[1]*Proceedings of the Woman's Rights Conventions Held At Seneca Falls and Rochester, N. Y., July and August, 1848*, (1870; rpt. New York: Arno, 1969), p. 6.

[2]Wendell Phillips, "Woman's Rights," *Speeches, Lectures, and Letters.* First Series, (Boston: Lee and Shepard, 1894), p. 16.

[3]Excerpt from William Henry Channing letter to Fourth Annual Convention of National Woman's Rights Association, 1853, *HWS*, I (1881), 130.

[4]Lucretia Mott address to N. W. S. A. Convention in Cleveland, 1853, *HWS*, I (1881), 143.

[5]Tracy Cutler at N. W. S. A. Convention in Philadelphia, 1854, *HWS*, I (1881), 380.

[6]Lucretia Mott at N. W. S. A. Convention in Philadelphia, 1854, *HWS*, I (1881), 380.

[7]William L. Garrison at Philadelphia, 1854, *HWS*, I (1881), 382-83.

[8]Thomas W. Higginson response to query from floor of the New York State Woman's Suffrage Convention, 1856, *HWS*, I (1881), 649.

[9]Grace Greenwood at A. W. S. A. Convention in New York City, 1870, *HWS*, eds. E. C. Stanton, S. B. Anthony and M. J. Gage, II (New York: Susan B. Anthony, 1881), 785.

[10]Catherine Beecher address to A. W. S. A. Convention in New York City, 1870, *HWS*, II (1881), 788.

[11]Mary F. Davis response to Beecher address in New York City, 1870, *HWS*, II (1881), 791.

[12]Mrs. Churchill response to Beecher address in New York City, 1870, *HWS*, II (1881), 792.

[13]Francis E. Abbot letter to E. C. Stanton, January 10, 1877, *HWS*, III (1886), 63.

Chapter VII

Local Conventions

Although we have limited discussion thus far to national conventions, state and local conventions were equally as important to the movement and equally effective forums for the woman's rights-religion debate. Since these conventions were often attended by the same men and women who frequented national conventions, arguments tend to be similar, and resolutions passed were very often but duplications of those adopted at national meetings. Even confrontations and debates reveal a distinct similarity to those found in the larger assemblies.

Yet local and state conventions deserve attention, if only to show the pervasiveness of the religion issue. The intent is not to review all local conventions (an impossibility here), but to select a few notable ones, which though unique in some respects, nevertheless display a concern which permeated local convention deliberations.

The best documented state woman's rights conventions were those held in New York State throughout the early days of the movement, yet the first official state convention was held in Akron, Ohio in May of 1851.

The religion question was one of the first issues addressed. Frances D. Gage, presiding officer of the convention, recognized its priority in her opening address to the convention. She conscientiously proclaimed that man's only claim to authority rested on usurped power and not divine decree as some had supposed.

Other addresses, reports and letters to the convention echoed

Gage's conviction. That of Hannah Tracy (Cutler) presaged her later arguments at national conventions. A newcomer to the woman's rights movement with her appearance at Akron, Cutler assured fellow Ohio feminists that woman was most assuredly the created equal of man; her present status was one of unjust victim of scriptural misinterpretation. This belief was one she would further develop until she would be considered one of the strongest defenders of a biblically-supported woman's rights policy in the feminist movement.

Letters to the convention were also important vehicles for the dissemination of the view of woman's created equality. They flowed into the Akron meeting from feminist leaders and woman's rights advocates throughout the Northeast—the socialist radical Henry C. Wright; Paulina W. Davis, leader of the Rhode Island feminists; Eliza Young, Illinois temperance leader; Elizabeth Wilson, feminist from Cadiz, Ohio; Elizabeth Cady Stanton and Amelia Bloomer.

Stanton, never one to shrink from placing the pulpit on her list of legitimate feminist concerns, informed the Ohio feminists that not only was it proper for women to be businesswomen, teachers, doctors and artisans, but it was just as proper for them to be preachers. Woman was best fitted for the ministry, she wrote, "for all admit her superior in the affections, high moral sentiments, and religious enthusiasm; and so long as our popular theology and reason are at loggerheads, we have no need of acute metaphysicians or skillful logicians; those who can make the most effective appeals to our imagination, our hopes and fears, are most desirable for the duties of this high office."[1]

Amelia Bloomer's letter shared Stanton's insights and appeared to continue where the Stanton letter ended. Bloomer contended that the continued subjection of women by rehearsal of the divine decree argument owed much of its success to the present apathy of women.

> They (women) have been taught that God created them inferior, and designed them to occupy an inferior and subordinate position, and to rebel against man's rule was to rebel against

God. Many minds are so impressed with this belief, that not-
withstanding the hardness of their fate, they feel that they
must meekly bow their necks to the yoke which the Great Master has laid upon them. They never stop to ask if or why this
is so, or to inquire so much at their hands.[2]

The first state convention at Akron addressed the religion
question as one of priority. It was the single most important ideological question to be answered, and they answered it as thousands of
their fellow feminists would—as a fallacious question based on faulty
premises.

The first New York state convention was held in New York
City, September 6-7, 1853. It was a particularly lively meeting. The
presense of an active opposition caused it to be regarded in the
annals of the woman's rights movement as "the mob convention."
Once again, the religious argument was the instigator of much of
the disputation.

During the convention speakers were hooted down by angry
opponents. Participants were often threatened, and delegates were
mobbed by irate crowds until some began to fear for their lives.
Yet even though property was destroyed, the New York Police
Department refused to interfere and stood passively by.

William Lloyd Garrison, who was to create considerable havoc
the following year at the national convention in Philadelphia, took
much of the crowd's abuse. As direct as always in his remarks, he
appeared to thrive on the chaos and pandemonium which upset so
many of the other members. Claiming himself a human rights man,
he attacked the pulpit's occupants mercilessly, accusing them of a
hostility which he deemed sought to subvert a movement which was
just, right and supported by God himself. His fiery rhetoric lashed
out at pulpit and press alike.

Show me a cause anathematized by the chief priests, the scribes,
and the pharisees; which politicians and demagogues endeavor
to crush, which reptiles and serpents in human flesh try to
spread their slime over, and hiss down, and I will show you a
cause which God loves, and angels contemplate with admiration.

Such is our movement. Do you want the compliments of the satanic press, *The New York Times, Express*, and *Herald*? If you want the compliments of such journals, you will be bad enough to take a place among the very vilest and lowest of the human race. They are animated by a brutal, cowardly, and devilish spirit.[3]

As the arguments grew more vehement, others entered the fray in defense of woman's rights, particularly her right to speak publicly. Charles C. Burleigh demanded to know whether God had given aspirations which, if gratified, were sinful. He thought such a contention was ridiculous. William H. Channing asked why it was acceptable for Jenny Lind to sing, Fanny Ellsler to dance and Fanny Kemble to read Shakespeare before large, mixed audiences, while it was unacceptable and transgression for women of the caliber of Lucretia Mott, Antoinette Brown, Abby Kelley Foster and Ernestine Rose to speak the simple truth publicly. No one could speak for women, he insisted, except woman herself.

Again and again the assembly was interrupted by stamping feet and laughter from the audience who attempted to drown out the feminist speakers. Finally, Dr. H. K. Root of New York City stepped to the rostrum. Amid cheers and applause, he argued against woman's right for elective franchise. Women could not vote, he contended, for three reasons. While the second reason argued the law of physical force and the third that voting by the female sex placed women in competition with men and thus would consequently disrupt domestic tranquility, it is Dr. Root's first reason which commands our attention.

Arguing the validity of the Genesis myth, Root told the now attentive audience that the Garden account spoke directly to the question then under consideration. Quoting Genesis 3.17, he claimed that, like Adam in the Garden of Eden, modern man was being asked to relinquish his judgment to woman. To do so, he warned, was to invite a catastrophe, just as such a decision had in the Garden narrative. Mankind could ill-afford another disaster of that sort, he asserted.[4] The galleries exploded with wild cheering.

Other speakers followed. Some reaffirmed Root's thesis;

others just as forcefully opposed it. It was a verbal battle between pro-feminists and anti-feminists, with the audience applauding their favorites. The debate itself occupied the major portion of convention time; yet, when the convention drew to a close, neither party had significantly altered the stance of the other.

When the New York State Suffrage Association met the following year in Albany on February 14, the debate continued. Similar arguments were again voiced, although it was accompanied by less violent behavior on the part of the audience. However, the presence of atheist Ernestine Rose generated great sensation and condemnation in the local press, as it had at the national convention in Syracuse in 1852.

Though surprisingly well-received by convention attendees, the local *Albany State Register* lashed out at both Rose and the convention itself. In its editorial it questioned whether the public "should sanction or tolerate these unsexed women, who make a scoff of religion, who repudiate the Bible and blaspheme God; who would step out from the true sphere of the mother, the wife, and the daughter, and taking upon themselves the duties and the business of men, stalk into the public gaze, and by engaging in the politics, the rough controversies, and trafficking of the world, upheave existing institutions, and overturn all the social relations of life."[5]

The paper laid much of the blame for the convention deliberations at the feet of Ernestine Rose, whom the paper claimed was a foreign propagandist and a "ringleted, gloved exotic." The newspaper admitted an inability to understand why educated American women would tolerate a woman whose efforts were designed to "obliterate from the world the religion of the Cross—to banish the Bible as a textbook of faith, and to overturn social institutions that have existed through all political and governmental revolutions from the remotest time."[6] The paper even went so far as to insinuate that legal action be taken against Rose.

It is a credit to the rival *Albany Knickerbocker* that such slanderous journalism did not go unnoticed. In an article of March 8, 1854, the *Knickerbocker* charged *The Register* with wilful misrepresentation. Stanton and Brown were no more anti-God or anti-religion than the editor of *The Register*, the paper claimed. It went still further in its criticism, suggesting *The Register* acquaint itself with the issues before engaging in such generalized condemnations. While not in full agreement with those issues itself, the *Knickerbocker* cautioned fair play and a truthful assessment of the issues from its competitor.

When the state convention met the following year at Saratoga, New York, the debate had still not been resolved. However, the disagreements were congenially voiced. The most noteworthy challenge came from a clergyman who accused the Reverend Antoinette Brown of misapplying biblical texts. He dissented from her view that Genesis 4.7 alluded to Cain and Abel and was compatible with the language of Genesis 3.16, where subordination was implied for woman (Eve).

Despite the clergyman's insistence that she was wrong, Brown held her ground, arguing as others like the Grimkes had done earlier, that neither verse could be construed to sanction the authority of one individual over another, whether Abel over his brother Cain or man over woman. Neither implied divinely-ordered subordination in any form whatsoever.

The specifically designated woman's rights conventions were not the only conventions which entered the controversy. Other conventions, which met to address other social issues, were not immune and were quickly drawn into the debate. Temperance conventions provide good examples.

Undoubtedly one of the reasons they found themselves addressing the issue of woman's political, social and ecclesiastical rights was the fact that so many women involved in the woman's movement also participated in other social reform movements, seeing the various crusades as interlocking in their demands. But the obvious reason, of course, was the fact that women who publicly engaged in social and political reforms found themselves in a position identical to the abolitionist women before them—they had to justify their right to speak openly on such matters. Thus one finds

Elizabeth Stanton addressing the Woman's State Temperance Society in Rochester, New York, June, 1853. Although she acknowledged temperance as the Society's primary concern, she was nevertheless constrained to assert that it was a woman's rights society as well, wherein it was proper to claim "it is woman's duty to speak whenever she feels the impression to do so; that it is her right to be present in all the councils of Church and State."[7]

Other temperance leaders shared Stanton's conviction; and, in later years, important temperance women like Abigail S. Duniway of Oregon and Frances E. Willard, President of the Woman's Christian Temperance Union, would prove effective spokeswomen for the broad concerns evidenced by the woman's movement.

They, like others, believed woman's rights to be an integral and necessary part of woman's drive to cure social ills and to halt intemperance in American society. There could be no more telling a statement of this belief than Duniway's address to the Oregon State Temperance Alliance in February, 1872:

> Give women the legal power to combat intemperance, and they will soon be able to prove that they do not like drunken husbands any better than men like drunken wives. Make women *free*. Give them the power the ballot gives to you, and the control of their own earnings which rightfully belong to them, and every woman will be able to settle this prohibition business in her own home and on her own account. Men will not tolerate drunkenness in their wives; and women will not tolerate it in husbands unless compelled to.[8]

For the women the success of social reform movements was prefaced by the essential demand that woman be allowed to exercise their equality in both state and church. The various issues, often seen as separate by their opponents, were inseparable in their own minds. Thus, national, state and local conventions, concerned with slavery, suffrage, temperance and numerous other social and legal reforms, effectively succeeded in bringing the basic demand for woman's equality into the public eye where it could no longer be ignored. And with it, they brought the biblical argument as well.

Debated strenuously within the movement, it would also be carried beyond convention halls to the very seat of government, eventually to the doorstep of theology and beyond to the pulpit itself. Within a relatively short amount of time, the biblical argument would pass beyond simple derogations by the pulpit and press to be addressed by some of the finest theological minds in the country, both within and outside the feminist ranks and both pro and con.

Notes

[1] *The Proceedings of the Woman's Rights Convention Held At Akron, Ohio, May 28 and 29, 1851* (1851; rpt. New York: Burt Franklin, 1973), p. 33.

[2] *Ibid.*, p. 36.

[3] William L. Garrison address to "Mob Convention," New York City, 1853, *HWS*, I (1881), 549.

[4] H. K. Root address to "Mob Convention," New York City, 1853, *HWS*, I (1881), 560.

[5] Editorial of Albany State Register following State Convention held in Albany, New York, 1854, *HWS*, I (1881), 608.

[6] *Ibid.*

[7] Haper, *Op. Cit.*, p. 92.

[8] Abigail Duniway address to Oregon State Temperance Alliance, February, 1872, *HWS*, III (1886), 772.

Chapter VIII

The Female Exegetes

In 1891 the National Council of Women met in Washington, D. C. An entire conference session was devoted to the role of women in the church. Topics included the deaconess movement, ordination in denominations, and the position of women in the Methodist Episcopal Church.

Formal papers were presented by noted feminists. Susan B. Anthony read the paper submitted by Elizabeth Cady Stanton titled "The Matriarchate, or Mother-Age." The Reverend Anna Howard Shaw, ordained minister of the Methodist Protestant Church and constant companion of Anthony after 1888, presented another titled simply "God's Women." Still another was delivered by Kate Tannatt Woods, editor of the *Ladies Home Journal* and Vice President of the National Woman's Press Association, with the self-explanatory title "Women in the Pulpit."

Although each paper contained important insights which reveal the many biblical understandings then held by women to justify their claim to full equality, Anna Howard Shaw's paper was a masterful attempt not only to review the long struggle already endured, but also to set in perspective the task which lay before the women. The truth of her words must have been acknowledged by many who attended the conference.

Shaw maintained that the woman's movement, like all reforms, had progressed in two distinct stages. The first stage, which the women had now passed beyond, was one in which ridicule and scorn characterized the opposition. During this stage the task of the women's righters had been one of steadfastness and endurance, bearing the derision and "aloneness" felt by all great reformers.

The second stage, which Shaw insisted they now experienced and had for a number of years, was characterized by an aspect of the movement which had demanded a good deal of attention and energy within the reform—a scholarly response to the religious question. Important to all reform movement in Shaw's estimation, it was a time when one

> ... must meet all the obstacles reared by religionists, by theologians, and by a class of people who are always afraid that religion born of God emanating from God, the soul and life of the world, will be overthrown by a few of God's simple human children; and these people fearing that God—I speak reverently—shall not be able to hold His own against a few, think they must stand up in defence of God and the great principle and soul-life of His Being, and of our being.[1]

The truth of her statement is readily discovered upon investigation of woman's activity throughout the Nineteenth Century, particularly those years following the Civil War. Women found that issuing convention resolutions and addressing public assemblies was not sufficient; they soon turned to the task of biblical exegesis. Biblical and theological attacks were to be met by well-constructed arguments of their own.

Often lacking scholarly training and prerequisite skills, they nevertheless possessed a fierce determination and zeal which is commendable, if not incredible at times. Firmly resolved in their belief that woman's alleged inequality and present position of political, social and religious impotence was antithetical to divine will, logic and Christian doctrine, woman's rights advocates refused to relent, waver, compromise or collapse in the face of their often more educated foes.

There was, to be sure, no uniform plan of attack, no single argument advanced or accepted by all feminists. Not only were diverse arguments employed, but diverse methodologies as well. Some questioned the integrity of Christianity or attacked the traditionally held belief that the Bible was an inspired book. Others challenged biblical literalism or accused male translators of prejudices which resulted in gross misinterpretations harmful to women. Still others questioned the application of supposed first century scriptural pronouncements for contemporary situations and the universality of biblical commands. A few even proclaimed certain biblical passages forgeries, included at a later date to guarantee male power and ecclesiastical position. The women found unity only in the conviction that the Bible was not, or need not be, the adversary their opponents made it out to be.

The women, as might be expected, dealt rather exhaustively with the Genesis account of creation. Although opponents often referred to it simply to bolster their arguments from Pauline admonitions and there is an amazing dearth of material to support any contention that they dealt with it to the same degree as they did Pauline materials, feminists noted it repeatedly in their arguments, concentrating a great amount of exegetical energy in making the Garden myth presentable to woman's rights advocates.

Most women in the woman's rights struggle when confronted with Genesis 1-3 maintained a belief voiced ably by the Universalist minister Phebe A. Hanaford in her book *Daughters of America or Women of the Century:*

> Every woman is a daughter of Almighty God, as every man is his son. Each was created in the divine image, and for each the path of duty and destiny is the same. ... He had given to neither power over the other. Man was not made subject to woman, nor should woman be subject to man. Neither men's rights nor woman's rights should be considered, but human rights,—the rights of each, the rights of all.[2]

One of the strongest supporters of this view was church historian Ellen B. Dietrick. Realizing that historical criticism was gaining respectability among biblical scholars and now widely employed, she rejoiced because of its ultimate benefit for women: "Now that every two-penny journal of Christendom has taken the Garden of Eden myth as a standing object of ridicule, the cornerstone of the ecclesiasticism built thereupon is, indeed, crumbling, and the subjection of woman to man maintains its tenure by a

thread whose brittleness no sagacious person can fail to see."[3]
She may have overstated the case, but one cannot ignore the fact
that the new historical criticism did work to woman's advantage.

For Dietrick, neither the Bible, nature nor history established
or supported a theory of creation in which the Creator had divided
domestic and political functions according to sex. Any argument
based upon such a theory was intellectually unsound and thus
logically indefensible. Those who employed it did so not from a
position of reason, but rather from egoism and malice. For Dietrick,
the latter alone explained woman's opposition.

Dietrick's commentary on Genesis as found in the *Woman's
Bible* noted the two distinct and contradictory stories in Genesis
1-3—Genesis 1.1-2.4 and Genesis 2.4-3.24. Not only did they record
two quite different terms for God, but they also contained differing
attitudes toward women. The first account, which she termed the
Elohist story because of its use of the term "Elohim" for God, was
decidedly more favorable to women. It portrayed male and female
"man" as simultaneously created and enjoying dominion over the
earth. It also contained no recitation of the "fall."

Since both could not be considered true, it was left to woman's own judgment which would be granted more credence. For
Dietrick, any intelligent woman would opt for the first account. The
second account, in Dietrick's opinion, "was manipulated by some
Jew, in an endeavor to give " 'heavenly authority' " for requiring
a woman to obey the man she married."[4]

Stanton also acknowledged the two dissimilar accounts of
creation. And, like Dietrick, she dispensed with the second account,
insisting it was "some mysterious conception of a highly imagina-
tive editor" or the production of "some wily writer, [who] seeing
the perfect equality of man and woman in the first chapter, felt it
important for the dignity and dominion of man to effect woman's
subordination in some way."[5]

Stanton agreed with other exegetes who avowed that woman
was created simultaneously with man and commanded with him to

exercise rulership over the created world, but she interjected a unique element into the debate. If God had created male and female in his image, then it was incumbent upon biblical scholars to impute a feminine element to the Godhead, she reasoned. The term "Elohim" for God, divine plural, confirmed for Stanton this contention. It was therefore quite proper in her estimation to address God as either heavenly Mother or heavenly Father.

Methodist Frances E. Willard also addressed the Genesis account, though never as forcefully as either Dietrick or Stanton. Rather than toss out huge portions of scripture, she disclaimed biblical literalism which allowed her to ridicule claims for male superiority based upon it. She sought to discredit both literalism and its arbitrary application by opponents.

If there was any validity to the literal interpretation of the Genesis account, opponents must take into account the fact that Adam, warned against eating of the tree of knowledge before Eve's creation, also sinned, was dismissed from the Garden and, if literalism was advanced, should make "it his personal duty, day by day, actually to " 'eat his bread in the sweat of his face.' "[6] Taken literally, the scripture revealed that woman was created *after* Adam was commanded not to eat of the tree of knowledge of good and evil, i. e., woman was not present when the restriction was voiced. This in itself was, according to Willard, just cause to reevaluate opponents' insistence that woman was to be regarded the greater sinner. Lillie B. Blake arrived at the same observation in her contribution to Stanton's *Woman's Bible*. However, it should be noted that although Eve was created subsequent to the command given Adam in the biblical account, she was nevertheless aware of it and even quoted it to the serpent.

A good case might even be built for woman's superiority in Creation, Willard contended. Restating an argument proposed by both proponents and opponents of woman's equality as early as the turn of the century, Willard argued that the evolution theory of creation—that God proceeded in creation from the lesser to the higher forms—sustained woman's claim as the loftiest member of the created order.

How serious Willard and others were in their claim of female superiority is questionable, but there is little doubt that Willard ever hesitated to advance an argument which ridiculed the logic of opponents. In this case biblical literalism worked at cross purposes with an evolutionary concept of creation, and Willard demanded that opponents who entertained both be aware of the flagrant contradiction in their position.

Logic, women charged, demanded something quite antithetical to subordination. According to Abby Morton Diaz, author of *Only a Flock of Women*, creation assured quite the opposite position for women.

> As women are held accountable beings, equally so with men, and, equally with men, endowed with moral perceptions, equally with men bound to obey the voice of conscience, they should be free, equally with them, to decide questions of duty and of rights, whether these questions are of acquiring knowledge, of teaching, of preaching, or of voting. Men and women stand in equal nearness to their Divine Source, and are equally likely to become subjects of divine inspiration. There should be no arbitrary restrictions.[7]

So, too, Anna Howard Shaw maintained that the creation account confirmed woman's equality rather than disparaging it. The term "Adam" was a generic one. In a rather difficult to follow passage in her address to the National Council of Women she elaborated upon this point.

> The race has believed all this time that Adam was Mr. Adam, and not Mrs. Adam at all. Eve was not Mrs. Adam because she was the wife of Mr. Adam than Adam was Mr. Adam because he was the husband of Mrs. Adam; not a bit. They were each Adam, and neither of them alone was Adam. They were Adam together. You can never have a male Adam or a female Adam. You must have a male and female Adam, and you have manhood and womanhood,—humanity.[8]

Women also refused to believe that the "fall" altered their inherent equality. Instead, they often found Eve's conduct in the

Genesis narrative worthy of admiration rather than scorn. Such a position was taken by Lillie Blake, Elizabeth Stanton and Lucinda B. Chandler.

Blake found Eve deserving of commendation when she did not yield immediately to the Tempter but instead quoted the divine command to him, ultimately succumbing only because of his promise that knowledge would follow the eating of the fruit, not power nor wealth. Like Murray who argued before the turn of the century, both Blake and Chandler saw Eve's motivation not as one of greed, but rather as a sincere quest for individual betterment—a noble pursuit.

Less noble, for Blake, was Adam's behavior in the affair, for he stood silently by in the midst of crisis, offering no objection nor any word of warning. Later, he whined his innocence before God while pointing the finger of blame at Eve. All this leads Blake to conclude that Adam's conduct was nothing less than cowardly. Chandler, too, reflecting on the New Testament's profession of male superiority and Calvin's belief that man did not err but merely succumbed to female enticement, found Adam's enhancement and Eve's debasement absurd. For Chandler, Adam not only remained a dastardly spectator while Eve responded impressively to the temptation, he must also be portrayed as a "weak creature" who was "overcome by the allurements of his wife."[9]

Stanton shared the same belief, and, like Blake and Chandler, voiced admiration for the nobility of Eve's motivation. She thought the Tempter possessed of the same admiration and exalted opinion of Eve in that he sought to lure her not with luxuries or promises of pleasure, but rather with access to wisdom.

The "curse" following the "fall" is also qualified by both Chandler and Stanton. Stanton saw it, as evidenced in pain during childbirth, as lessened, if not erased, by proper diet, dress and exercise. Maternity, she argued, was not necessarily a curse, but could indeed be a blessing. She failed to understand the logic of churchmen who spoke of maternity as a disability, then readily chanted The Magnificat in their cathedrals without realizing their inherent relatedness. Chandler concurred, acknowledging that pain in childbirth was not a universal. Thus its existence could not be construed as a punishment but a "physiological problem"[10] easily mitigated with the use of modern anesthetics. She also reasoned that if its existence could be controlled by human medicine, it could not be regarded as a divine punishment; such amounted to human negation of divine will.

Blake, like the earlier Grimkes, saw the "curse" as a simple prediction, although she went beyond the Grimkes in the development of her argument. Sarah Grimke had seen it as prediction because she saw the masculine claim to superiority as the natural consequence of male strength exercised in the struggle for power following expulsion from Paradise. Victory naturally went to the physically stronger male. God knew such a struggle would occur with man as its victor; He simply acknowledged this in his statement to the transgressors.

Blake understood the predictive aspect of the "curse" also in terms of the triumph of physical strength, but she also saw it in the context of circumstance. Whereas in early times physical power was an all-important factor in human survival and thus not without validity, the evolution of humanity tended to minimize that validity. If once man held valid claim to superiority on the basis of physical strength, he no longer could voice such a claim. Blake even envisioned a time when the severity of labor would be so minimal that woman would naturally be freed from oppression. For Blake, necessity as well as masculine lust for power had produced woman's presently deplored status.

No female exegete ever saw the "curse" as cancelling woman's created equality. God had simply related that which was inevitable—man would rule over woman. He would do so neither by moral nor divine right, but rather by virtue of his superior strength and the dictates of circumstance.

Opponents' arguments formulated on the Genesis accounts of creation were, for the female exegetes, weak, illogical and patently false. In their minds, no intelligent female would be convinced of female inferiority on the strength of them.

The New Testament was the true battlefield in the contest for recognition of woman's divinely established equality. And it is in the exegesis of New Testament passages so often quoted against them that the female exegetes excel.

As women sought to discover New Testament justification for the equality, they, unlike their opposition, carefully reviewed Jesus' position in the gospel records. Their opponents concentrated almost exclusively on what was then considered entirely Pauline material. Their failure to include gospel references in their detailed condemnation of woman's claim to equality will appear obvious.

As women searched the gospels for support, they were not diappointed. They found in Jesus' teaching and comportment nothing which denied women equality. Instead, they were forced to conclude the opposite—that Jesus affirmed their equality with man and elevated woman's status far above that allowed by his contemporaries.

One of the first spokeswomen for this view was Mary Dodge (Gale Hamilton) in 1867. In her book *Woman's Wrongs: A Counter-Irritant*, a response to the Reverend John Todd's *Woman's Rights*, she wrote:

> What gospel is this? Honor and dignity and happiness consist not in truth, integrity, self-sacrifice, self-command, benevolence, communion with God, and likeness to Christ, but in marriage and motherhood and housekeeping! Where is the warrant for such affirmations? Not surely in the words of the Master. Christ propounded no such doctrines. . . . He looked upon woman, he treated woman, as a human being. Nothing that he ever said could be construed into a concession of her inferiority to man.[11]

Frances Willard discovered the same, and discredited the view that Jesus' choice of male disciples alone proved woman's inferior station. For Willard, such a move on Jesus' part was purely logical. The age dictated it, for only masculine impartation of the message would be tolerated at that time. Since the message was all-important, Jesus merely selected the most reasonable means to insure a hearing.

This being the case, Willard concluded that "no utterance of his (Jesus) marks a woman as ineligible to any position in the church he came to found; but his gracious words and deeds, his impartation of his purposes and plans to women, his stern reproofs to men who did them wrong, his chosen companionships, and the tenor of his whole life and teaching, all point out precisely the opposite conclusion."[12]

Ellen B. Dietrick shared the Dodge-Willard conviction, arguing that although Jesus had repeatedly sustained his behavior and person with reference to scripture, he had not once alluded to the Genesis myth, the "fall" or to any divine decree ordering woman's subjection. Even Stanton, who denied Christ's divinity in an attempt to show that as human he was more worthy of imitation and reverence, reached the same understanding. So, too, did Stanton's friend Chandler who, in an article for Stanton's *Woman's Bible*, maintained:

> Jesus is not recorded as having uttered any similar claim that woman should be subject to man, or that in teaching she would be a usurper. The dominion of woman over man or of man over woman makes no part of the sayings of the Nazarene. He spoke of the individual soul, not recognizing sex as a quality of spiritual life, or as determining the sphere of action of either man or woman.[13]

The women exegetes, it must be noted, cited both specific examples and the general tenor of Jesus' teaching found in the gospels to sustain their beliefs. His teaching of one moral code equally binding upon men and women demolished any theory claiming masculine lordship for Dietrick. Such a code was manifested in particular pronouncements of Jesus related to divorce, adultery, punishment for sexual crimes and the pursuit of knowledge. The latter issue proved to be of immense concern to Nineteenth Century feminists, and the account of Mary and Martha in Luke 10.38-42 was quoted numerous times in the writings of female biblicists.

Dodge mentioned it in 1867, insisting that "Martha is the model woman of men, but Jesus praised Mary."[14] Dietrick also saw Jesus' rebuke of Martha for busying herself about the house rather than listening to his message as a singular event. No where else in the gospels did Jesus speak so harshly to a woman, and he did so at this time because Martha, unlike her sister Mary, neglected a chance to cultivate her mind and broaden her intellect.

An identical view is found in Shaw's aforementioned address to the National Council of Women in 1891. There is no doubt that Shaw's position as a minister influenced her treatment of the story. For Shaw, it is no mere knowledge which is Jesus' concern, but rather woman's learning theology. "There was the Mary who sat at the feet of the Lord learning theology of Him: and the only reproof the Lord ever gave a woman was not given to Mary, the theological student, but to Martha, the woman who worried about her housework, and wanted Mary to give up theology and go into the kitchen and cook the dinner,"[15] Shaw informed her audience.

If gospel passages like those mentioned above were to prove advantageous to the woman's argument, there were numerous passages in the epistles, at the time almost exclusively attributed to Paul, which were fuel for opposition arguments—I Corinthians 11.2-16, I Corinthians 14.34-35, I Timothy 2.8-15, Ephesians 5.21-33, Colossians 3.18-19, and I Peter 3.1-7. The women, although they agreed among themselves that the passages were not sufficient to enforce either their subjection or silence, dealt with the troublesome texts differently. Although not always mutually exclusive, one may discern three major patterns of attack. A fourth approach seems to be uniquely that of Ellen B. Dietrick. For the purpose of understanding them, I have somewhat arbitrarily separated them.

As the women faced Pauline verses arrayed against them, they often had difficulty salvaging Paul from amid his verbiage. Some women made no attempt to save him, and he was forthrightly condemned. And in some cases the Bible itself was also discarded. This position, condemning of Paul and/or the Bible, represented the disqualification of the scriptures as inspired and thus instructive. Among those who advocated such a stance were Matilda J. Gage, Josephine K. Henry, Sarah Underwood, Lucinda Chandler and, of course, Elizabeth Stanton.

Underwood maintained that the centuries old insistence that the Bible was an infallible revelation of God had not only worked to woman's disadvantage, but also ridiculed reason and common sense. Any belief in woman's equality could not look to the Bible for support, according to Underwood, for the Bible, far from liberating women, had "left the slave in chains, and the woman in fetters."[16] Henry took an almost identical view, arguing that woman's inferiority and subjection was a persistent theme throughout the scriptural record. No scriptural book was exempt; all contained the same degrading theme—woman's subordination to man.

Both Underwood and Henry looked to science and reason for woman's elevation rather than scripture. The century's scientific treatises had quite obviously not escaped their notice. Such is clear in a letter written by Henry to Elizabeth Stanton.

> When Reason reigns and Science lights the way a countless host of women will move in majesty down the coming centuries. A voice will cry, "Who are these?" and the answer will ring out: "These are the mothers of the coming race, who have locked the door of the Temple of Faith and thrown the key away; 'these are they which came out of great tribulation and have washed their robes and made them white in the fountain of knowledge.'[17]

It is noteworthy that the above remarks were addressed to Stanton, most definitely a sympathizer. Many of the most critical comments directed against the scripture come from her pen. She not only used higher criticism and rejected biblical literalism, but attacked the central doctrine of biblical inspiration. Her radicalism in this regard often set her apart from, and indeed against, many other female exegetes. It was also this radicalism which precipitated the controversy following publication of her *Woman's Bible*.

For Stanton, who stated her views clearly and concisely, no amount of rationalizing could erase the fact that the Bible taught principles adverse to women. In her introduction to the *Woman's Bible* she summarized her evaluation of what scripture actually taught regarding woman's place and role in society.

> The Bible teaches that woman brought sin and death into the world, that she precipitated the fall of the race, that she was

arraigned before the judgment seat of Heaven, tried, condemned, and sentenced. Marriage for her was to be a condition of
bondage, maternity a period of suffering and anguish, and in
silence and subjection, she was to play the role of a dependent
on man's bounty for all her material wants, and for all the information she might desire on the vital questions of the hour, she
was commanded to ask her husband at home. Here is the Bible
position of woman briefly summed up.[18]

Such sentiments as these Stanton found both demeaning and
humiliating. Yet of even greater concern to Stanton was the fact that
such proposals of woman's inferior status emanated not from divine
will, but rather were products of masculine haughtiness and arrogance. The Bible was for Stanton a book composed by arrogant
men; that it was inspired was absurd. Her view finds its best expression in a letter written to the editor of *The Critic* and in response to
criticisms directed against her *Woman's Bible*.

The first step in the elevation of women under all systems of
religion is to convince them that the great Spirit of the Universe
is in no way responsible for any of these absurdities. . . . "The
Woman's Bible" comes to the ordinary reader like a real bene-
diction. It tells her the good Lord did not write the Book; that
the garden scene is a fable; that she is in no way responsible for
the laws of the Universe.[19]

Such opinions alienated Stanton from what might be considered the mainstream of female exegesis. In fact, Stanton experienced
great difficulties in persuading women to help her in writing the
work initially. Some women felt the book largely unnecessary;
others felt it would be of little or no benefit. Still others proclaimed
it downright sacrilegious. Carrie Chapman Catt, a leading feminist
who had initially agreed to serve on the committee preparing the
book, eventually saw that it would disturb those in the struggle
holding religious convictions and immediately withdrew from the
project. Later, Catt was to prove one of its strongest opponents.

Even Susan B. Anthony declined to participate in the undertaking. Stanton would write later of Anthony's unwillingness to
support the project in her autobiography *Eighty Years and More*:

"My beloved co-adjutor, Susan B. Anthony, said that she thought it a work of supererogation; that when our political equality was recognized and we became full-fledged American citizens, the Church would make haste to bring her Bibles and prayer books, creeds and discipline up to the same highwater mark of liberty."[20]

Condemnation of her radical position culminated, of course, in the simple issuance of a resolution of censure by the National American Woman Suffrage Association in 1896. See Chapter Five. One can appreciate this step by the women in the movement in light of growing vociferation on the part of anti-suffragists. One, Helen Kendrick Johnson, did what many in the movement feared would happen—she linked the *Woman's Bible* with the Association, even issuing a pamphlet denouncing it. The pamphlet entitled *Woman's Progress Versus Woman Suffrage* maintained that "education as well as religious decency received a blow from these professed friends of woman's progress when the authoritative members of the Association issued the " 'Woman's Bible.' "[21]

Stanton's religious radicalism continued to rankle members within the movement well after 1896. As late as 1930 when Alice Stone Blackwell appraised Stanton's activities, she was to write in less than commendatory phrases.

> Mrs. Stanton was really more interested in attacking orthodox religion than in promoting equal rights for women. In the early woman's rights conventions, she had loved to introduce some ultra-radical resolution that she knew could not pass, and it amused her to watch the fluttering in the dove-cotes that followed. The fact that such a resolution had been offered was always used as a crudgel afterwards by the enemy.[22]

Blackwell is undoubtedly less than just in her evaluation of Stanton, but there is little doubt that Stanton did prove to be a thorn in the side of the woman's movement on several occasions or that she often stood apart from the majority on issues. However, she was never totally divest of supporters, and her insights remain both original and comprehensive. The *Woman's Bible* taken alone attests to this.

If Stanton, Underwood and Henry exemplify the radical faction in their attack on scripture, the moderate faction would be exemplified by Matilda Gage and Lucinda Chandler. They took a more tempered view of the scripture which though it openly condemned Paul did not go to the length of disclaiming the entire biblical record. Gage proclaimed Paul's teaching divisive, particularly his teaching that Adam was not the first in sin and woman not a part of the original creation idea, but an afterthought. Such teaching, Gage insisted, divided the human race into two contending parties—one male; the other female. Chandler's argument paralleled Gage's. It was Paul's assertion that woman introduced sin into the world and suffered subjection as a result which had poisoned both state and church. Paul was judged accountable for the subjection and oppression of women by both civil and canon law. Both women did dismiss what they thought to be Pauline error or malice; neither rejected the authority of scripture per se.

Most of the women, however, did not go to the extreme of condemning the scriptural record or discounting Paul's genius. Instead, the sought to interpret and apply the offending verses without seriously compromising either the integrity of the record or Paul. It would prove a difficult task, for how was one to reconcile the alleged Pauline passages condemning woman's participation in the church with such passages as that found in Galatians 3.28—"There is neither Jew nor Greek, there is neither slave nor free, there is neither male nor female; for you are all one in Christ Jesus"?

One of the most obvious approaches was to argue that such regulations must be understood as parochial restrictions, limited to a particular time and situation and thus not applicable to present day circumstances. One of the most outspoken women for this line of reasoning was Lucretia Mott, who argued quite boldly "that all the advice given by the apostles to the women of their day is [not] applicable to our own intelligent age; nor is there any passage of Scripture making those text binding upon us."[23] She was supported in this contention by the Reverend Antoinette Brown Blackwell, who deplored the fact that earlier, cruder regulations had continued to be imposed upon later generations. For Brown, such early behaviorial norms could in no way be considered authoritative.

Although a number of scholars adhered to the theory of parochial limitation per se, there was often disagreement as to where the exact boundary of limitation lay and the criterion to be utilized in determing it. For Abby Morton Diaz, the boundary was determined by the exercise of simple common sense. As woman faced the admonitions declarative of her subjection (Ephesians 5 and Colossians 3), she was not to respond unequivocally to them, insisted Diaz, but exercise a measure of discrimination and honest judgment. Diaz also cautioned against relinquishing either conscience or individual responsibility to be swept up in a sort of blind obedience to traditional principle. In other words, the simple employment of individual reason and common sense ordered that the texts be nullified, for unquestioning adherence to them might eventually contradict the very directives of the gospel message itself.

> But shall a woman obey her husband to do wrong? Of course not. How will she know wrong from right? By her conscience. But the right to obey her conscience gives her the right of decision, and the right of decision makes the text of no avail, and if one text can be set aside, just as well can another.[24]

Frances P. Cobbe also found the passages in Ephesians and Colossians nonapplicable to the Nineteenth Century. They were invalid because they spoke directly to the social constructs of the First Century Mediterranean world, not modern-day America. Only this observation could explain Paul's support of the institution of slavery and his apparent conviction that woman was the subordinate of man. Those who chose to quote such submission passages in their arguments were, for Cobbe,

> . . . bound to attach the same authority to a parallel passage in another Epistle, wherein the same apostle commands slaves to obey their masters, and actually sends back to his chain a runaway who in our day would have been helped to freedom by every true Christian man or woman in America. The whole tone of early Christian teaching, indeed, was one of entire submission to the "powers that be," even when they were represented by such insane despots as Tiberius, Caligula, and Nero. In our day, men habitually set aside this apostolic teaching, so far as it concerns masters and slaves, despots and subjects, as

adapted only to a past epoch. I am at a loss to see by what right, having done so, they can claim for it authority, when it happens to refer to husbands and wives.[25]

The cry for woman's silence in the church, more than any other single suppressive demand, drew a flurry of response from the feminists. The women who hinged their exegesis on the argument from parochialism refused to accept the admonition to silence in I Corinthians 14 and I Timothy 2 as general precept; instead, they claimed that it was contravened by local circumstance. Paul's concerned utterance for woman's silence in the church was purely a response to parochial situations in the churches of Ephesus and Corinth. This fact would be abundantly clear when the passages in question were rightly interpreted and understood insisted feminist scholars like Frances E. Willard.

"Rightly understood" the verses would be seen as having been addressed to eliminate confusion in the local assemblies in Ephesus and Corinth. They were ultimately only concerned with the maintenance of good order, nothing more. The context of I Corinthians 14 appeared to sustain such an interpretation, for Paul's intent throughout the chapter was to curb disruption in the meetings of the Corinthian congregation. Phoebe Palmer, a Methodist and one of the leading lights of the Perfectionist movement, stated the feminists' position well.[26]

> Under what circumstances was this prohibiton given? . . . Surely it is evident that the irregularities here complained of were peculiar to the church of Corinth, and in fact, we may presume, were not even applicable to other Christian churches of Paul's day, much less Christian churches of the present day, as no such disorders exist. The irregularity complained of was not the prophesying of women, for this the apostle admits, and directs how the women shall appear when engaged in the duty of praying and prophesying. But the prophibition was evidently in view of restraining women from taking part in those disorderly debates, which were not unusual in the religious worship of those days.[27]

Much of the ensuing controversy centered about the Greek word "λαλεω"—to speak. A number of leading female exegetes preferred to translate it "to babble" or "gabble" as did both Lucy Stone and Frances Willard although most of the detailed exegeses related to this term were formulated by male exegetes sympathetic to the feminist position. See the following chapter.

Beyond the argument from parochialism and often intimately interwoven with it was the feminist attack on biblical literalism and, consequently, faulty scholarship. One of the strong expositors of this view was Frances E. Willard. In a major work, *Woman in the Pulpit*, she attempted to disprove literalism as a realistic means of interpreting scripture. Not only did she see the inconsistency of exegetical interpretations as discrediting the credibility of the literalist approach, but she maintained that anyone who followed the rigid rule of literalism had logically to admit that the Bible was riddled with contradictions. In support of the latter contention she devised a table of conflicting verses.[28]

Paul	Other Scriptures	Paul
I Tim. 2.11	Judges 4.4-5	Gal. 3.28
I Cor. 14.34	Joel 2.28-29	I Cor. 11.5
I Cor. 14.35	Lk. 2.36-38	Phil. 4.3
I Tim 2.11	Acts 18.26	Rom. 16.3-4
I Cor. 14.34-35	Acts 9-10	I Cor. 11.11
I Cor. 11.3	John 1.1, 3	Rom. 16.1
Eph 5.23	Jn. 14.9; Col. 2.9	
	Jn. 10.30	

If any of these verses were taken literally, Willard claimed, they could not be effectively reconciled with the other passages. Paul, in effect, contradicted himself numerous times in a sort of intellectual schizophrenia hardly worthy of comment much less canonization. The only solution for Willard lay in viewing the passages in their context and by determining their intent.

Another advocate of this approach was Ellen B. Dietrick, author of *Woman in the Early Church Ministry*. Although she was later to incorporate an extremely unique approach to the Pauline problem, which will be noted subsequently, there is no doubt that she stood firmly with the anti-literalist exegetes. Indeed, she argued vehemently that biblical literalism had fostered and now maintained the entrenched prejudices toward women. She called for woman's rescue from such deplorable scholarship as that evidenced by the literalists. Her words, condemning and austere, charged that woman would never gain the liberty of self-ownership and self-government

> ... without delivering man from a style of biblical exegesis which is unworthy of a manly and intelligent twelve-year-old boy, and this deliverance will be a benefit to the entire human race, man himself not excepted. It is true that the worst examples of the prejudicial interpretation of the Bible are found in the works of the older commentators, but young men, especially in illiterate and libraryless Southern states, are still stupidly following in the track of the Rev. Thomas Scott and commentators of that stamp, and pinning their faith, on the woman question, to the mediaeval-minded Rev. Horace Bushnell, a man fifty years behind the present standard of knowledge in Europe and America.[29]

The call for sound scholarship and, more particularly, feminine scholarship was a pervasive one in the movement. It was readily voiced by Willard, though never in words as harsh as those of Dietrick. In 1888, Willard lamented the fact that male exegesis so often issued in sentiments prejudicial to women and urged more women to actively undertake the task of exegesis: "We need women commentators to bring out the woman's side of the book; we need the stereoscopic view of truth in general, which can only be had when woman's eye and man's eye together shall discern the perspective of the Bible's full-orbed revelation."[30]

Still another anti-literalist was Ursula N. Gestefeld. One of the best statements of her position is in a letter written to Elizabeth Stanton wherein she developed the thesis that biblical literalism retarded Christain growth. She claimed that under the burden of such irritation neither sex was free to achieve utmost benefit from the other, nor could they prove truly useful to the community.

When faced with particular New Testament passages intimating their subjection, the anti-literalists, like the parochialists, refused to accept them as crippling denunciations of their claim for recognized equality. Many alined with Frances Willard and feminist Catherine Stebbins, both of whom thought the subjection theory was fundamentally the product of male-dominated biblical scholarship. The monoplizing of theological inquiry and biblical translation by men had resulted in the imposition by men of their own selfish theories upon the scripture, which had a debilitating effect on Christian theology.

Willard was even more explicit in her criticisms. Her exegesis led her to believe that Paul required no more nor less subjection on woman's part than he required of all Christians. The word "subjection" was used repeatedly by Paul, calling Christians to be subject to one another; and, in Ephesians 5.21, he addressed *men*, admonishing them to submit themselves "one to another in the fear of the Lord." To argue that in one place the same word meant something quite different than its use in another place was a tenuous argument for the keen-minded defender of logic Willard.

She applied a similar argument in dealing with II Timothy 2.2—"And the things that thou hast heard of me, the same commit thou to faithful men, who shall be able to teach others also." Opponents had charged that this verse confirmed their belief that only men were instructed to engage in teaching. Willard thought otherwise; the term "men" was used in other contexts where it could only be interpreted generically. "But the word translated " 'men' " is the same as that in the text, " 'God now commandeth men everywhere to repent,' " and even the literalists will admit that women are, of all people, " 'commanded to repent!' "[31] wrote Willard with subtle though evident wit. She simply demanded to know by what rule male scholars determined to translate the term "men" one way in certain contexts and another way in other contexts. The most obvious answer for Willard was a rule born of their own prejudice.

Anna Howard Shaw was another anti-literalist who faced particular verses with the charge that the scriptures had been victimized by faulty translation and even faultier translators. One verse which drew her immediate attention was I Timothy 2.15—"She (woman) shall be saved in childbirth." It had been traditionally interpreted by men as advocating motherhood as woman's unique route to salvation. Such an assertion was absurd in Shaw's estimation.

> Most of us regard this passage of the Scripture as meaning that she shall be saved by the coming of the Child,—shall be saved by the coming of Jesus Christ. She shall be saved because Jesus Christ came into the world to save not man alone, but woman also. Women shall be saved because of the coming of Him who is the Emancipator of the race, woman included. Believing this, we think the discussion which has been raised upon this line is a mere makeshift; it has nothing to stand upon.[32]

As can be seen, the feminists' devotion to understanding scripture in its historic-cultural context and/or their refusal to entertain belief in the literal interpretation of scripture supplied them with a strong foundation for their exegetical method. They employed both criticisms consistently and well, as they dealt again and again with specific passages thrust at them by opponents who held such verses to be proof-positive that women had no legitimate claim to full equality in either church or state.

However, the anti-literalist and parochialist stances entertained by the female exegetes did not exhaust the repetoire of approaches employed by the feminists. Another approach which bears note is the unique argument advanced by Ellen Dietrick. While it gained few adherents at the time it was advanced, it needs mention, for it has a decidedly modern ring to it and is much more compatible with recent twentieth century scholarship than nineteenth century feminist views.

Whereas many feminists chose to rescue Paul from condemnation by charging that he had been mistranslated, misunderstood or misappropriated, Dietrick took a more radical tack. In effect, she simply denied that Paul had written the offending verses: "In view of *the whole* of what is given us as Paul's life and letters, we must pronounce the woman-despising passages palpable forgeries and very bungling forgeries at that."[33]

Who then was responsible, if not Paul? Dietrick thought the guilty parties "Unscrupulous bishops, during the early period in which a combined and determined effort was made to reduce women to silent submission, not only in the Church, but also in the home and in the state."[34] The genuine Paul had encouraged the ministry of women, Dietrick insisted. Indeed, the real Paul's only reference to the Genesis myth was in Romans 5.12 where *Adam* is labelled the culprit, the one man through whom sin entered the world.

Dietrick's justification for such a stance is fuzzy at best. One is only left to conclude that in her desire to retain Paul untarnished, deal with the problem of Pauline inconsistency, and maintain woman's inherent equality she realized something had to give. The easiest solution to the conundrum was to rid scripture completely of views which deprecated either Paul indirectly or women directly. Yet, we must be fair and note that although her rationale is obscured, she was undoubtedly on a sound exegetical track when she chose to evaluate the offending verses in the context of the full Pauline corpus.

In the summary, it must be said that although the female exegetes devised no concerted plan of attack but rather a variety of approaches encompassing several distinct exegetical methods, they nevertheless all sought to secure greater freedom for women in the life of the church. Some proved daring in their efforts; others remained cautious and somewhat hesitant lest they concede too much. In any event, their efforts would have a long-term affect on the woman's movement and serve as an effective means for stimulating biblical scholarship, both favorable and unfavorable to their cause.

Notes

[1]Anna Howard Shaw, "God's Women," *Transactions of the National Council of Women*, ed. Rachel Foster Avery (Philadelphia: J. B. Lippincott, 1891), p. 243. Hereafter cited as *Transactions*.

[2]Phebe A. Hanaford, *Daughters of America or Women of the Century* (Augusta, Me.: True and Company, 1882), pp. 19-20.

3Ellen Batelle Dietrick, *Women in the Early Church Ministry* (Philadelphia: Aflred J. Ferris, 1897), pp. 70-71.

4Ellen B. Dietrick commentary on Genesis 1-3, *Woman's Bible*, E. C. Stanton and others, comps. (1895-98); rpt. New York: Arno, 1972), p. 18.

5Elizabeth Stanton commentary on Genesis 1-3, *Woman's Bible* (1895-98), pp. 20-21.

6Frances E. Willard, *Woman in the Pulpit* (Boston: D. Lothrop Company, 1888), p. 33.

7Abby Morton Diaz, *Only a Flock of Women* (Boston: D. Lothrop, 1893), p. 58.

8Anna Howard Shaw, "God's Women," *Transactions* (1891), p. 244.

9Lucinda B. Chandler letter to E. C. Stanton, *Woman's Bible* (1895-98), p. 166.

10*Ibid.*, p. 167.

11Mary Dodge, *Woman's Wrongs: A Counter-Irritant* (1868; rpt. New York: Arno, 1972), p. 185. [The reprint is published together with John Todd's *Woman's Rights* (Boston: Lee and Shepard, 1867), and is a reply to the arguments advanced in that work.]

12Willard, *Op. Cit.*, p. 41.

13Lucinda B. Chandler letter to E. C. Stanton, *Woman's Bible* (1895-98), pp. 164-65.

14Dodge, *Op. Cit.*, p. 187.

15Anna Howard Shaw, "God's Women," *Transactions* (1891), p. 247.

16Sarah Underwood letter to E. C. Stanton, *Woman's Bible* (1895-98), p. 191.

17Josephine Henry letter to E. C. Stanton, *Woman's Bible* (1895-98), p. 198.

18Elizabeth Cady Stanton, "Introduction," *The Woman's Bible*, E. C.

Stanton and others, comps. (1895-98; rpt. New York: Arno, 1972), p. 7.

[19]Elizabeth Stanton letter to the editor of *The Critic* in support of the *Woman's Bible*, *Up From the Pedestal* (Chicago: Quadrangle, 1968), p. 119.

[20]Elizabeth Cady Stanton, *Eighty Years and More* (1898; rpt. New York: Schocken Books, 1973), p. 392.

[21]Helen Kendrick Johnson, *Woman's Progress Versus Woman Suffrage* (New York: New York State Association Opposed to the Extension of the Suffrage to Women, 1904), p. 5.

[22]Alice Stone Blackwell, *Lucy Stone: Pioneer of Woman's Rights* (Boston: Little, Brown, 1930), p. 230.

[23]Lloyd C. M. Hare, *The Greatest American Woman: Lucretia Mott* (New York: Negro Universities, 1937), p. 204.

[24]Diaz, *Op. Cit.*, p. 139.

[25]Frances P. Cobbe, *Duties of Women* . . . (Boston: George H. Ellis, 1881), pp. 124-25.

[26][Although Palmer was extremely liberal in interpreting the role of women in the church, she conceded that "the sort of teaching here alluded to, stands in necessary connection with usurping authority. . . . And though the condition of woman is improved, and her privileges enlarged, yet she is not raised to a position of superiority, where she may usurp authority, and teach dictatorially, for the law still remains at the beginning. It is an unalterable law of nature."] *Promise of the Father or a Neglected Speciality of the Last Days Addressed to the Clergy and Laity of all Christian Communities* (New York: W. C. Palmer, Jr., 1872), pp. 7-8.

[27]Palmer, *Op. Cit.*, pp. 6-7.

[28]Willard, *Op. Cit.*, pp. 27-28.

[29]Dietrick, *Women in the Early Church Ministry*, *Op. Cit.*, pp. 88-89.

[30]Willard, *Op. Cit.*, p. 21.

[31]*Ibid.*, p. 34.

32Anna Howard Shaw, "God's Women," *Transactions* (1891), p. 248.

33Dietrick, *Women in the Early Church Ministry, Op. Cit.*, pp. 106-07.

34Willard, *Op. Cit.*, p. 37.

Chapter IX

Limited But Sure Support

The female exegetes were not without the support of a significant number of male scholars. Mott's view regarding the parochialism of the biblical record gained acceptance, to a greater or lesser degree, from such respected theological minds as scholar Edward
Lyttelton, The Reverend William Deloss Love of Andover, Lutheran Theodore E. Schmauk, Methodists David Sherman and John O.
Foster, and Congregationalist Charles Torrey. Some, it should be
noted, entertained the view even though they remained strong
opponents of woman's right to participate in the ministry itself.
Still others argued its validity from an integrity of scholarship
position and not from a basic belief in female equality.

Methodists Foster and Sherman maintained that the apostles
did not deal with particular questions facing the nineteenth century
American woman, e.g., possession of the ballot, right to education,
etc. In Shermans words,

> The believer in the elevation and rights of woman, on opening
> the New Testament where he would naturally expect to find
> some recognition of his views, will find no discussion of the sub-
> ject, and yet the book is pervaded by principles which tra-
> verse the whole field and sanction his most advanced ideas.
> The reason for the silence is to be found in the fact that the
> world was not ready for the discussion. In the East, where
> the Gospel was first promulgated, woman held a low place on
> the social scale, public sentiment had become familiarized to
> her humiliation, and many preliminary steps would be required
> before reaching the climacteric points of discussion today.[1]

Both men were willing to concede that all support for

woman's equality hinged upon those "pervasive principles," for they contained the germ of any biblical argument favorable to woman's rights. The fact that the Gospel and apostolic witness had addressed woman as a responsible being worthy of both admittance and mission is the church and dignified status in the family logically anticipated, contrary to much popular sentiment, the great questioning which now drew the women's attention. The principles were all important for Sherman and Foster, while particular biblical practice and precept were not.

William Deloss Love, working from a similar assumption, took a slightly different approach. He formulated a favorable, though tempered argument for woman's right to preach and share in the decision-making powers of the church almost entirely on an insistence that local church customs in the apostolic age should never be construed as anything more than simple custom. Such culturally conditioned admonitions as those found in the gospels could not be regarded as binding upon nineteenth century womanhood.

Times had changed, and a recognition of this fact was imperative. For Love, such things as woman's silence in church assemblies were necessary in the apostolic age to distinguish Christian women from the more base and immoral women of the day, but any reasoning grounded in a set of similar convictions in modern times was no longer reasonable. Christian women could now speak publicly without appearing either immoral by doing so or introducing confusion to the minds of unbelievers regarding their Christian status. Women could teach and preach, if such was necessary and desired, with feminity neither deteriorated nor compromised by such activity.

Although Love still objected strongly to woman's assuming authority over man, he conceded, "While her relation to man has not changed, the customs expressive of that relation and appropriate to it have partially altered, so that the same degree of silence and retirement requisite in the apostolic age is not now demanded."[2] The customs, i. e., silence and veiling, had passed away, but Love was still unwilling to concede that the central principle of subjection had also become inoperative.

A distinctly similar position was entertained by The Reverend Charles Torrey of Ohio who, expounding on the custom of veiling in particular, argued that it was proposed to insure "modesty and reverence but to these as interpreted by the habits of the age."[3] Each age decided what was fitting and proper Christian decorum; one age did not dictate to the other.

Edward Lyttelton, more of a feminist than either Love or Torrey, developed another variation on the same theme. He preferred to apply the same conviction by utilizing an argument reminiscent of that employed earlier by Sarah Grimke—the argument from Pauline prejudice. In an article for *The Contemporary Review* entitled "Woman's Suffrage and the Teachings of St. Paul," Lyttelton asserted that Paul's teaching could not be fully understood unless one was cognizant of the fact that both rabbinical teaching and social customs of the time had greatly influenced Paul's thought. No one who was an honest scholar could fail to see that Paul was hindered by his early training in Jewish circles and hampered by the social mores of the world in which he lived.

> Few problems of greater interest could be presented for solution to a Jewish scholar than to determine how far St. Paul remained to the end of his life under the influence of Gamaliel, and how far his vigorous and divinely illuminated mind shook itself free from the intensely material and narrow prejudices in which the training of a young Pharisee must have been steeped. But it seems to me tolerably evident that, on the subject of the position and conduct of women, he was, till far on in his life, more under the dominion of Rabbinical prepossessions than on any other subject of which he treats in his Epistles.[4]

Modern research and historical criticism, Lyttelton maintained, were necessary to determine which precepts were to be invested with greater authority and which with lesser. Whatever could be considered transitory must be regarded as no longer supportive or feasible justification for modern-day practice and restriction. Lyttelton recognized immediately that the spirit of Pauline thought was unsympathetic to woman's present course of action and demand, but he also realized that culturally-determined directives and regulations were also culturally bound. For the sake of intelligibility Paul needed to speak as he had. Not to have done so would have been both bewildering and nonedifying to his contemporaries. In Lyttelton's words, "The power of the divine inspiration acting upon a human being is shown in its most impressive form when there is evidence of a wonderful but yet orderly *growth* (his emphasis) in power of character and width of view; and while to point out that on this one question St. Paul was a child of his time, is in no way to impair his authority as a teacher, it is only by recognizing his limitation that we can truly appreciate the greatness of the convert from Pharisaism who could write the Epistle to the Romans."[5]

One of the most pronounced male applications of what might be termed the Mott Thesis is found among advocates of woman's right to participate in church decision-making. Theodore E. Schmauk, again a man one can never truly place amid the ranks of woman's righters, argued rather effectively that apostolic precepts were conditioned by the social milieu of their birth. Despite his rigid stance against women occupying the pulpit or engaging in the formal ministry of the church, Schmauk nevertheless agreed that law and custom had changed to the point "where heathen conceptions of authority have disappeared under the influence of the Gospel in the state," and where such did indeed exist, "they (heathen conceptions of authority) ought not to surface in the family, and still less in the Church itself."[6]

Schmauk's views were best presented in an article for the July, 1899 issue of *The Lutheran Church Review* wherein he sought to show that Paul was exposed to a culturally determined view of authority which a growing sense of individualism, evidenced in history and brought to fruition among Reformation scholars, had eclipsed.

Schmauk claimed that Christianity had been instrumental in the rejection of an absolute, unlimited authority which had brutalized earlier societies. Now limited authority which recognized the worth of the individual and was inculcated in democratic forms of government prevailed. It did so because men had seen fit to throw off the shackles of pagan law, practice and attitude, this in both church and state. Schmauk then raised the question why women should not be allowed to do the same.

Like Love, Schmauk never carried his understandings to what might be thought their logical conclusion—woman's right to full equality of action and position in church and state. Instead he remained mentally chained to the supposed biblical pronouncements of woman's subjection and man's rulership, while refusing to believe that such male prerogative denied woman a right to voice or vote in the church's decision-making. Yet even here he remained unwilling to allow them participation in cases involving doctrinal and disciplinary dispute. Subjection remained in force; it simply "... does not debar women from voting in the congregation, nor make the husband an absolutely despotic ruler over her in earthly affairs. Even though the wife is to be subject to her husband as the Church is subject to Christ, even though man is the woman's head as fully and completely in every respect as Christ is the head of the Church, she still has many liberties and rights, and among them—voting."[7]

Methodists had used a rejection of New Testament precept nine years earlier when faced with the same question. Although they employed dissimilar arguments, they reached summarily the same conclusion as Schmauk. In the March, 1891 issue of *The Methodist Review*, there appeared an article appropriately entitled "The Eligibility of Women not a Scriptural Question." Its author, not acknowledged by name, faced the question of woman's membership in the General Conference of the Methodist Episcopal Church, an issue then pending before the laity of that denomination.

Though careful to set down the biblical arguments of both proponents and opponents of the measure, the author denied that the scriptures provided a definitive answer to the question. At the same time however, he was willing to reverse his position "if it is true that they (the scriptures) speak as plainly either for or against woman's right to assist in the legislation of the Church as they do for such doctrines as incarnation, atonement, regeneration, sanctification, resurrection, and a judgment."[8]

The Methodist Church, the article affirmed, had always held

to the position that neither Christ nor his apostles prescribed a specific form of church government. Therefore, it was logically assumed that any scrutiny of scripture in this regard would be futile and offer no resolution of the issue. Any question of church government rested ultimately in the hands of the church; woman's eligibility as delegates to the General Conference was simply a question of church government, solution resided within the province of the church alone.

Like his Lutheran counterpart Schmauk, this Methodist author was also unwilling to contenance woman's ordination or any formal participation by women in the church's ministry. Unlike the question of delegation, this was a scriptural problem and therefore well beyond consideration of church policy. His conservatism on the matter seems incongruous with later demands in the same article that one discard as irrelevant to the question those supposed Pauline verses relegating women to a position of subordination in the family, as well as the treatment of the meanings apparent in each verse. No doubt, the author's position reflected the spirit of the times, in which many proved amazingly agile at entertaining ideas which were pulled up short of their logically reasoned consequences.

Subjection applied only to the family structure, not church government, the article stated. Yet even in the family Paul's commands did not deny woman a legislative function, only an executive function. The latter, of course, was reserved by scripture to the male alone. In regard to the church, application of Pauline thought must be tempered as well, for the directive admonishing woman's silence in the church (I Corinthians 14.34) did not address the question of church government at all, but merely reproved social disorder in a particular church. Those who chose such texts to sustain an argument excluding women from participation in the governing body of the Methodist Church both strained and misapplied Pauline intent. Thus, the article concluded:

> We are not to decide whether the New Testament admits woman's eligibility to legislative rank in the Church, nor should the question by any legerdemain be made to revolve around that point. It is not a question of exegesis or interpretation that the Church is to decide, but a simple question of whether

woman's eligibility shall be recognized by law, which the General Confernece is competent to enact, because there are no scriptural barriers or instructions on the subject. Conference action is legal action, pure and simple. It is not sitting in judgment on the Scriptures, because the Scriptures are not in the case.[9]

The Methodist Review article was not without challengers however. On March 5, and again on March 12, 1891, *The Christian Advocate* issued editorial condemnations. Betraying a fear that woman's voting in church assemblies was opening the floodgates to an attack upon male domination of the pulpit, *The Advocate* stated that although the Methodist Church recognized, and was correct in its recognition, that the New Testament set forth no apostolically designed church order, the New Testament was also not devoid of authoritative principles related to church government.

The Review rebutted in a tone that was both apologetic and firm. It began by assuring its fellow Methodist journal that it was in no way advocating or encouraging woman's admission to the formal ministry of the church. That was scripturally unthinkable. It advised any woman entertaining such rebellious inclinations to be promptly retaught the New Testament.

However, *The Review* did reaffirm its stance that the New Testament proposed *no* principles outlining proper forms of church government. Its positon on the matter was unequivocal: "Had it been the plan of the apostles to establish church government on certain principles, or to give the Church a legislative constitution, to be operative throughout the ages, they would have at once settled certain questions that not only perplexed their own times, but are still the sources of discussion because they failed to resolve them."[10]

The Review closed its defense by assuring both its readers and *The Christian Advocate* that woman's eligibility rested solely upon her membership in the church, Methodist polity and the principle of lay delegation, and the *absence* of any scriptural inhibition in the matter. It could not, and should not, be dealt with outside of Methodism: "It is imperative upon us to say that the root of the whole matter is in Methodism itself, and in nothing else. It is a Methodist question, within the domain of our law, to be decided without external influence, without reference to the past, except to the history of Methodism itself, and without reference to the future, except to the welfare and development of Methodism."[11]

As can be seen, all of the above arguments agreed in principle and in part with that of Lucretia Mott, but few proceeded from the same spirit. For instance, all argued that the questions regarding the rights of women could not be fashioned solely from biblical dictate, yet few would have maintained that such opened the way for the realization of woman's full dignity in the church. Whatever the shortcomings of the above arguments, they do serve to show that form criticism, or its immediate predecessor, had come to the woman's rights controversy, i. e., the Bible needed to be understood with reference to both the culture and time it reflected.

Male support came not only to the parochialists among the women exegetes, but also to the anti-literalists. Edward Lyttelton carefully coupled his early form critical argument with an attack on biblical literalism and plenary inspiration. Throughout his written work he continued to maintain that previous attitudes binding biblical scholars had changed. No longer was the biblical exegete bound to a "theory of inspiration, to which the Church has never committed herself, that every sentence, in the New Testament at least, was of equal value, and derived in an equal measure from heaven."[12]

Although Lyttelton acknowledged that the popularity of historical criticism did not automatically insure its correctness, he also pointed out that literalism, whatever its popularity rating at any given time in history, had never been consistently ascribed to by the church nor made the basis of christian conduct. Those who claimed otherwise had grossly overlooked or purposely ignored the evidence of church history.

If women were not to teach, why, asked Lyttelton, did even the most conservative Christians of the day allow women to teach their own children, engage in congregational singing or conduct sunday school classes. Either Paul's general concern or denotation of the word "teach" meant something quite different than what literalism would indicate, or Christians were guilty en masse of transgressing divine decree. At the same time, if Paul was indeed encumbered by contemporary custom or denounced something different from what was presently considered teaching, and modern practice seemed to imply such was the case, then modern biblical scholarship and research needed to admit that fact.

Practically speaking, Christians had already done just that, for they had disregarded precepts, which literally understood should have sentenced the Christian woman to muteness within the walls of the church. Lyttelton simply called for truthful admission, for "anything, surely, is better than to go on profession a literal adherence to all the New Testament injunctions while, at the same time, ignoring some of them without knowing why."[13]

Even before Lyttelton's charge of hypocrisy, another scholar had sided with the feminists and attacked biblical literalism as a viable approach to biblical study. Congregationalist Charles Torrey, in an article for *The Congregational Quarterly*, April, 1867, charged, as Lyttelton would do twenty-nine years later, that if Paul was to be taken literally in his command for woman's silence in the church, it would convict the entire church in nineteenth century America. Women no longer appeared veiled nor did they sit silently during congregational worship. They taught both children and adults in church school classes throughout the country.

Torrey saw resolution of the discrepancy in terms of an either/or proposition:

> The only answer is, either "We are wrong, and ought to reform immediately;" or, "We serve in newness of spirit, and not in the oldness of the letter." The reasons for the injunction have ceased, and of consequence it is not now binding. *Ratione cessante, cessat lex.*[14]

Torrey wrote that he found it difficult to comprehend why some men could ridiculously quote Paul literally to hold women in subjection while, at the same time, encouraging them to break Pauline dictate, and intending as persistently to encourage them to continually do so in the future. The inanity of such a position was illustrated by Torrey in a story which bears recitation.

> Some twenty-five years since, when General Harrison was candidate for the presidency, he had a narrow escape from injury, by his horse falling with him into a deep tunnel. An opposition newspaper, intending to burlesque the story, repeated it with additions, representing him as checking his steed in mid air, and by a prodigious feat of horsemanship, leaping him back to upper ground without waiting to reach the bottom. This feat seems here to find a parallel.[15]

Adherence to a position of biblical literalism was, for Torrey, akin to stopping a horse in mid air and reversing direction. Such a stunt was not only manifestly ridiculous, but clearly impossible. Woman was limited, according to Torrey, only by her intrinsic talents and propriety. To argue otherwise, particularly from affirmation of biblical literalism, was frivolous. He concluded that if one chose to persist in such a belief, one should then eschew hypocrisy by carrying out their literal understandings in practice, i. e., women should be made to sit mute in the sanctuary enclosed in a heavy veil. Anything to the contrary must be considered hypocrisy of the rankest sort.

Feminists also found male scholars who echoed their sentiments with regard to the creation accounts in Genesis. Methodist Benjamin T. Roberts restated fellow Methodist Willard's position in his book *Ordaining Women*. Not only did he find the Genesis account nonmenacing toward women, but he claimed that the evolution theory of creation in and of itself was enough to destroy any argument positing woman's inferiority. For Roberts, it would take an amazing feat of mental gymnastics to assert woman as the last, and thus noblest, of God's creatures, while concurrently affirming her inferiority.

Male supporters concurred with the female assessments advocating the equal creation of the sexes, often relying on Adam Clarke's exposition of Genesis 2.18 wherein he maintained woman "to be a perfect resemblance of the man, possessing neither inferiority nor superiority, but being in all things like and equal to himself."[16] Unlike the women however, men found it difficult to treat "the fall" as lightly as their female counterparts were want to do.

Whereas women scholars saw in "the fall" no sanction for the relegation of women to stations of subjection, male exegetes often did. B. T. Roberts, liberal thinker that he was regarding woman's right to full equality, refused to believe that "the fall" had not affected or altered woman's created equality. Though woman was created with the rights and prerogatives of man and nothing was said of subjection before "the fall" itself, it became impossible for Roberts to ignore woman's punishment for her role in that transgression. Genesis 3.16 could only be understood as a clear statement that woman's desire was to be to her husband and that he should rule over her.

Roberts, like other male advocates and even Hannah Crocker in 1818, could hold that woman was created equal, punished by subjection to man for her part in the garden rebellion, and still entitled to full participation in the life of the church and state. He did so in the belief that fulfillment of the promise in Genesis 3.15 negated the subjection. The Christ event provided such a fulfillment, and the New Testament record attested to that fact. Roberts cited Galatians 3.13, Galatians 3.28 and Matthew 19.14 as evidence.

Another supporter of this position was L. T. Townsend who stated his position concisely in a contributing article to Willard's book *Woman in the Pulpit*:

> If Christianity bids us lift the curse from man, in the same breath it must bid us lift the curse from woman; and that is what will restore her original rights, when she, as queen, was bidden, with man, as king, to have dominion over the earth. Paradise in Eden was lost by sin; it is being regained throughout the earth by the coming of Christ.[17]

The women's appraisal of the gospels and Jesus relationship to women also did not go unnoted by male scholars. James Donaldson, somewhat of a skeptic about religious and scriptural benefits accorded women, nevertheless was forced to admit that women occupied a surprisingly prominent position in the gospels in an article for *The Contemporary Review*. Though he remained throughout his life a pessimist with regard to Christianity's service to women, Donaldson found impressive Jesus' willingness to relate to women as persons rather than inferiors.

His article for *The Contemporary Review* cites numerous gospel incidents which Donaldson insisted served as evidence of Jesus' enlightened attitude toward women and, thus, confirmed women's equal stature with man. He entered into profound conversations with women, e. g., the Samaritan woman at the well, the Syrophoenician woman who wrung from him the healing of her daughter, the discourse with Mary and Martha. He also travelled and mingled with women, a behavior unheard of in his day. His first appearance following the resurrection was to Mary Magdalene, and it was to her that he entrusted the first Easter message.

Jesus exhibited, for Donaldson, genuine respect and great gentleness where women were concerned. His confrontation with the Samaritan woman revealed respect well beyond that tolerated by his contemporaries; his treatment of the woman taken in adultery showed gentleness beyond that expected or shown by the males who gathered to stone the unfortunate woman. For Donaldson, Jesus was seen as a man unique for his day, and even uniquely different in his attitudes from most male Christians throughout the generations of the church.

The suspected Pauline passages, as might be expected, drew much attention from male exegetes, and often they directed entire articles to exegesis of particular texts. Edward Lyttelton illustrated his argument from Pauline prejudice by addressing I Timothy 2 and I Corinthians 11, wherein woman's subjection is tied to the Genesis account. Lyttelton advised his readers that the passages could not be correctly understood unless one acknowledged that Paul, as was then customary, presupposed a very literal interpretation of the story. Genesis was historical fact for Paul; and because he held such a veiw, it was impossible for him to assert that woman was the equal of man. The book of Genesis clearly stated for Paul that woman was made for man and that sin had entered the world through the unfortunate manipulations of the woman. Paul's logic was clearly clouded by the sentiments of the time in which he lived.

Times had changed however. Lyttelton claimed that even if one conceded that sin did enter the world through the disobedience of Eve, it would not necessarily follow that woman was then to be accorded a permanent position of submission. Such would not be the logic of modern scholars. Yet, for Paul, who thought in accord with fellow scholars of his age, this modern option was not a viable alternative. He had been conditioned to believe that the Garden myth left a permanent mark on the relationship between the sexes. Though he was often more liberal in his outlook than his rabbinical counterparts, he nevertheless was so immersed in similar thought forms that he often borrowed their phraseology.

Such parallels in Paul's writings and the rabbinical works of his day led Lyttelton to the conclusion that "St. Paul was not only tinged but saturated with Jewish ideas. Especially in regard to the duty of submissiveness to husbands he does not seem to have departed at all from the conventional opinions of the time. He borrowed the very expressions of the Rabbis, and like them justifies his approval of existing customs by somewhat recondite references to the Old Testament."[18]

The Pauline admonition for woman's silence in the church produced some of the most systematic studies. Certainly one of the most complete was prepared by Harmon Loomis. Its attack on traditionally held belief resulted in difficulty getting it published. After several unsuccessful attempts to secure a publisher, Loomis finally succeeded; it appeared in the April, 1874 issue of *The Congregational Quarterly*.

Loomis, like others, was greatly troubled by what appeared to be a contradiction in Paul's writing, if not the New Testament itself. Were women both encouraged to speak and admonished in the next breath to keep silent? Was Paul against Peter? Against the prophet Joel? Against himself? Loomis answered a resounding "no!" He was convinced that no contradiction whatever existed in the biblical record. Contradiction was, in fact, totally eradicated once one rightly translated the crucial Greek word λαλεω.

In his study, Loomis declared that Paul used no less than five Greek words—λαλεω , λεγω , ειπω , ειρω , and φημι —translated "speak" or "say". In the disputed passages only two appeared—λαλεω and λεγω —and of those " λελεω " was the word most often employed.

> In the noted I Cor. xiv, λαλεω, in some of its forms, occurs twenty-four times, λεγω only three times. There seems to have been a state of things in that Corinthian church that made that word, λαλεω, singularly apposite and appropriate, so that the apostle could think of no other word so adapted to the confusion and disorders.[19]

In its classical sense the word meant to speak, talk, prate, prattle, babble, chatter, or twitter and was generally the complementary Greek word for the Hebrew "dabar." Both dabar and λαλεω were used one of five ways, according to Loomis, and never to denote common conversation. It meant: a) mere use of the voice conveying no definite thought; b) in the sense of counselling or communing together; c) to express implication rather than a clear thought or truth; d) to wrangle or discuss in a confused, non-edifying manner; and e) in allusion to what had before been stated without resorting to repetition.

Thus Loomis concluded his argument by asserting that Paul was talking about confusion, commanding *men and women alike* to cease their unconstructive din and babble.

> The context shows it to be only temporary (the command), and from a certain kind of talk not edifying to the church (λαλια), the babble of foreign tongues. By what rule of logic is it partial and temporary in one case (for men), and general and perpetual in the other (for women)? The confusion had been made principally by the men, and the apostle's rebukes were chiefly to them, with the reason for it, in the 33rd verse, which is connected with the preceding verse by a " γαρ " (for) God is not the author of confusion, but of peace, as in all churches of the saints.[20]

The Reverend S. B. Goodenow of Illinois, writing in *The New Englander*, also felt that the question of good order was paramount in Paul's thinking but thought the issue of subjection of equal importance. Noting that the phrase "they are commanded" was an interpolation of the translator and that Paul's most intimate concern was the elimination of chaos, Goodenow argued that woman could speak, but only when order was not jeopardized nor man's supremacy challenged. The latter contention was supported by Goodenow through his own translation of I Corinthians 14.34-35. The verses, in his mind, should have been translated as follows: "Let (your) women in the churches (thus) hold their peace (or restrain their speech), for it has not been permitted (or assigned) to them to speak, save (or as much as) to be in subjection; as also the law says. And if they wish to find out something, let them ask their respective men at home; for shaming it is to (or with) women to talk (it thus) in church."[21]

A somewhat similar view was expounded by Professor George H. Gilbert of Chicago Theological Seminary and The Reverend William Deloss Love of Andover. Gilbert discredited all arguments which only partially conceded the right of women to speak in the church, i. e., only in small circles or in particular, non-worship services of the church bodies. The verses in I Corinthians did not allow for such distinctions.

Paul in the same book testified to the fact that women were definitely allowed to both pray and prophesy in Christian gatherings of the New Testament church. Thus, both I Corinthians 14 and I Timothy 2 were, for Gilbert, primarily concerned with the question of subjection. It was this regulation, and this alone, which the Corinthian women were challenging in their behavior. "The speaking which is prohibited is that which transgresses the limits of proper womanly subjection. One thing is pretty certain: if Paul in chapter 11 (Corinthians) did not think praying and prophesying necessarily at variance with woman's subordination to men, he did not think so when he dictated chapter 14. Therefore, what he prohibits in chapter 14.34-35 cannot be praying and prophesying."[22] Goodenow's views, published in the July, 1893 issue of *The Biblical World*, appear to affirm an equality when in fact they do not. A woman may speak in

the church but not without the express consent of male superiors;
her "equality" is not an equality at all.

For Goodenow, women were guilty of a breach of womanly
dignity and/or crassly interrupting the proceedings to the general
confusion of the entire assembly. They were thus forbidden to continue such activity but were not, at the same time, excluded from
participating in any of the exercises of public worship. Goodenow
maintained that the passages understood in this way saved Paul from
the accusation of self-contradiction.

William Deloss Love offered still further commentary on the
Gilbert-Goodenow thesis. For Love, Paul's concern addressed only
woman's abandonment of the law of subjection. Woman's speaking,
in and of itself, did not necessarily violate such a law; only the methods and attitude displayed would effectively do that.

Love, it might also be noted, dismissed all arguments from
translation of the word " $\lambda a \lambda \epsilon w$," parochialism and maintenance of
good order. The pronouncement applied to all churches and all
women. The women were not babbling incoherently nor being disruptive; they were challenging masculine perogative, and such could
not be tolerated. The husband's headship over the wife was an
established principle not to be dismissed. Paul was merely upholding
that inexorable principle, not persecuting women.

One readily notes that the support offered by several male
supporters fell far short of the positions and understandings voiced
by the women exegetes. They are supportive however in that they
raised serious questions regarding the traditionally rigid stances
then in force. The fact that they were not rabid feminists does not
exclude the fact that they helped drive forward the wedges of
feminine scholarship. In their attempts to draw defensive perimeters
they were forced to concede a good deal; in effect, they provided
an uncertain yet sure support for the women.

Notes

[1]David Sherman, "Introduction" to John O. Foster's *Life and Labors of Mrs. Maggie Newton Van Cott, the First Lady Licensed to Preach in the Methodist Episcopal Church in the United States* (Cincinnati: Hitchcock and Walden, 1872), p. xxxv.

[2]William Deloss Love, "Women Keeping Silence in Churches," *The Bibliotheca Sacra*, 35, No. 137 (January, 1878), 41. [Another supportive article which sought to show that Paul's admonitions were to be parochially applied and thus did not restrict women from voting was John Hooker's short tract *The Bible and Woman Suffrage*, Hartford: Case, Lockwood and Brainerd, 1874.]

[3]Charles W. Torrey, "Women's Sphere in the Church," *The Congregational Quarterly*, 9, No. 2 (April, 1867), 166.

[4]Edward Lyttelton, "Women's Suffrage and the Teaching of St. Paul," *The Contemporary Review*, 69 (May, 1896), p. 681.

[5]*Ibid.*, p. 688.

[6]Theodore E. Schmank, "A History of Authority, and of the Right to Rule, in Christian Society, in its Bearings on the Woman Question," *The Lutheran Church Review*, 18, No. 3 (July, 1899), 543.

[7]*Ibid.*, p. 550.

[8]"The Eligibility of Women not a Scriptural Question," *The Methodist Review*, 73 (March, 1891), p. 287. [Although the article does not bear the author's name, it is no doubt the editorial work of J. W. Mendenhall.]

[9]*Ibid.*, p. 291.

[10]"The Ground of Woman's Eligibility," *The Methodist Review*, 73 (May, 1891), p. 459. [Again this article appears to present the editorial stance of J. W. Mendenhall. The reader is also referred to the March 5 and March 12 issues of *The Christian Advocate* for additional information on the debate.]

11*Ibid.*, p. 457.

12Lyttelton, *Op. Cit.*, p. 681.

13*Ibid.*, p. 682.

14Torrey, *Op. Cit.*, p. 167.

15*Ibid.*

16Adam Clarke, *The Holy Bible . . . With Commentary and Critical Notes Designed as a Help to a Better Understanding of the Sacred Writings*, I (London: Joseph Butterworth and Son, 1825), n. pag.

17L. T. Townsend contributing article to F. E. Willard's *Woman in the Pulpit* (1888), p. 162. [Another excellent article in support not only of woman's simultaneous creation with man and Christ's removal of the burden of the curse, but also of woman's commendable role in the life of Israel and the early church is George Hays' pamphlet *May Women Speak? A Bible Study by a Presbyterian Minister.* Chicago: Woman's Temperance Publication Association, 1889.]

18Lyttelton, *Op. Cit.*, p. 685.

19Harmon Loomis, "Women in the Church. May They Speak in Meetings?" *The Congregational Quarterly*, 16 (April, 1874), p. 271.

20*Ibid.*, p. 272.

21S. B. Goodenow, "Voice of Women in the Church," *The New Englander*, 26 (1877), p. 129.

22Geroge Gilbert, "Women in Public Worship in the Churches of St. Paul," *The Biblical World*, NS 2 (July, 1893), p. 46.

Chapter X

Women in the Early Church

The woman's movement produced not only accomplished biblical exegetes, but church historians as well. They appraised the role of women in the history of the church and, summarily, arrived at two distinct, seemingly opposed, conclusions. For some, Christianity had provided women with progressive advantages and elevated them above the status of surrounding pagan women, granting to women dignity previously denied members of the female sex. For others, less in number but persistent and vociferous in their opinions, Christianity had always demanded nothing less than woman's enslavement; and church history, far from revealing a developing dignity accorded women, attested to woman's continued debasement by theology-wielding religionists. Both parties substantiated their claims well.

Among the feminists who argued that the Christian faith uplifted rather than demoralized women were such scholars as Frances E. Willard, John O. Foster, C. C. Shackford, David Sherman, William Henry Milburn, Phoebe Palmer, Benjamin T. Roberts and J. L. Spalding. They continued to maintain that wherever one might point in the history of the church to sustain an argument intent upon showing that the church forged woman's shackles and denigrated her personhood there were other, more important, factors which revealed that Christianity had indeed loosened the bonds of feminine slavery and contributed to woman's physical, mental and spiritual welfare. Christianity was for them not only a vital force, but *the* vital force in woman's progress throughout the pages of history.

Frances E. Willard was certainly one of the foremost champions of this view. She remained outspoken in her defense of the

Christian faith and its advantageous affect on woman's position, although she did prove open-minded enough to concede that there were times when practices in the church had resulted in the belittling of womankind. Still she declined to confirm Christianity itself as the villian; selected abuses, in and of themselves, could never be construed as sufficient evidence to undermine the overall integrity of the faith. Despite any cited incidents to the contrary, Christianity's impact was decidedly positive for woman's advancement.

Phoebe Palmer, an earlier and definitely more conservative feminist than Willard, agreed with this view. Her argument was both simple and logical; one only needed to contrast the postion of women in christianized countries with those lacking Christian influence. Although it is obvious that in her attempt to emphasize the role of Christianity she deemphasized or ignored other important contributing factors, her argument is not without validity. Her statements manifest a call to exercise common sense in the matter.

> That the general principles of Christianity are calculated to exalt woman is a fact too obvious to need comment. Where Christianity is not acknowledged, men are barbarous in their treatment of the female sex. Might is right, and man, wholly depraved, manifests his supreme selfishness by making woman his slave. But where Christianity is acknowledged, though it be a general acknowledgment of its principles, there woman is honored and her opinions regarded, and a breach of courtesy towards the sex is summarily condemned as unchivalric and disreputable.[1]

Her idealism, so apparent in all her writings, came to the fore in this argument as well. Her inner city mission work in New York defies any claim that she was out of touch with the debasing conditions experienced by many American women; thus, her statements must be viewed almost entirely in the context of her deep spiritualism, which manifested itself in her leadership in the "holiness movement" and its call for entire sanctification. Christianity was for her an opportunity for human perfection; it necessarily could not be a vehicle for human debasement.

Similar sentiments were voiced by J. L. Spalding in an article for the *North American Review*[2] and William Henry Milburn. Both men developed a thesis wherein Christianity was viewed as granting women a status far beyond that granted to women in Jewish, Teutonic and Roman societies. The distance between Christendom and pagan cultures was incalculable; woman's progress, a factor in the discrepancy between cultures, was undeniably dependent upon the Christian gospel. The source was Christ himself, who, for Milburn, was woman's greatest single champion: "He was the first to appreciate her woes and wants; he was the first to offer the remedy for her wrongs; his gospel is the only philosophy which recognizes her value, and which points out her true sphere; his spirit is the only guide to lead her to duty and blessedness."[3]

Milburn's words might still be said to imply a rather limited and conservative appreciation for woman's worth and position, and how extensively he interpreted woman's "sphere" remains questionable. Yet there is little doubt that Milburn assumed Christianity to be the foundation upon which women had progressed and would continue to progress.

C. C. Shackford, in an article for *The Monthly Review and Religious Magazine*, also argued from this basis of contrast between pagan and Christian cultures. His comparison of the ascent of women in Christendom to their counterparts in Asia was very illuminating. To contrast woman's deplorable condition in India under Hinduism forced Shackford to conclude that "the forms of self-reliant women gleam out upon us in the history of every Christian nation."[4]

Even the Middle Ages were not at all bleak for women according to Shackford. Contrary to the opinions of many nineteenth century feminists, Shackford insisted that they were years in which women were accorded new respect. During those so-called bleak years women had reached new heights by healing the sick, becoming fountainheads of charity and compassion and even confounding theologians with their wisdom. To women he gives credit for converting barbarian kings, and his impression is such that he views women as the indispensable instruments in the conversion of Europe itself.

Yet Shackford's image of woman in the Middle Ages is not one of power but of piety. They are reservoirs of tenderness and virtue who are consistently depicted in art as holy, chaste and objects of man's highest adoration. It is their piety which stands forth in sharp contrast to the cruelty and violence which characterized the age. His noble, almost idolatrous, appreciation of women, whatever its merit, was unsettling to feminists of the nineteenth century, as it still is to women of the twentieth.

Two scholars who were not quite as flowery as Shackford in their conclusions were John O. Foster and David Sherman, both of whom would become Methodist bishops. Like fellow Methodist Willard, neither was blinded to the injustices toward women evident in Christian church history. They acknowledged that women had certainly suffered at the hands of tyrannical clerics and perished beneath the weight of oppressive church dogma. At times, they maintained, the church had mercilessly and mindfully exploited women, but within the history of the church also lay woman's social, as well as spiritual, salvation.

They disagreed with Shackford in his evaluation of the Middle Ages. For Foster and Sherman these years could only be characterized by untold villainy toward women. The Reformation and, as might be expected, Methodism were the two single movements which had done the most for woman's cause and fostered an enhancement of her worth and merit.

An even more tempered evaluation was presented by Benjamin Roberts, who, like Sherman and Foster, was rooted in American Methodism. In essentials he agreed with both Foster and Sherman, but he did not do so with the same sense of wholehearted conviction. In his book *Ordaining Women*, published in 1881, he was to write: "Though Christianity has greatly ameliorated the condition of woman, it has not secured for her, even in the most enlightened nations, that equality which the Gospel inculcates."[5]

Although the above-mentioned scholars spoke with differing degrees of convictions and with not always compatible lists of reasons, they succeeded in presenting a reasonably united defense for the protection of Christian integrity. Their views also proved enduring. As late as 1949 their words would be echoed in Mary Beard's book *Women as a Force in History.*

> From the flowering of Christianity in the later ages the idea of human equality was never absent. It is true that many Christian writers and teachers, recognizing the force of woman in society, inveighed against woman, declared her a source, if not the source, of evil in the world, and proclaimed in bitter language that she ought to be in all things subject to man. But such teaching was utterly different from the contention that as a matter of fact woman had been throughout the past subject to man and still was. Moreover it is possible to assemble from other Christian teachings quotations giving entirely different views of woman; and in any case the doctrine of human equality continued to be asserted amid the storms and strains of centuries.[6]

Such conclusions as those presented by these protectors of Christian integrity, whether enthusiastically or with great reserve, were unacceptable, even incomprehensible, to women like Elizabeth Stanton, Matilda J. Gage, Abby Morton Diaz and New Testament scholar Ellen B. Dietrick. They were joined in their position by James Donaldson, who would voice some of the most condemning accusations against the church.

For these feminists Christianity had consciously fashioned and fitted the shackles now binding women to inferiority. Far from liberating woman, Christianity had heaped upon the sex burdensome dogmas with such cunning that women still struggled to throw them off. It had crippled her mentally and abused her physically; the church stood indicted for the most horrendous crimes perpetrated against women.

Angrily, Abby Morton Diaz voiced her conviction, and that of fellow feminists as well, when she wrote:

> Being at one and the same time the instructor of the office, the selector of the candidate, the candidate, the elector and the incumbent, he (man) proceeds according to his Mohammedan, or his Buddhistic, or his Christian, or his Hebrew, or his savage, or his civilized ideas to mark out woman's sphere—tell her what are her duties, her needs, her capabilities, how to be womanly,

how she can make him happy, what in her will meet his approval, in what ways she can serve him, what he will and will not
allow her to acquire. He has constructed her creeds for her, and
mapped out her heaven and hell. He has made her his toy and
his slave. He has made himself her law maker, judge, jury,
jailer and executioner. He has burnt her; put her to torture;
given her to wild beasts, and thrown her into the water by the
hundred sackfuls. He has been her sole attendant in imprison-
ment, has had sole charge of every public institution in which
woman has been placed.[7]

These sentiments, expressed so forcefully by Diaz, resound in
the writings of women like Matilda Gage and Elizabeth Stanton,
both of whom proclaimed that Christianity had not beneficially
altered man's attitude toward woman or woman's position in society.
Instead, Christianity had succeeded in doing just the opposite. Woman, rather than gaining greater freedom under the aegis of Christianity, saw what freedom she did possess wrenched from her, either
abruptly or gradually over the span of centuries. Whatever the speed
of her degradation, the villain was unmistakeably the church, or
broadly speaking, religion.

For Stanton and Gage, Christianity was but a part of a more
encompassing movement to usurp woman's freedom. Centuries
before Christianity appeared on the scene there had been concerted
efforts to deny feminine dignity. Christianity had merely threw its
power and prestige behind the age—old trend to insure woman's
removal from social and political power.

By the middle of the nineteenth century, Johann J. Bachofen
had published his controversial work *Mutter-recht* which, in essence,
maintained that the earliest form of societal organization had been
matriarchal and matrilineal. While Bachofen faced great difficulty in
acquiring support for his views in certain sectors of the intellectual
community, he gained two enthusiastic supporters in Matilda Gage
and Elizabeth Stanton. Both women appropriated the Bachofen
thesis in their writings and saw it as supportive of their arguments for
woman's equality. Stanton was without a doubt the most vocal
adherent of the Bachofen view,[8] though Gage devoted an entire

chapter to supporting the matriarchate in her book *Woman, Church and State*, published in 1893.

For both women, Christianity restricted the freedom women had experienced under older civilizations, where they insisted the matriarchate was much in evidence and easily discernible. Gage outlined the primary intent of her book *Woman, Church and State* as an attempt to "prove that the most grievous wrong ever inflicted upon woman had been in the Christian teaching that she was not created equal with man, and the consequent denial of her rightful place in Church and State."[9] So adamant was Gage in this conviction that she informed fellow feminists that she had no faith in any religion whatever which received revelation only through man and did not grant man and woman an exact equality of religious rights.

Stanton was equally vehement in her negative appraisal of Christianity. Writing in an article for the *North American Review*, she set forth her views acidulously.

> A consideration of woman's position before Christianity, under Christianity, and at the present time, shows that she is not indebted to any form of religion for one step of progress, or one new liberty; on the contrary, it has been through the perversion of her religious sentiments that she has been so long held in a condition of slavery. All religions thus far have taught the headship and superiority of man, the inferiority and subordination of woman. Whatever new dignity, honor, and self-respect the changing theologies may have brought to man, they have all alike brought to woman but another form of humiliation. History shows that the condition of woman has changed with different forms of civilization, and that she has enjoyed in some periods greater honor and dignity and more personal and property rights than have been accorded her in the Christian era. History shows, too, that the moral degradation of woman is due more to theological superstitions than to all other influences together.[10]

Evidence abounded, or so the two women argued, in the extant records of earlier civilizations. Such cultures, thought to supply this evidence, were carefully and thoroughly reviewed by Gage and Stanton and conclusions drawn.

In ancient Egypt they discovered indications that women carried on commercial enterprises without male interference, were treated equally with men in the marriage relationship and had freely engaged in such activities as writing and composing. Egyptian women had occupied the throne, and, as priestesses, performed the holy offices of religion. In both of the latter capacities cited women could be seen as directing civilizations and determining national destinies. Far from chained to domestic roles, the Egyptian woman was given access to education, with colleges expressly founded for the intellectual advancement of the female. According to Gage, so far in advance of Christian civilization were such sentiments prevalent in ancient Egypt that Christian women could boast of nothing comparable until the nineteenth century. Stanton was quick to note that even such recent developments had not come about without insult and overt ridicule.

Similar findings were recorded for Greek, Roman and Teutonic cultures. Roman history not only attested to a female priesthood and literati, but "the pages of Roman history are gilded with the honor shown to women, and the civil laws for wives and mothers were more liberal in some respects than those in Christian countries have ever been. The rights of property that were willingly secured to women by ancient Roman law, were wrung out of the English Government by the persistent efforts of women themselves, only three years ago."[11]

Although we might be want to charge the women with a rather superficial appraisal of Egyptian and Roman history, they did serve to caution against the equally superficial and simplistic views often voiced by Christianity's enthusiastic defenders. And their evaluations were not without credibility, nor without supporters. Donaldson lent his support by agreeing in print with their views regarding the status of Roman women.[12] For Donaldson the fact that Roman women appeared in public unveiled, studied philosophy and literature, participated in political movements and even argued their own lawsuits confirmed their enlightened status in the Roman world.

Teutonic culture was also ripe with benefits accorded woman. Such was confirmed, for Stanton, by no less an authority than the

Roman historian Tacitus. The Teutonic mind had furthered woman's esteem; and, in Stanton's estimation, much of what had been traditionally credited to the influence of the Christian gospel should rightly have been ascribed to the Teutonic spirit.

> It is only in countries where Germanic ideas have taken root, that we wee marks of any elevation of woman superior to that of Pagan antiquity; and as the condition of the German woman in her deepest paganism was so striking as to challenge the attention of Tacitus and his contemporaries, it is highly unreasonable to claim it as an achievement of Christianity.[13]

Both Christianity's critics and Christianity's supporters addressed specific events and practices in church history which they thought to be adverse to women. Critics did so with a vengeance; defenders with remorse. It also must be noted that often on particular issues the champions of Christian integrity crossed over to join the ranks of Christianity's severest critics. At such times, it is often difficult to discern one group from the other; only when one draws back to survey their general framework of idea and belief is differentiation possible.

With few exceptions, feminists believed that women did occupy office and perform administrative functions in the early church. Even skeptics of the caliber of Gage and Stanton were convinced of this fact. Stanton, though she repeatedly challenged scholars to prove that Christianity had ever worked in concert with woman's growing independence from male domination, concluded, however reluctantly, that women had held prominent positions in the church for several centuries after the Christ event. Subsequent canonical restrictions against such activities on the part of women testified as much. Even Gage affirmed that "woman was officially recognized in the early services of the church, being ordained to the ministry, officiating as deacons, administering the act of baptism, dispensing the sacrament, interpreting doctrines and founding sects which received their names."[14]

Others, not easily nor often persuaded by the religious opinions of either Stanton or Gage, nevertheless shared their opinion that women played an active role in the life of the early church. Among them were Frances Willard, Phoebe Palmer, Lydia M. Child, John Foster, L. T. Townsend, Benjamin Roberts and William Deloss Love. One surprising, and thus noteworthy, exception was the feminist scholar James Donaldson who, for the most part, remained remarkably close in his observations to those expounded by radical feminists like Gage and Stanton.

Donaldson refused to believe that the first three centuries of Christendom evidenced any favorable affect on the position of women. In fact, he argued, quite an opposite point of view, maintaining that Christianity had both depreciated their character and restricted the range of their activity. No greater contrast could be drawn to show the wide range of feminist opinion in this matter than to place Donaldson's views beside those of Ellen B. Dietrick, the foremost proponent of woman's participation in the early ministry.

Woman's rights advocates grounded their arguments for woman's early participation in the church firmly in the New Testament record. While opponents rushed to their testaments to disprove woman's claim to ecclesiastical power and to school themselves in Pauline anathemas, feminists scoured the same scriptures to discount their disapprovals. They did so not only to disclaim their adversarys' wrongful interpretations of Pauline materials, but also to show that it was not a simple question of what Paul said or did not say but also what women did or did not do in the context of the early church.

For many feminists the gospels revealed that woman possessed the rights of ministry. L. T. Townsend found numerous instances in which such a claim proved valid.

> Though Christ did not call women to stand among his original twelve travelling companions (he had respect for the existing customs of society, and may thereby have escaped scandal), still in the presence of the multitude he drew from Martha the same testimony he required of the twelve (Jn 11.21-27). He declared his commission to the woman at the well of Samaria, with an emphasis and a particularity hardly equalled in any of his public addresses, and that woman became the first preacher of Christ outside the Jewish commonwealth (Jn 4.4-42). They

were women whom angels from heaven and Christ himself first
commisioned to preach the Lord's resurrection from the dead
(Mt 28.7-10, Lk 24.9-11).[15]

For Phoebe Palmer, too, there was no doubt whatsoever that
women performed clerical duties in the early centuries of the Christian church. Paul's admonitions, she contended, confirmed rather
than outlawed woman's public prophesying. The same understanding was also voiced by William Love. With reference made to I Corinthians 11.5, Love found it unthinkable that "the apostle would
take the pen of inspiration and write about the right method of
doing a thing when it was not to be done by any method."[16] Townsend provided additional support, declaring that Paul had mentioned
at least twelve women whom he recognized as ordained ministers of
the Gospel of Christ. Paul had designated them deacons, using the
same term ($\delta\iota\acute{a}\kappa o\nu o\varsigma$) that he applied to himself and Apollos and
the same word, prophesy($\pi\rho o\sigma\eta\tau\epsilon\acute{\iota}a$), that he employed when referring to the apostles.

Palmer was also convinced that Junia, mentioned in Romans
16.7, was a preacher, and she quoted the corroborative opinions of
the early church fathers to sustain her conviction. Benjamin Roberts,
fully aware that some commentators insisted that Junia was of the
feminine gender, shared Palmer's view, maintaining that Junia was
female and exercised a preaching ministry. His proof was also secured
from the writings of the church fathers, most noteably Chrysostom.

John Foster concurred and refused to believe that Paul had in
any way curbed woman's preaching: "Whatever may be the meaning of praying and prophesying in respect to the man, they have
also the same meaning in respect to the woman. So that some women
at least, as well as some men, might exhort, comfort and edify. And
had there not been such gifts bestowed on woman, the prophecy of
Joel could not have had its fulfillment."[17] See Joel 2.28-32. For
Foster, women were both last at the cross and first at the tomb. Indeed, the first Christian sermon on the continent of Europe was
preached at a woman's prayer meeting, and the first convert a
woman (Acts 16.13). The apostles had several times saluted female
laborers who had worked untiringly beside them. But, for Foster as
for others, the gravest injustice had been done to Phoebe. Romans

16.1, which popular understanding translated "I commend unto you Phoebe, our sister, which is a servant of the church which is at Cenchrea," had been prejudicially translated. "Our translators have hardly done Phoebe justice in translating διάκονον, servant, and προστάτις succorer for the former is the term for deaconess or ministra, and the latter is patroness, being radically the same word as is rendered " 'he that ruleth,' " in chapter 11.8"[18]

Roberts lent added support to the selfsame argument. Διάκονος was translated minister in all instances except one, argued Roberts—when it referred to the woman ?hoebe. Her ecclesiastical position was that of deacon or minister of the church at Cenchrea, a fact which could not be clearer nor more conscientiously presented in the biblical record.

Lydia M. Child, in the second volume of her *Progress of Religious Ideas*, wrote of the simplicity of organization in the early church, noting particularly the appointment of deacons. Although male and female deacons may have performed somewhat different tasks, Child insisted that women were appointed to the same office. The word "deacon" in Greek meant "to serve" or "to minister." Roberts once again offered further support, stating that deaconess was simply a woman who possessed the functions and discharged the duties of deacon. An even more vigorously worded argument came from the pen of Ellen Dietrick. She claimed that every deacon, regardless of sex, was, in the primitive church, an "apostle, servant, minister, prophet, evangelist, presbyter or bishop, and originally no one of these were, by virtue of the name " 'apostle,' " more important than another."[19]

Dietrick's argument deserves special attention. She more than any other advocate of woman's role in the early church developed her argument to its fullest extent. She not only included Phoebe within the diaconate of the early church but Priscilla as well. Priscilla, the theological instructor of Apollos, may also have been the founder of the church in Rome, although Dietrick was willing to concede that such a conclusion remained open to question. What she refused to deny was Priscilla's position as a true deacon of the church. She was always, for Dietrick, a deacon in the truest sense of that term, for "Paul, hailing Priscilla by the current term which specially active apostles and bishops used in addressing other specially active workers in the apostolate, " 'Helper in Christ Jesus,' " eulogizes her as one known, gratefully, by " 'all the churches of the Gentiles,' " and recognizes a Church of Rome as established in Priscilla's own house."[20]

Dietrick not only presented her own view, but discredited the views of many opposing commentators. She refuted Chalmers' commentary which insisted that if Priscilla did teach Apollos, it must have been in regard to temporal things only, while Aquila her husband offered him spiritual insight. In like manner, she also discounted Chalmers' contention that if Priscilla did help Paul, it must have been solely in the teaching of women and children. Such conclusions were utterly preposterous; Paul himself pronounced Priscilla his own equal—Acts 18.26 and I Corinthians 3—and was extremely emphatic about it.

According to Dietrick, Paul not only pronounced Priscilla a fellow apostle and fellow bishop (Romans 16.3-5), but commended Phoebe, a Greek woman, as a minister (diaconos), which Dietrick interpreted either presbyter, bishop or apostle. She expressed not the least hesitation about the bishopric status of Phoebe, who was the bishop of the church at Cenchrea and "both a powerful and useful overseer in the episcopate."[21]

Dietrick also refused to limit woman's participation in the early diaconate to but two exceptional women. She maintained that there were countless other women serving in the same or similar function. Again Paul was her chief witness, for he "indicates the equality of male and female apostles by mentioning in one and the same category Priscilla and Aquila, Andronicus and Junia, Mary, " 'who bestowed much labor among you,' " Amphis, Urbane, Tryphena and Tryphosa, Persis, Julia, Rufus, Hermas, and so on, mingling male and female apostles indiscriminately."[22]

Philippians 4.3—"I entreat thee also, true yoke-fellows, help those women who labored with me in the gospel, with Clement also, and with my other fellow laborers, whose names are in the book of life"—also fueled feminists' arguments. Dietrick herself maintained that the Greek word translated "labored" was derived from the competition for prizes in the Greek games and referred to women who *publicly* struggled to attain "the prize of the high calling of God in Christ Jesus."

Roberts agreed, insisting that the Greek word συνηθλησαν (labored with) came from Greek words for "together" and "to strive" as in an athletic contest. Thus, there use in the biblical context could only refer to those women who strived openly and vigorously by Paul's side. Willard not only concurred with the findings of Dietrick et. al., but launched an attack of her own against their critics. She derided those who affirmed both apostolic succession for a male priesthood and an early church hierarchy of organization. Little warrent could be found to sustain either practice, while, at the same time, there was an abundance of evidence that women did preach in the early church; Phoebe was but the foremost example. How could one build elaborate structure and dogma for such things as apostolic succession on nebulous biblical support and, concurrently, ignore woman's participation in the ministry, which fairly lept from the pages of Scripture; the apparent illogic astounded the eminently logical Willard.

Although feminist positions occasioned a variety of opinions and approaches, I think it safe to assert that all would have applauded L. T. Townsend's challenge:

> Such is the evidence for the statement that women are authorized by our Lord, in the Gospels; they are authorized by the apostles in the Acts; they are authorized by Paul, in the Epistles; and they are authorized by the prevailing custom of the church throughout its early history. If in all this there is not authority, we would like to be informed as to the kind and amount of authority that would be satisfactory to those who, on these grounds, are fighting the admission of women to the Christian ministry.[23]

A respectable number of feminists were also convinced that women continued to play vital roles in the church well beyond the apostolic age. Palmer wrote not only of eminent female martyrs, but also of church historian Eusebius' mention of the Philadelphian prophetess Potominia Amnias and other equally distinguished women. Dietrick, Willard and others recorded the fact that Pliny the Younger, in his second century letter to the Emperor Trajan seeking advice in regard to Christian prisoners, reported that he had found *women in the ministry of the church.*

Such scattered, but undeniable, evidence of woman's prominence led Dietrick to suppose that women

> ...continued in the ministry through the fourth and the succeeding century, as we know from the references to them made by Basil, Chrysostom, Gregory of Nyrsa, Theodoret and Sozomen, and, indeed, they have always and everywhere, since Jesus began his teaching, continued working in the ministry, the only difference being that whereas they had originally worked in honorable equality with men, after that evil triumph of which just men should be ashamed, they toiled in obscure positions under the domination of men.[24]

Supporting an argument that women had been active functionaries in the church posed a recognizable dilemma for woman's righters. Assuming that women had held prestigeous and vital positions, how was one now to explain their almost complete impotence in ecclesiastical circles? The all too apparent regression needed to be accounted for, and convincingly.

The women were unanimous in one belief—women had relinguished their attained power reluctantly; it must have been forceably taken from them. However, when and how such occurred was once again a subject which generated diversity of opinion.

Stanton and Gage found themselves again in agreement. Both women traced woman's removal from ecclesiastical rank to a series of church councils dating from the fourth through the ninth century. At the Council of Elvira, circa 305, restrictive canons forbade women to write in their own names to fellow lay Christians or to receive personal letters addressed solely to themselves. Sixty years later at the Council of Laodicia, Canon Eleven specifically denied woman's right to ordination and further prohibited women from entering the altar area. At the Council of Orleans in 511 A. D., twenty-six clerics declared women too frail to serve in the diaconate, and they were subsequently expelled from that office. At the Council of Macon in 585 A. D., one of the most damning debates took place as sixty-nine bishops debated the question, "Does woman have a soul?" Although the question remained moot, the bishops deserve an ever so slight commendation for halting the debate and thus not classifying women with brute creation and allowing her to retain her membership in the human race.

The ninth century witnessed further restrictions imposed on women. At the Council of Aix-la-Chapelle, 816 A. D., abesses were forbidden priestly functions; and at the Council of Paris, 824 A. D., complaints were voiced against women who continued to serve at the altar and dispense the sacrament. This series of canonical regulations uncovered by Stanton led her to conclude "that for centuries women preached, baptized, administered the sacrament, and filled various offices of the church; and that ecclesiastics, through prohibitory canons, annulled these rights."[25] The point which Stanton wished to make concerned the logic behind these councilar regulations. They would be supremely nonsensical if they did not address activities which women then were presently engaged in; to assume that clerics spent councilar time developing regulations which defended against the spectacularly impossible was a stupidity that even Stanton would not countenance for church ecclesiastics.

Yet, tracing canonical promulgations did not explain the change in attitude which must have prefaced such actions; it could only expose the results. The feminists reached no concensus on this even more difficult question. Some explained it solely in terms of Christian negativism toward sex and the growing acceptance of the doctrine of original sin; others saw it as simply another manifestation of male egoism, corruption and lust for power. Still others attributed the changed position of women in the church to the theological popularity of certain church fathers whose thoughts depreciated woman's worth and labelled her responsible for sin, and almost every other disaster known to humankind. She became, in effect, the universal scapegoat.

J. Donaldson maintained that Paul's attitude toward women,

which he took to be overwhelmingly negative, resulted in a growing depreciation of the institution of marriage. This, together with the expanding popularity of the Christian faith, led ambitious clerics to curtail woman's ecclesiastical freedom and bind her once again to physical and spiritual serfdom, wrenching from her in the process all prominent stations she had formerly held in the church. This drive to horde ecclesiastical power by depriving women of it allowed women but two roles in the church, according to Donaldson. They could choose to die for the faith, as did Perpetua and Felicitas and Blandina of Lyons, or they could serve as deaconesses, a role which was severely circumscribed.

Donaldson, with classic sarcasm, contrasted the glory heaped upon the female martyr with that normally accorded women of the day.

> Every honour was heaped after death on the women who thus suffered for Christ's sake, and their ashes and other relics were supposed to exercise a sanctifying and miraculous influence; but during their lives it was their duty to stay at home and manage the affairs of their household and not meddle in teaching or any spiritual function.[26]

In actuality, the only official sanctioned channel for women to gain masculine respect and self-esteem necessitated exposure to seemingly endless rounds of torture and, of course eventually, death.

Donaldson, contrary to the majority of feminist historians, did not see the office of deaconess as a true office in the first three centuries of the church. Instead, he argued, it did not become a common position in the church until well into the third century when circumstances demanded its existence. Unlike other scholars, Donaldson declined to recognize the deaconess as serving a real spiritual function in the church; she neither preached nor taught. Her sole function consisted of ministering to the temporal needs of women, praying and performing other acts of piety.

Donaldson also acknowledged another avenue for woman's spiritual pursuit in the early centuries of the church. If dissatisfied with her exclusion from ecclesiastical office, she could always start her own sect. This avenue had been traversed several times by the more strong-willed women of the age; and it was only the heretical sects, Donaldson averred, which gave women any possibility of exercising priestly or leadership roles. Here they often played leading roles and continued to maintain a measure of freedom and prestige which more orhtodox circles denied them. Thus Simon Magnus has Helene, Montanus has Maximilla and Apelles has Philumene.

With characteristic pessimism, Donaldson concluded that orthodoxy belittled women: "The highest post to which she (woman) rose was to be a door-keeper and a message-woman, and even these functions were taken away from her during the Middle Ages."[27] Woman's choices in the early church were really quite simple for Donaldson: she could die and thus gain reverence for her ashes; she could commit her life to the role of spiritual boot-black; or she could opt for heresy and thereby retain some of her dignity.

Dietrick, often as acerbic as Donaldson in her responses, not only claimed that women were a vital part of early church ministry, but also protested against any contention that women docilely stepped down from prominent offices in the church. Theological modifications had occurred to be sure, and they alone were responsible for robbing women of rightful, dignified places in the church. The Trinitarians and, more expressly, the North African Tertullian were singled out by Dietrick as the prime culprits. She had little praise for either; she lashed out at both with venom. She deplored the Trinitarians because she insisted they had promulgated an

> . . . absolutely silly theory (borrowed in germ, from obscure Asiatic myths by the Jews, and widely republished by the ignorant Tertullian) that the female sex is the primal cause of all human evil, and that mankind is threatened with an eternity of horrible pain on account of a mythical deed attributed to the mythical "first woman" of the human race. It is, of course, as all the reasoning world at last knows, a theory born in the empty skulls of ignorant, cowardly and selfish sensualists, who found it easier to condemn all womankind, than to control the passions which inclined them to place themselves in the power of some artful and designing woman. It is a theory worthy of the brainless moth which dashes itself, again and again, into the

flame that, bit by bit, burns it to death. Something better
might be expected of men.[28]

Her language simply bristled with anger; and if such is possible,
Tertullian fared still worse. He was described by Dietrick as "a
middle-aged man, who, having run the gamut of the vices common to
sensual men in great cities, had become an insipient woman-hater,
and, having exhausted life in one extreme, was easily plunged into its
opposite, contempt for the rational joys of life and great expecta-
tions of rewards to be gained after death through such contempt."[29]

Tertullian, for Dietrick, was simply a much overlauded man,
who purposed nothing less than an entire reconstruction of Christianity and got away with it. Dietrick is sure that had it not been for
the machinations of Tertullian the church would have continued to
reverence a wedded episcopate and maintained an equality of the
sexes in regard to rights, duties and privileges.

Dietrick found Tertullian's work *Prescription Against Heresies*
rife with his own personal idiosyncrasies and replete with prejudicial
tirades against women. Thus, when the church popularized Tertullian, it popularized the dogma that sex and depravity were synon-
omous and woman guilty first cause of such depravity.

Why Dietrick centered her attack so completely upon Tertullian leaves room for speculation. Surely she could have found
equally inflamatory rhetoric in the writings of other early theologians. Most assuredly she grants to the heretical Tertullian an influence which might easily be refuted. Her emotional outbursts becloud
much of her reasoning unfortunately, and we are but left to conclude
that she was either more familiar with Tertullian's works or, for some
reason, found them particularly offensive.

Less virulent, but equally committed to the belief that woman's power had been stolen from her, were Benjamin Roberts and
Kate Tannatt Woods. Woods, a member of the Woman's National
Press Association, spoke before the National Council of Women in
1891. In her address, "Women in the Pulpit," she laid the blame for
woman's ejection from the church's ministry on an increasingly

corrupt priesthood and a growing ambition in high places. Roberts voiced an identical notion and thought the reinstatement of the priesthood, together with masculine pride and corruption, sufficient to explain the gradual but sure removal of women from respected offices in the church. With the resurrection of the priesthood, proud and aspiring men assumed priestly prerogatives. In the process they assigned women lower places in the Christian ministry, finally dropping them completely from it.

Notes

[1]Phoebe W. Palmer, *Promise of the Father* (New York: W. C. Palmer, Jr., 1872), pp. 361-62.

[2]J. L. Spalding, "Has Christianity Benefitted Woman?" *The North American Review*, 140, No. 342 (May, 1885). [Spalding, arguing against the Stanton article of the same name, thought Stanton erroneous in her contentions that early civilizations had reflected a greater social, political and economic benefit for women. Instead, he argued that all pre-Christian history was based on the law of superior strength, which was decidedly disadvantageous to women.]

[3]William Henry Milburn, *The Pioneer Preacher* (New York: Derby and Jackson, 1858), p. 158.

[4]C. C. Shackford, "Woman, Historic and Prehistoric," *The Monthly Review and Religious Magazine*, 43, No. 1 (January, 1870), 60.

[5]Benjamin T. Roberts, *Ordaining Women* (Rochester, New York: Earnest Christian Publishing House, 1891), p. 16.

[6]Mary Bard, *Woman as Force in History: A Study in Traditions and Realities* (New York: Macmillan, 1946), pp. 148-49.

[7]Abby Morton Diaz, *Only a Flock of Women* (Boston: D. Lothrop, 1893), pp. 136-37.

[8]Elizabeth C. Stanton, "The Matriarchate," *Transactions* (1891). [Stanton argued that elements of the matriarchate continued until the sixteenth century when "Luther eliminated the feminine element wholly from the Protestant religion and brought the full power of the Church to enforce woman's complete subjection, . . ." (p. 141).]

[9]Matilda J. Gage, *Woman, Church and State* (Chicago: Charles H. Kerr and Company, 1893), p. 12.

[10]Elizabeth C. Stanton, "Has Christianity Benefitted Woman?" *The North American Review*, 140, No. 342 (May, 1885), pp. 389-90. Hereafter cited *NAR*.

[11]*Ibid.*, p. 390.

[12]J. Donaldson, "The Position of Woman Among the Early Christians" *The Contemporary Review*, 56 (September, 1889).

[13]Stanton, *NAR, Op. Cit.*, p. 391.

[14]Gage, *Woman, Church and State, Op. Cit.*, p. 51.

[15]L. T. Townsend article for Willard's *Woman in the Pulpit* (1888), p. 149.

[16]William Deloss Love, *St. Paul and Women* (New York: Fleming H. Revell Company, 1894), p. 128.

[17]John O. Foster, *Life and Labors of Mrs. Maggie Newton Van Cott* (Cincinnati: Hitchcock and Walden, 1872), p. 308.

[18]*Ibid.*, p. 312.

[19]Ellen B. Dietrick, *Women in the Early Christian Ministry* (1897), pp. 26-27.

[20]*Ibid.*, pp. 27-28.

[21]*Ibid.*, p. 30.

[22]*Ibid.*

[23]Townsend in Willard's *Woman in the Pulpit* (1881), p. 152.

[24]Dietrick, *Op. Cit.*, p. 51.

[25]Stanton, *NAR, Op. Cit.*, p. 395.

[26]Principal J. Donaldson, *Op. Cit.*, p. 437. [The reader is also referred to *The Magazine of Christian Literature* (November, 1889.]

[27]*Ibid.*, p. 440.

[28]Dietrick, *Op. Cit.*, p. 55.

[29]*Ibid.*, p. 34.

Chapter XI

Celibacy and Witch-hunting

Feminists who argued the erosion of woman's position in the church and her ultimate removal from any vital function or office viewed such a removal not as a conclusion, but rather as the beginning of what was to become a constant and persistent pattern of abuse. The church would in the ensuing centuries repeatedly harass and victimize women, and the ultimate justification for such activities would rest on the mere charge that women were women.

Two practices which were thought by feminists to depreciate women in the eyes of the world with the greatest degree of devastation were the enhancement of celibacy and the deplorable practice of witch-hunting. Both were practices considered neither noble nor necessary, resting on faulty assumptions and misguided theology. The former took away spiritual dignity and robbed woman of social and intellectual equality; the latter took her life in untold numbers.

Many women claimed that both practices could be traced to the same source—the church's acceptance of the doctrine of original sin. In their view, Paul had laid the biblical groundwork for such a doctrine while the church elaborated it and applied it wilfully to degrade and curtail the influence of women. Paul was once again singled out as the villian. Women like Matilda Gage who were overtly contemptuous of Paul and spared few words in condemnation of him could with little difficulty hold his teachings responsible for the growing contempt with which the church regarded woman. Gage with her friend Stanton went so far as to charge that this doctrine could be easily singled out as a principal cause for the church's plunge into the Dark Ages.

Yet, once again feminist opinion was divided. J. Llewelyn Davies was to write of the beneficial effects of celibacy on the station and appreciation of women. Not given to the grandiose statements readily found in the writings of women like Gage and Stanton, Davies, quite simply, divided New Testament insight from church tradition. In so doing, he found that the New Testament contained "no such praise of virginity, in comparison with marriage, as became nearly universal in the fourth century and after."[1] At the same time, however, he found no such similar discrepancy in regard to the subjection of women, especially wives.

Davies' contention was not to condemn celibacy per se, but to expose and condemn its wrongful use to sustain abusive insight and practice. Although Davies acknowledged that asceticism had led the church off on a wrong track with deplorable consequences, he nevertheless thought Christian attitudes toward marriage and celibacy instrumental in improving the actual condition of women and bringing them closer to an equality with men. "It is a glory of the Fathers in general to have insisted that sexual virtue was binding in a man as in a woman, and to have made feminine sanctity an object of devout admiration,"[2] he wrote in an article for *The Contemporary Review*.

Davies was not alone in his insistence that the practice of celibacy had accorded a measure of dignity to women. J. L. Spalding wrote a supportive article a year later in *The North American Review*. On the premise that nothing exalted woman more than real belief in the sacredness of womanly virtue, he maintained, "The exaltation of perfect chastity is the most emphatic assertion of the truth that woman does not exist simply for man; that the sphere of her activity is not bounded by the duties of wife and mother."[3]

Gage and Stanton's insistence that celibacy "plunged the church into the Dark Ages" and Davies and Spalding's opposite conclusion that celibacy had enhanced the sphere of women reflect the extremes of the feminist response to the issue. It might also be argued that they reflect a narrowness of insight and appreciation of the dynamic which surrounded the problems generated by the issue of celibacy vis a vis the status of women.

In my research I found only one woman who approached the issue from a broader perspective which went beyond the bounds of Christianity itself. Lydia M. Child, in her two-volumed work *The Progress of Religious Ideas*, sought to view the issue as one which could not so easily be attributed solely to ill-willed theologians and ecclesiastics in the Christian church. Instead, she insisted that the belief proceeded from the "almost universal prevalence of the idea that Matter was the origin of evil, . . . that Matter was considered a feminine principle, and that Spirits were attracted downward into union with it, whereby visible forms were produced."[4] The important aspect of Child's view is that although she never denied that woman's responsibility for sin was a commonly held opinion by Christian fathers and detrimental to women as a result, she argued for a root cause beyond Christianity and even Judaism. Christian theologians were not so much sinister as gullible.

Support for her argument came from her discovery that the sacred books of several religions pictured the First Mother as a figure who introduced sin into the world by enticing the First Father. If the idea had a greater claim to universality than most feminists were willing to grant, then, for Child, women who limited their confrontation of the issue to attack upon figureheads in the church were guilty of ignoring the underside of the iceberg. It is unfortunate that nineteenth century feminists did not more fully explore this avenue of thought.

Feminists contented themselves with reviewing how women came to be viewed as the chief instrument of sin in Christian theology. For the women a great deal hinged on the church's acceptance of the doctrine of original sin which feminists acknowledged as not fully developed until the fifth century. In their assessment its chief architect was unquestionably Augustine. In the minds of many feminists the process was a simple one; the consequences horrendous. When the church accorded Augustine theological preeminence and subscribed to Augustinian theology, it, at the same time, assented to the doctrine of original sin, which then became an integral part of the structuring of canon law.

As part of canonical regulation, it provided the theological basis for numerous persecutions aimed primarily at women, fostered further restrictive legislation regarding women, and perpetuated attitudes which judged woman as little more than temptation to be shunned by the truly pious. With woman regarded as the introducer of sin into a paradisaical world, man was now thought justified in appointing himself as the legitimate and necessary enforcer of her curse. The theological consequences were devastating, and Donaldson probably should not be totally discounted as given to dramatic overstatement when he charges that man had successfully and effectively removed "human being" when defining woman. Woman, indeed, became a creature deserving special consideration and qualification when discussing her being or assessing her historical role. Her adjudged wickedness severely qualified her humanity; her very being as woman became grounds for suspicion and, ultimately, grounds for her victimization.

The theological foundations provided by scholars like Augustine and particularly the belief in original sin produced a growing negativism toward sex and an attendant enhancement of celibacy. This, in turn, generated a number of specific practices which served to proscribe woman's sphere of influence. In the words of Elizabeth Stanton, it succeeded in making "woman an afterthought in the creation, the author of sin, in collusion with the devil, sex a crime, marriage a condition of slavery for woman and defilement for man, and maternity a curse to be attended with sorrow and suffering that neither time nor knowledge could ever mitigate, a just punishment for having effected the downfall of man."[5] Relations with women were labelled unclean; and celibacy, which most feminists considered an unnatural condition, became increasingly more virtuous.

In this context of theological thought the women claimed that a hierarchy of sacredness logically found roots. Not only did it succeed in dividing clergy from laity, but also man from women. In the developing gradation of sanctity, women would be accorded the lowest rank. Her sin was her sex, and marriage a state which could now be regarded as inferior. Gradually clerical marriages became restricted, entirely phased out in major branches of Christendom by the thirteenth century. Superior holiness was accorded those who remained unmarried, and man was taught that the celibate risked less danger of infestation by demons.

Feminists spared few words in their ridicule and condemnation of both the theology and the practices built thereon. Frances E. Willard thought such beliefs a "denaturalizing heresy" and charged that man had "defrauded manhood and womanhood, in the persons of priest, monk and nun, of the right to the sanctities of home." Such theologically corrupt thinking had, for Willard, "invented hierarchies, enthroned a fisherman as God's viceregent, lighted inquisitorial fires, and made the Prince of peace a mighty man of war."[6] For women like Willard a deluded theology opened the floodgates for erroneous doctrines and practices. Her Protestant bias, of course, cannot be overlooked, but her general contention was always that women were to be viewed as the chief victims of theological license. If the theology was corrected, woman's equality would logically be granted acceptance.

Feminist historians did of course recognize that disparate evaluations of marriage existed in the early centuries of the church, one of which clearly valued the institution of marriage without considering it but the lesser evil. Tradition in the Anti-Nicene period remained unyielding in its assertion that it was both unlawful and heretical to forbid marriage. Even the "incipient woman-hater" Tertullian had described the happiness and blessedness possible in marriage.

Yet, concurrent with this view which esteemed marriage there existed another which despised and rejected marriage, opting instead for an ascetic lifestyle opposed to marriage on principle. Such a view regarded marriage an unfortunate result of "the fall" itself and its continuance but an extension of the evil which had brought sin into the world. The flesh, its appetites and passions, was soon intoned as the source of human corruption. The gratification of fleshly desires became the occasion for grave sin. Marriage was not exempt from this appraisal; and, although marriage was never officially nor overtly condemned, it was considered as opportunity for carnal indulgence best avoided by those who wished to retain moral and spiritual purity.

This negative assessment of marriage was supported by and furthered an equally negative view of woman. The term "woman" became almost synonymous not only with sin, but with the term "sex" as well. In some early church theologies the three terms can be used interchangeably without doing serious injustice to the thoughts of many early church theologians.

Nineteenth century feminists claimed that it was this adverse evaluation of marriage which gained popularity and gradually triumphed over the older, more positive view of marriage. In due course, they insisted, it shaped church dogma and discipline to the detriment of women. The measure of favor shifted in the eyes of the church from marriage to celibacy, which would in time be regarded as the highest condition to which both men and women could aspire. The growing popularity of celibacy, some feminist historians maintained, could be readily detected as early as the third century when some openly withdrew into monastic celibacy.

Woman's righters perused the writings of early church fathers in hopes of finding some alleviation for the derision heaped upon the female sex. They were woefully disappointed. Statement after statement provided little basis for hope while consistently sustaining a depreciatory view of woman. She was not only given detailed instructions by the Fathers as to what she might wear and what she might legitimately do, but was repeatedly the brunt of invectives calling her vain, profane, and a sex both to be pitied and despised. For Tertullian she was the "devil's gateway." For Clement of Alexandria it was a shame for woman even to reflect upon her own nature. Gregory Thaumaturgus thought woman incapable of any form of chastity and doomed to licentiousness, and St. Chrysostom called her both a "deadly fascination" and a "painted ill."

While most nineteenth century feminists argued for a strong connection between glorification of celibate life at the expense of an appreciation of the institution of marriage and the resultant derogation of women, other feminist scholars sought to expound an even more comprehensive view of its destructive influence. Donaldson wrote of its affect upon family life after noting it strange that children were so seldom mentioned in second and third century writings. After scouring the writings of the church fathers, he concluded with this alarming statement: "Christians had come to the belief that the world had enough of children, and was fully stocked, and that every birth was a cause of sorrow and not of joy."[7]

Still others noted that a significant consequence of nega-tivism toward marriage and sex, and thus women, produced a differ-ing code of morals contingent upon a person's sex. With the sup-posed existence of a superior and inferior sex, man and woman now possessed different rights under both civil and canon law, with wom-an held accountable to a much stricter moral code than her male counterpart. Penance was required of her for sins lightly passed over when the sinner was masculine. Many crimes involving women were punished with a severity unmatched when the same crime was perpetrated by a man.

This prejudicial view of justice on the basis of sexual distinc-tion served to destroy woman's self-respect and fueled additional ecclesiastical and civil legislation, which produced even greater social, intellectual and spiritual crippling. Matilda Gage maintained that the difference in moral codes had an adverse affect on both man and the church as well, for "man has lost fine discrimination between good and evil, and the Church itself as the originator of this distinction in sin upon the trend of sex, has become the creator and sustainer of injustice, falsehood and the crimes into which its priests have most deeply sunk."[8]

For Gage and others, celibacy, rather than producing purity of life, produced instead criminal activity, and vices of the basest sort and constituting the grossest breaches of morality were now charged of numerous clerics. The church's teaching, debasing mar-riage, sex and women, had succeeded only in subverting the moral character of the Christian world. Gage insisted that the previous fifteen hundred years evidenced a sad commentary on Christian morality and could be directly traced to the promulgations on celibacy with its attendant debasements of women, sex and mar-riage.

Many feminists refused to believe that the Reformation had eased woman's burdens or altered ecclesiastical attitudes toward women. Luther, although he spoke of "the priesthood of all believ-ers" and eschewed clerical celibacy, had done little to significantly ameliorate woman's status. Although he had married the former nun Katherine von Bora and had spoken in laudatory terms of the institution of marriage, he nevertheless retained the old theory of woman's inequality. He thought wisdom in woman something to be deplored and continuously reaffirmed the age-old opinion of woman's position of subordination. Woman, for Luther, was a creature to be ever obedient to man, employed for his benefit and responsible to him in both her thoughts and activities.

Whatever hope might have been extended to women as a result of reformation ideals was scuttled by Luther himself when he abandoned monogamic principle to consent to the bigamy of Elector Philip of Hesse. Without consulting either wife it appears, he, along with six other reformers, decided the scriptures did not condemn polygamy and that it had justly been practiced in times past by noted dignitaries of the Church. Thus on the bases of political expediency and an uncritical acceptance of tradition, Luther, in one fell swoop, further degraded woman's dignity in a decision which would later have far-reaching consequences in Christendom. Nineteenth century feminists were quick to point out the difficulty involved in refuting Mormon polygamy when the most esteemed Protestant scholar had sanctioned it.

The feminists concluded that women would have to challenge both the theological undergirdings which sustained celibacy as well as supply theological and biblical alternatives if they were ever to assume a rightful place in both church and state. The problem was a root one; institutional change demanded a more fundamental theological change to be effective. Gage spoke for many feminists when she wrote that "as long as the church maintains the doctrine that woman was created inferior to man, and brought sin into the world, rendering the sacrifice of the Son of God a necessity, just so long will the foundation of vice and crime of every character remain."[9] Dietrick shared the same conviction and argued that the only way natural equality and dignity could be restored to the sexes was to demolish completely the theological structures which sustained the view that woman was made for male possession and celibacy a state of superior purity. Indeed, it might be said that the general thrust of feminist theology was against this insidious doctrine that woman was an inferior being and chief sinner.

The second practice feminists singled out as a heinous affront to women was witch-hunting, which they also linked to the doctrine of originial sin. Like celibacy, witch-hunting found its theological justification in the basic denigration of women which resulted from the proclamation of woman's baseness and proclivity to sin. Feminists, like Stanton, declared that the church's contempt for women, manifested in ecclesiastical canons and born of Pauline sentiments and the expressed hatred of church fathers, fostered the deplorable practice of witch-hunting, which, in time, destroyed man's respect for woman and legalized the burning, drowning and torturing of thousands of women. For Dietrick it was the nadir of woman's degradation in Christendom when "public sentiment (guided by ecclesiastics) . . . condemned thousands of poor creatures to be tortured and publicly burned alive at the stake for their imaginary league with Christendom's imaginary devil!"[10]

Stanton, unable to separate the acceptance of Christian dogma from the demise of the Matriarchate, wrote in her address to the National Council of Women of the disasterous results:

> Women and their duties became objects of hatred to the Christian missionaries and of alternate scorn and fear to pious ascetics and monks. The priestess mother became something impure, associated with the devil, and her lore an infernal incantation, her very cooking a brewing of poison, nay, her very existence a source of sin to man. Thus woman, as mother and priestess, became woman as witch. The witch trials of the Middle Ages, wherein thousands of women were condemned to the stake, were the very real traces of the contest between man and woman. Christianity putting the religious weapon into man's hand made his conquest complete. But woman did not yield without prolonged resistance and a courageous final struggle. Driven from the home, an outlaw and a wanderer everywhere, ostracized by the State, condemned by the courts, crucified by the Church, the supreme power of the mother of the race was conquered only by the angel of death, and the Dark Ages tolled her funeral knell.[11]

With little difficulty, woman's rights advocates discerned that the clergy comprised the ranks of those who became the most skilled witch hunters. They were the predators who hunted down women by the tens of thousands, only to torture, try and condemn them for claims whose only real existence resided in the minds of the clerics themselves. If blame was to be ascribed, the church once again stood condemned as the chief offender in the eyes of most feminists.

It made little difference if the clerics involved were Catholic or Protestant in their religious convictions. Luther had extended no compassion for alleged witches. Instead, he had vowed to burn them all. John Knox had stood idly by at the public executions of witches, lifting not a finger on their behalf nor uttering a word in their defense. Even John Wesley, as late as 1768, had declared an abandonment of belief in witches akin to renouncing scripture itself. Protestant England, far from disagreeing with its more Catholic neighbors, had boasted of its legislation against witchcraft, parliamentary act making it officially a felony. And the Protestant Pilgrims carried with them the same convictions to the shores of Massachusetts, with leading Puritan divines like Richard Baxter and Cotton Mather loquacious about beliefs in witchcraft.

Woman's rights advocates recognized that witchcraft and punishments for practicing the diabolical arts were not restricted either spacially or temporally to Christendom. Yet many were convinced that procedures changed for the worst under the enthusiastic direction of the church. Feminist scholars cite numerous examples. Matilda Gage insisted that torture was employed to extract confessions from supposed witches initially under the reign of the Christian emperor Charlemagne. Later its forms would demand all the technological skills medieval man could muster.

One of the most damning examples cited by feminists hinged upon Christendom's growing acknowledgment of the importance of sexual distinction. Unlike paganism wherein witches and wizards alike were stoned to death, Christianity, with its pronounced teaching that woman was the greater sinner, rarely uncovered a wizard though with phenomenal ease discovered literally thousands of practicing witches. According to Gage, paganism protected pregnant women with a rigid legal structure, while in Christian countries it was not uncommon for expectant mothers to be burned at the stake. Gage records one disgusting case in which a mother gave birth in the midst of the flames only to have the child tossed back into the fire by a nearby priest who saw his action as ridding the world of yet another heretic. Whether the incident is fact is difficult to ascertain; documentation is often lacking in Gage's work. She, however, clearly saw the abusement of such women as the direct result of the promulgation of the dogma of celibacy after the Lateran Council of 1215 and furthered by the Inquisition's link to the state in the fourteenth century.

According to Gage, ecclesiastical law and practice was more exacting than civil law. The use of red hot irons to gain confessions from offenders charged with the practice of witchcraft was abandoned by secular courts in the fourteenth century, although such instruments remained in use for another century and a half in ecclesiastical courts. While civil courts recognized the ability to withstand torture as proof of innocence, church courts accepted no such precept. Accused witches were tried and tortured again and again for the same crime in church courts until all resistance was broken and the victim succumbed. Gage insisted that no legal structure at all protected women in Christian countries. Even the great Magna Charta, lauded by men for centuries as the harbinger of true freedom, did nothing for women unless protest was made on their behalf by a husband.

So much a part of the mindset of the day was the assumption of woman's inferiority and guilt that in common understanding witchcraft implied a feminine offender. This together with the superstitious atmosphere that dominated the era made it relatively easy for contemporaries to imagine a woman who had deliberately sold her soul to the Devil, wished to harm others, engaged in satanic revelries and sought to carry out all sorts of diabolically evil commands. In the popular imaginaiton of the time women, already under theological condemnation, found themselves the most obvious candidates for the role of scapegoat.

Witchcraft was essentially a female sin in the eyes of the church. Inquisitor Spengler's book *The Witch Hammer*, a sort of How-To book for locating and identifying witches, contained a lengthy section which sought to prove that women were more susceptible to satanic advances and the practice of sorcery. In fact, it "declared the very word *femina* meant one wanting in faith."[12] Although Gage's statistics are once again open to question, she argued that the proportion of witches to wizards gradually increased. At an early date the proportion was set at one hundred to one until, by the reign of Louis XIII, it was thought to be more like 10,000 to one.

Although accurate extant records are not to be had, it can be safely asserted that tens of thousands, even hundreds of thousands, of women perished at the hands of church clerics who were intent upon riddling the world of witchcraft and salving their own fears. Gage cites numerous figures in her book *Woman, Church and State* although she gives no reference for her statistics other than the vague phrase "it is computed from historical record." However, even if such numbers are inflated, they are worthy of mention if only to reveal the perspective evidenced by an influential nineteenth century feminist.

Gage claimed that 100,000 witches were destroyed in France alone during the reign of Francis I, while 500 perished in a single month in the city of Geneva and 400 were burned in a single hour in the French city of Toulouse. According to Gage's "computation from historical record," nine million persons were condemned and executed as witches or wizards in the three hundred years following 1484. At the rate of 10,000 witches to one wizard that means 8,999,100 women lost their lives as accused witches in this designated period alone.

The question which remains lurking behind all the statistics is the question why. In part that question has been addressed and partially answered by supposing that theological logic stemming from the base assessment of women facilitated an easy translation of chief sinner to chief instrument of diabolical evil in the popular mind of the era. Yet feminist scholars did not halt their investigation at this point, but imputed to the church a series of sinister reasons which they maintained the church itself refused to articulate. While the church professed that its actions rested on the sincerity of conviction in its persecution of witches, woman's righters sought and found more malefic motives for its actions. Again Gage proved to be the main architect in this regard.

One of the most often cited reasons for the consistent condemnation of women as witches is that of sheer greed. Property of condemned witches, and often that of their families, was subject to confiscation by the church, with a share divided between prosecutor and judge. Whatever questions might be raised about the relationship of women to property wealth, many feminists were convinced that the rewards reaped by the church were sufficient to perpetuate a lust for power and wealth on the part of the church, which caused it to prey upon society's most helpless members—women, and often children.

Another reason revolves around the issues of beauty and ugliness, youth and age, although it would seem that possession of any of the above attributes made little difference to the actual fate of an accused witch. For either alternative there was sufficient reason for suspicion, despite obvious contradiction. Beauty in itself was good reason for suspicion. Devils were said to prefer the most beautiful of women, and regulations were enforced against women to minimize their attractiveness. For instance, women were ordered to cover their hair lest such overt displays of beauty be seen by demons who might then lure them into satanic seduction.

Just as youth and beauty were no guarantees against a charge of witchcraft, their opposites, age and ugliness, offered even less protection. The old, ugly and particularly the insane fell under immediate suspicion. Abnormal behavior resulting from senility was often the basis for an accusation of diabolism.

The apparent contradiciton is somewhat mitigated if one keeps in mind the identification of women with sexuality itself. Gage offered an interpretation for the persecution of elderly women by noting just this underlying assumption: "We see a reason for this hatred of old women, in the fact that woman was chiefly viewed from a sensual stand-point, and when by reason of age or debility, she no longer attracted the physical admiration of man, he looked upon her as of no farther (sic) use to the world, and as possessing no right to life."[13] While Gage does not expressly state that the same logic was employed to cast suspicion on the young and beautiful, it remains undeniably evident. If the church repeatedly affirmed that a woman's sex was her sin, then her sexuality could with relative ease be envisioned as the single most important factor in her sinning. And through a rather perverse application of logic it determined her very being and thus her reason for being. Both its noted absence or presence provided man with justification for her debasement and condemnation.

Accusations for witchcraft also enabled husbands to dissolve a burdensome marriage with minimal difficulty. With no legal recourse herself, a woman could be accused of practicing the diabolical arts by her husband for the slightest displeasure or most unregenerate of reasons. Her death at the stake made time-consuming legal procedures unnecessary. The extent to which this method of terminating a marriage was utilized is impossible to determine, but mention is made in history of wives dragged before inquisitors by ropes tied about their necks.

Even more prominent in the arguments of feminists in some respects is their insistence that the church was motivated by a fear of women and the knowledge they possessed or were thought to possess. Gage, and she was not alone in her belief, came to believe that "the witch was in reality the profoundest thinker, the most advanced scientist of those ages. The persecution which for ages waged against witches was in reality an attack upon science at the hands of the church."[14] Gage maintained that medieval women had secured knowledge in the presently recognized fields of chemistry and medicine and even cites Paracelsus statement that he had attained all his knowledge from these so-called witches. According to Gage it was this advanced knowledge which frightened the church, which supposed that such knowledge could only have been derived from satanic sources.

It would be an injustice to discount Gage's thesis as simply another dramatic gesture constructed to serve the interests of nineteenth century feminism and heap more derision on the church. While such notions are clearly a concern for Gage, there is little doubt that beneath the grandiose lies a noteworthy kernal of truth.

Women did procure and use herbs in treatment of diseases in the Middle Ages to be sure. Even pain-killing drugs like belladonna were employed by medieval women to lessen the pain accompanying the birth of a child. And it is true that such practices occasioned censure by the church.

The alleviation of pain during childbirth was itself regarded as a travesty of divine decress which sought to uphold the curse voiced in Genesis that women should give birth in travail.

> The use of mitigating herbs assailed that theory of the church which having placed the creation of sin upon women still further inculcated the doctrine that she must undergo continual penance, the greatest suffering being a punishment in nowise equal to her deserts. Its teachings that she had therefore been especially cursed by her Maker with suffering and sorrow at this period, rendered the use of mitigating remedies during childbirth, dangerous alike to the "wise woman" and the mother for whose relief they were employed.[15]

In the shared perspective of numerous feminists the denial of knowledge to women was an inseparable part of the church's suspicion of science. Even when such knowledge was employed in the interests of compassion and benefit, the clerics placed male-interpreted dogma above a concern for the welfare of women. The general picture painted by such feminist historians and their sympathizers is one of a church gripped by dogmas built upon theological deadwood, which made simple compassion extraneous, and sustained by preying on the fears and superstitions of the age. By maintaining its dogmatism and fuelling prevalent fears it stood to gain both power and wealth. A more corrupt portrait could not have been painted than that painted by Matilda Joselyn Gage in *Woman, Church and State*. While many feminists refused to engage in the degree of condemnation evidenced in the writings of such women as Gage and Stanton, few attempted to absolve the church of blame. Redeeming qualities might be pointed out by women such as Frances Willard, but in the eyes of nineteenth century feminists the church was recognized as an undeniable instrument wilfully used to denigrate women.

The persecution of witches had dire social and religious consequences above and beyond loss of life and property, and even suppression of valuable knowledge. It created an atmosphere in which morality itself was threatened. Friends betrayed friends; family members turned against each other, often seeking only to remove the taint of suspicion from themselves. Selfishness and fear supplanted love. In the words of Matilda Gage, "Mercy, tenderness, compassion were all obliterated. Truthfulness escaped from the Christian world; fear, sorrow and cruelty reigned pre-eminent."[16]

The social fabric itself was rent as thousands of women committed suicide rather than face the horrors of public accusation and torture. Even if she were not executed, the alleged witch carried a stigma which made her virtually a social outcast to be shunned by any self-respecting citizen. The damage it did to women was incalculable, whether viewed from a male or female perspective. Many women confessed, preferring death to life, and it is impossible to assess how many women actually came to believe in their own guilt. Gage records the case of one English woman on her way to be burned who absolved her judges of guilt by saying she much preferred to die than to live on in disgrace, spurned by both parents and her husband. It is hard to believe that such sentiment is exceptional, and infinitely easier to suppose that women entertained a greater sense of worthlessness and a heightened sense of their own sinfulness.

Some feminists however viewed the witch-hunting phenomenon and the accompanying atmosphere it produced as a stimulus rather than a deterrent. They claimed that it brought about a silent rebellion wherein the female peasantry of Europe slipped off into the forests to ridicule and mock their oppressors. Out of these secret assemblies came the foul Black Mass, its officiating priest none other than the church's chief victim—woman. Her prayers understandably called for a deliverance from man and scorned the institutions which not only abused her humanity, but robbed her of life itself.

In summary, it made little difference how the women ordered themselves on the question of Christianity's beneficial affects on womankind. All found that when weighed in the balances, the church was ultimately found wanting. Though the scales tipped more violently for some than others and they responded with greater emotion and anger, feminists agreed that injustices had been perpetrated against women under the banner of Christianity. The theological presuppositions which undergirded both the practices of celibacy and witch-hunting were irrefutably the single most blatant cause for woman's denigration. The criminality of theology was most apparent; church history simply reflected its equally criminal application.

Notes

[1]J. Llewelyn Davies, "Christianity and the Equality of the Sexes," *The Contemporary Review*, 46 (August, 1884), p. 226.

[2]*Ibid.*, p. 233.

[3]J. L. Spalding, "Has Christianity Benefitted Woman?" *The North American Review*, 140, No. 342 (May, 1885), p. 406.

[4]Lydia M. Child, *The Progress of Religious Ideas Through Successive Ages* (New York: James Miller, 1855), II, 351.

[5]Elizabeth C. Stanton, "Has Christianity Benefitted Woman?" *NAR*, 140, No. 342 (May, 1885), p. 396.

[6]Frances Willard, *Woman in the Pulpit* (Boston: D. Lothrop Company, 1888), p. 46.

[7]J. Donaldson, "The Position of Woman Among the Early Christians," *The Contemporary Review*, 56 (September, 1889), p. 446.

8Matilda Gage, *Woman, Church and State* (Chicago: Charles H. Kerr and Company, 1893), p. 109.

9*Ibid.*, p. 93.

10Ellen B. Dietrick, *Women in the Early Christian Ministry* (1897), p. 62.

11Elizabeth Stanton, "The Matriarchate," *Transactions* (1891), p. 227.

12Gage, *Woman, Church and State, Op. Cit.*, p. 224. [Spengler insisted that the Latin word "femina" came from *fe*, meaning faith, and *mina*, meaning minus.]

13Gage, *HWS*, IV (1902), p. 765.

14Gage, *Woman, Church and State, Op. Cit.*, p. 243.

15*Ibid.*, p. 242.

16*Ibid.*, p. 274.

Chapter XII

A Reform Against Nature

Woman's penetrating look at the church's history and her defensive exegesis of scriptural texts did not go unchallenged. Some of the most prominent biblical scholars and theologians of nineteenth century America scurried to their Bibles, commentaries and church history texts in an attempt to refute the implications of feminist scholarship. Most prominent among the scurriers was the distinguished Congregational theologian Horace Bushnell.

Bushnell thought it biblically unsound to challenge woman's subordinate role, although he insisted that subordination must never be confused with inferiority. Woman's subject status did not necessarily infer woman's inherent inferiority. In fact, Bushnell had a tendency to idealize and idolize woman. She was, for him, the epitome of piety and delicacy, yet she possessed none of the qualities required to successfully exercise rulership.

Suffrage for women, Bushnell declared, would only degrade women and, at the same time, jeopardize the security and sanctity of marriage. Arguing that only unprincipled women would vote if given the opportunity, Bushnell brushed aside suffragists as simply women who rejected femininity and betrayed an unhealthy desire to become men. He went as far as to label the entire woman's movement a reform against nature, disseminating his views in a book bearing the title *The Reform Against Nature*, published in 1869.

Bushnell's rigidity of view regarding the place and role of women in society also encompassed a rejection of women who sought clerical professions. Although "anything which belongs to the quickening, and edifying of assemblies in the Spirit may be left open

to them (women); only when we come to matters of church administration and presiding rule, these do not come within their juris-
diction. They cannot, in true Christian order, be made pastors, or
presbyters, or bishops; not one of the apostles ever heard of such a
thing."[1] The same held true for the legal and medical professions in
Bushnell's thinking. While large areas of service remained open to
women in such areas, the women possessed no right of administration in either area.

Fundamentally, Bushnell's argument rested on his exegesis of
the Creation account in Genesis. Woman's subordination was not
something devised by men and forced upon her, but a universal fact
which could not be altered as long as the world itself continued; it
was by divine appointment. Woman was not man's duplicate, but of
a subsidiary nature, both complementary and derivative. The "fall,"
with its subsequent and divinely ordered punishments, offered yet
further reinforcement to woman's subject status. Of the results in-
curred by the "fall" Bushnell wrote:

> Visibly the man has precedence and the woman a subordinate
> lot, only it is no more the sweet relationship or order and
> protective sympathy originally intended, but of one made
> hard and dry by the partly retributive extirpations of love and
> tenderness. And still, under so many repulses and discourage-
> ments, the desire of the woman is, none the less fixedly, to the
> man and to his rule, harsh as it is now become in its severity,
> and dismally distempered by the abuse of power.[2]

The New Testament did not repeal Old Testament edict
according to Bushnell. Instead, it had further sustained it. Although
he conceded that Paul may have been unduly harsh and, no doubt,
had been influenced by the callous temper of his times, Bushnell
still found the central intent of Paul's admonitions valid. The central
intent of Paul was, of course, his attempt to stop Christian women
from scandalizing the gospel by their unabashed audacity.

Bushnell rejected all feminist claims that Paul or any apostle
would have condoned woman's present cry for equality. Such a
thought was an abhorrent transgression of good biblical scholarship.

> The assertion of their political equality with men would have shocked any apostle, or other scripture writer, and an agitation by women, based on such equality, to secure the right of open contest with men for political office and power, would have been looked upon even as an offense against nature itself—an outrage on decency and order utterly abominable. The great question of female suffrage they decide only the more effectually without naming it, for indeed it was a thing unknown, whether as respects the rights of men or of women, and we hear them say, just what we have been seeing with our eyes, that men are the force element of the world, the imperative sex, and women the beauty element, called to reign by the more sacred title of obedience and trust; both in unity, to be one flesh, a complemented whole of ornament and strength.[3]

Woman's entry into the political sphere and her present claim to peerhood with man would not elevate her status nor remove her present depression and dishonor. Instead, for Bushnell, it would necessarily culminate in greater depression and dishonor; unable to function successfully in the realm of politics, woman would be forced into an even more helpless and hopeless prostration.

Bushnell's argument was not unique among feminist opponents. Nor was he the first to voice it. His argument is noteworthy only in that he was the most outstanding American Protestant theologian of his time, and his insights could not but influence scores of others. In a very real way he brought together in one text the central objections of numerous anti-feminists, some of whom had already publicly voiced their oppositon.

One cleric who had written against the woman's movement two years before the appearance of Bushnell's book was the Calvinist clergyman, John Todd. Using similar arguments as those employed by Bushnell, he asserted that God had not designed women to occupy the same sphere as men and warned feminists of the impending consequences of their present actions.

> If woman steps out of her sphere, and demands to be and to do what men do, to enter political life, to enter the professions, to wrestle with us for office and employments and gains, she must

understand that she will have to take the low places as well as
the high places of life. She will not be allowed to be a man and
be treated with the tenderness due to women. If she goes to
Congress, she must also go to the heavy drudgery of earth.[4]

Phrases like "proper sphere of women," "divinely-appointed
subordination" and "scandalizing the gospel" would appear and re-
appear in anti-feminist texts. Often they would be accompanied by
warnings—the women would suffer greater degradation, the family
would disintegrate, society would suffer internal moral collapse. In
short, Bushnell's words would echo throughout the century.

Bushnell had easily disposed of the woman's movement as
farcical, unnatural and dangerous. Woman's righters, on the other
hand, just as easily sought to dispose of Horace Bushnell. For Ellen
Dietrick he was a medieval-minded man, fifty years behind present
biblical scholarship. For a Professor Estabrook, a convert to the
feminist ranks, Bushnell proved *too* much. Estabrook, speaking before the American Woman Suffrage Convention in Detroit, 1874,
insisted that Bushnell's objections to woman's right to vote were
equally valid when used against nine-tenths of the men. Harriet
Robinson, in her book *Massachusetts in the Woman Suffrage Movement*, labelled Bushnell's book, and others like it, "nothing better
than rubbish, since in them there is no logical reasoning against
Woman Suffrage as a right."[5] Similar sentiments were voiced by
John Hooker, who, like Bushnell, was both a clergyman and resident
of Hartford, Connecticut. In an address delivered shortly after the
appearance of Bushnell's book, Hooker charged that Bushnell's views
were largely irrelevant to the issue at hand—suffrage. While he conceded that wives should be subject to their husbands in family matters, he refused to believe that Paul's admonitions were anything
more than parochial restrictions and that the Bible offered any instructions which denied women the right to vote.[6] Bushnell had
clearly read his own prejudices into scriptures.

Indeed, most feminists thought Bushnell's argument and
others of the same genre revealed not the strengths, but the weaknesses, of their opposition. Mary Dodge, in her reply to John Todd,
had put it another way: "A remarkable feature of the discussion is

the scarcity of reasons brought against female suffrage. There seems to be a sort of instinct against it, but scarcely anything that can be called a reason."[7]

Whatever feminist attacks against Bushnell, others found him and men like John Todd right on target. Numerous articles appeared in subsequent years, written by noted scholars and fully in accord Bushnell's understandings. Henry Van Dyke of Brooklyn, New York matter-of-factly stated in an article originally published in *The Homiletic Review* that woman's subordination, though not her inferiority, was "written upon the constitution of her nature, in the history of her creation, and in all Christian theology."[8]

Another prominent nineteenth century theologian, Daniel Wise, fearing that the century's women were bent upon transgressing the masculine sphere to their detriment hastened to advise them of the iminent danger which lay ahead in a work entitled *Young Lady's Counsellor*. For Wise, woman's righters were "modern agitators" and "invaders of ancient ideas" engaged in an ill-advised and vain crusade. Presenting their reasoning, he warned female readers who might be persuaded by such inflammatory rhetoric.

> The ballot-box, the hustings, the bar, the halls of legislation, the offices of state, the pulpit, are demanded as fitting arenas for the exercise of your talents. There ought to be no barrier in your way to any position in society whatever, merely because you are a woman. And you are wronged, injured and proscribed, so long as you are debarred, either by law or prejudice, from entering any sphere you may prefer. Such are the claims set up and advocated for your sex, by those who would have you not a woman, but an Amazon.[9]

As can be readily seen, much of the anti-woman's rights arguments hinged on what they chose to term the nature and sphere of woman. Wise rested his entire critique on the assumption that woman's nature offered "indignant protest" against such innovations and rebuked "the audacity of the modern innovators" who thought otherwise. The Bible was thought to spell out clearly the differing spheres and natures of the two sexes. Anyone who elected to ignore his or her distinctly created nature or chose to tramp upon the appointed sphere of the other endangered the sanctity of the home and the stability of all social institutions.

The social concern for a well-ordered society and maintenance of the family was inseparable from the theological concern to comply with divine directive in anti-feminist literature. God had ordered life, and male and female had been given differing functions and rights. To challenge such an ordering brought both social and theological disaster.

One of the best spokesmen for this view was the Reverend Morgan Dix, who published a series of six lectures in 1883 entitled *Lectures on the Calling of a Christian Woman, and Her Training to Fulfil It.* Under such lecture titles as "The Place of Woman in This World" and "The Sins of Woman Against Her Vocation," he set forth what he thought her proper sphere which, he insisted, "is a distinction made by the Creator Himself, stamped ineffaceably, not on the body only, but also on the soul and spirit; a distinction which no art, device, or practice can change or abolish."[10] Arguing that society depended on defense of the home, which he referred to as woman's "normal, primal seat," he informed his listeners that "the test and measure of a Christian woman is whether, and to what extent, she is qualified to help, order, comfort, and adorn her home."[11]

For anti-feminists of Dix' stripe, woman's nature, and thus her sphere, was adequately revealed in the scriptures for any who chose to consult them. The key text was of course the Genesis account of creation. Man was first formed; his task, to have dominion over the earth. Woman, formed out of man, was to be his "helpmeet." This particular account, one of two in Genesis, was singled out by feminism's opponents to assure themselves and convince others of a natural inequity which existed between the sexes.

If subordination was not directed here, asked L. P. Brockett, why had God not created another Adam. Methodist Bishop Hargrove thought the text obvious: "To say that the woman is " 'a helpmeet for man,' " is most explicitly and emphatically to affirm that a woman is not a man; and all attempts to make the woman a man, in the Church or elsewhere, is to pervert the divine intent and order."[12] A great deal rested upon the anti-feminists' interpretation of the single word, "helpmeet," a word whose pronunciation is often indistinguishable in the writings of some theologians from another highly descriptive relational term—slave.

Anti-feminists were not only convinced that woman's creation defined her as a being subject to man, but went to great lengths to elaborate on exactly what her "nature" might entail. Charles Duren, writing in the January 8, 1868 issue of *The Congregational Review*, carefully outlined his position that woman's subjection was determined by her order in creation and the qualities inherent in her nature. And lest his readers remain unsure of what inherent qualities might refer to, he clarified:

> Why did Satan tempt the woman, rather than the man? Because he had reason to suppose that he could more easily prevail. Her nature rendered her more pliable, more easy to be persuaded. She was not formed with those stern and strong qualities that more particularly pertain to man. Therefore she is fitted, not to lead, and command and reason, and teach, but to be in subjection, to be reliant. Her will is as strong as that of man; but it is controlled by feeling and impulse, rather than by reason. Her emotions are stronger; her understanding is relatively weaker.[13]

Duren concluded his article by warning his Congregational readers that woman was not a safe teacher, her reasoning power thwarted by emotional impulses. Guilty once of being deceived and leading man into sin, woman now, because of her very nature, was quite likely to repeat the offense, leading others again into sin and disgrace. It is, of course, difficult to reconcile the contradiction between woman as moral flame of home and society and sinful deceiver in public life. This author has long since abandoned such a task!

Yet whatever the illogic employed, anti-feminists continually reiterated the argument. Women shaped the character, integrity and culture of public men and maintained the sacredness of the home as helper, wife and mother, but a step out into public life turned her into a cunning predator according to Samuel Gilmore Anderson in a sermon entitled ."Woman's Sphere and Woman's Influence."[14]

Much the same reasoning was used by Presbyterian J. M. Stevenson. Arguing that there indeed was a divinely ordered hierarchy based on superiority of species, he proceeded to place woman somewhere near the bottom of this heavenly pyramid.

> When the catastrophe occurred which so disastrously changed man's relations to God, the law of headship and subordination between man an woman was not changed, but its terms were made more distinct, and the subordination empahsized, "Thy desire shall be to thy husband, and he shall rule over thee." (Gen. 3.6) And this increased subjection of woman's will to man's, is expressly on account of her priority in sin.[15]

It is not an overstatement to say that denominational journals devoted extensive space to anti-feminist views. The following articles are certainly not to be taken as the sum-total of such writings; they are a mere handful, but serve to set forth the central concerns dominating the anti-feminist literature of the time.

In the July, 1870 issue of *The Congregational Quarterly* the argument from differing natures once again made an appearance. The article entitled "The Biblical Position of Women" was authored by The Reverend D. R. Cady, who sought to prove that "the account of the creation of the first pair impresses one with this thought, that, as regards authority, rule, public duties, the position of the woman is secondary. That, constituted as she is, delicate, susceptible, shrinking from rude contact and strife,—she is unfit for leadership and public station."[16]

The same year another article appeared in the esteemed biblical journal *The Bibliotheca Sacra*. Its author was the Reverend A. Hastings Ross, who once again upheld the argument of differing natures for the two sexes. Convinced that scripture placed a limitation upon woman, Ross maintained that woman's subordination to man was in tune with the law of the entire animal kingdom. The male was created stronger than the female and thus aptly suited to serve as the protector of the much weaker female, and, at the same time, guaranteed all the benefits that such a relationship might entail. This was true in the animal kingdom as a whole and applied equally to that part of it called the human race.

For Ross, woman's limitation, evidenced in her subordination, was "not founded, as some other apostolic directions are either on some present exigency, or social custom, or changing propriety; but it is founded on something as permanent as the relation of the sexes, and the fact of the first transgression."[17]

Methodist Bishop R. K. Hargrove's article which appeared several years later in *The Methodist Review* proceeded from an identical set of assumptions. In fact, Hargrove took great pains to contrast male and female natures.

> If he (man) is distinguished for courage, she (woman) for fortitude; if he for strength, she for delicacy; if he for analysis, he for synthesis; if he for reasoning, she for intuition; if he for persistence, she for patience; if he for firmness, she for flexibility; if he for grandeur, she for gracefulness; if he for boldness, she for beauty.[18]

Anti-feminists remained insistent and outspoken in their contentions that woman's nature provided the greatest deterrent to any feminist attempt to assume roles heretofor restricted to the masculine sex. Like Bushnell had done earlier, they thought the woman's movement a doomed reform—a reform against nature itself.

F. Godet, in an article for the transatlantic journal *The Contemporary Review*, argued that woman's role, even in the church, was determined by her natural aptitudes, a fact, he asserted, even the apostle Paul had recognized. Godet summed up his views by setting forth woman's role in accord with what he thought to be her nature, although, like some others, he was forced to allow for exceptions.

> She (woman) is formed for motherhood, and to be the rallying point of the family. Her centre of action is the domestic hearth, of which she is the guardian angel. At the same time

her soul is richly endowed with feeling and affection. This gift
is at once her strength and her weakness. Capable of self-sacrifice even to heroism, she has not, like man, that judicial temper
which weighs impartially the two sides of a question; she
decides by instinct rather than by reflection, and her instinct is
easily confounded with passion, whether that of love, of jeal-
ousy, or of antipathy. Thus, a woman's penetration, though
often exceedingly keen, is easily disturbed. It was the woman
who was deceived, says the apostle. For this reason, he con-
cludes, she must neither teach, nor assume any authority
over man.[19]

In discounting the rationality of women, anti-feminists often
found that they had to qualify their views. History provided numerous instances of women who had indeed exercised leadership roles.
However, anti-feminists quickly noted that the exception did not
constitute the rule. Both Morgan Dix and F. Godet assured their
audiences that God had indeed granted exceptional gifts to some
women at appropriate times in history, and S. G. Anderson even
went so far as to list great women in history who, he claimed, stepped in to save the day when no great man was available.[20] Yet,
while a few women might possess high intellectual faculties and calm,
"masculine" judgment, anti-feminists thought such exceptions did
not merit modification of the position assigned by God to the entire male sex, and they certainly were not to be imitated by the
nation's women. The Reverend C. Cort spoke for many when, in an
article for the *Reformed Quarterly (Church) Review* entitled "Women as Preachers," he wrote: "Her (woman's) true welfare and safety
are to be found in imitating the pious and modest example of the
godly matrons of old rather than in presumptuously pressing into
positions in Church and State which God never intended that she
should occupy."[21]

Woman was destined by her nature to a subordinate role
according to feminist opponents, and it was this nature which was a
prime factor preventing her from occupying pastoral office in the
church. R. A. Fink, although he, too, admitted exceptions did exist,
wrote of woman's natural limitations in an article for *The Quarterly
Review of the Evangelical Lutheran Church*.

> Women are excluded, not for want of piety and zeal, nor, in some cases, at least, for want of talents and learning; but, in part, for the want of that robust constitution, that strength of body, that physical adaption to the work inseparably connected with this office (ministry). Their delicate frame is not calculated to perform the numerous and laborious duties required in the public service of the Church.[22]

When Fink was forced to concede that there might be some women who did possess a physical constitution capable of meeting the challenges and vigor of ministerial tasks, he fell back on the argument from biblical dictate. He simply declared that the apostle Paul clearly forbid such engagements to woman and averred that the precepts of the gospel were founded on the general characteristics of the sex, not exceptions from the general rule.

Added support for the argument came from Marcus Dods in an article "Women in the Corinthian Worship" for *The Lutheran Church Review*. For Dods, as for others, the subordination belonged not to the order of the Christian church, but was rooted in woman's very nature. God's image was most fully revealed in the man alone. It was man, according to Dods, whom God had chosen to subdue, rule and develop the world. Woman occupied a secondary status in creation and, thus, in the present age.

> And just as it appeals to our sense of fitness that when God became incarnate He should appear as man, and not as woman, so does it appeal to our sense of fitness that it is man, and not woman, who should be thought of as created to be God's representative on earth. But while man directly, woman indirectly fulfils this purpose of God. She is God's glory by being man's glory.[23]

Woman's merit was evidenced only if she upheld and served man, and this in a manner of abject devotion. God had ordained it so; the scriptures did not allow dispute in this regard.

It was woman's distinct nature which presupposed an equally distinct sphere of activity. As Samuel Anderson charged, "the words from Genesis constitute God's charter of woman's rights, duties and liberties."[24]

Woman was a unique creature, in some ways quite the opposite of man. "The woman [excelled] in the sphere of her feminine qualities, on the whole side of the sensibilities, the tender emotions, the quick insight into spiritual truths, the instinctive perception of right; the man [was] superior in the strength of his masculine nature, in comprehensiveness of understanding, in logical force of reason, in power of will,"[25] according to Cady.

Anti-feminists attempted to show that differing natures and spheres did not imply inferiority. In fact, scholars like Anderson argued a superiority of certain qualities in woman. She was pictured as more vituous and possessed of a greater degree of moral sensitivity, which, in turn, inclined her to be more religious. For Anderson, the qualities invoked in the gospel were clearly preeminent in a woman's nature. Therefore he could write, "The invincible power of the gospel is therefore the invincible might of womanhood."[26]

Charles Duren, too, had assured his readers that although woman was not the equal of man nor possessed of an equal right with man to rule or exercise authority, she nevertheless was not to be thought of as inferior. They were equal with reference to their respective spheres. According to Duren, woman's place was not in teaching, dictating or controlling; these activities were wholly unfeminine pursuits for a man (Duren) who understood femininity as synonymous with modesty, propriety and delicacy. Linus P. Brockett made the point equally well when he argued against the growing number of female public speakers in 1869. He insisted that all the intelligence and eloquence mustered by such female orators did not offset the fact that they "almost inevitably divest themselves of something of that maidenly modesty and delicacy which are such essential charms in the character of woman, ..."[27]

Daniel Wise had titled one of the major chapters of his book *Young Lady's Counsellor* "The True Sphere of Woman." In the chapter he argued that the Christian gospel "made delicate and trembling girls heroic martyrs; but it never produced a bold declaimer, an Amazonian disputant, nor a shameless contender for political and ecclesiastical rights." Nor did it "intimate that at the climax of its triumph it [would] remove her from her distinct and appropriate sphere."[28]

Wise, too, refused to believe that such indicated an inferiority. In fact, he challenged any reader to show him wherein the mission accorded the sphere of women was in any way beneath that of her more masculine counterpart. Her mission, he informed his young female readers, revolved about the home and social circle wherein she was to mold character with an unlimited supply of love and piety. Such a great work was not to be construed as inferior labor.

Three years after the publication of Wise's book, another book with similar purpose appeared. The book, *Representative Women*, written by George C. Baldwin, declared that Eve's surpassing sin was her desire to trespass the limits of her divinely appointed station. And, according to Baldwin, this was also the chief sin of women in the nineteenth century. In contrast, woman's greatest accomplishment lay in being a good wife and mother, nothing less and nothing more. It was woman, he reasoned, who could make or destroy a home, as it was woman who must ultimately be held accountable for her husband's success or lack of it.

It would be misleading to assume that only males held such views. A significant number of women ascribed to them with equal conviction. Among these women suspicious of the suffragist was Maria J. McIntosh. In 1850, she published a book broadly titled *Woman in America: Her Work and Her Reward* in which she, too, maintained that woman's place was in the home as wife and mother. She argued that a political inequality did exist between the sexes, ordained in Paradise itself and evidenced in the Creator's statement that man would rule over woman. The question of female equality was, to her mind, a question bordering on the inane. Arguing that the tasks of all moral and intellectual beings differed according to and in proportion to their differing physical and spiritual development received from their Creator and Moral Governor, she dismissed the question of equality: "Different offices and different powers—this is what we would assert of them (the sexes), leaving to others the vain question of equality or inequality."[29]

Augusta Moore was another female anti-feminist who shared the same conviction. Writing a quarter of a century after McIntosh, for *The Congregational Quarterly*, Moore insisted that woman was benignly fated to a sphere of activity inconsistent with any public endeavor: "As natural to the true woman as her love for beauty, [was] her instinct to shrink from public view. Her constitution, her nerves, her voice, all declare that the representative, the modal woman, was never made for public efforts."[30]

The sexes occupied equally important spheres of action which made any question of the relative superiority of the sexes a ridiculous and impertinent one. Man and woman were preeminent in their respective, divinely-instituted positions or spheres; either would be inferior if they chanced to encroach upon that of the other. Man was ordained for the rougher work of life and his sphere encompassed the broad arena of social and political conflict. Woman, on the other hand, possessed of a more gentle nature, found her realm in the home, which many anti-feminists portrayed as a haven where women decided the destinies of men and nations by sowing the seeds of piety, patriotism and maturity.

Woman's sphere, expressly determined by her nature, was the central concern of anti-feminist writers, and they often took great pains to delineate its boundaries. While the home and family proved the hub for woman's acitvity, many anti-feminists willingly acknowledged that it might extend beyond. Morgan Dix, in a lecture entitled "A Mission for Woman," wrote of their great service and sacrifice, making particular reference to the sisterhoods, and praised women as "ministering angels" ever engaged in "philanthropic pursuit."[31] The Lutheran R. A. Fink wrote from a similar set of convictions, arguing that although woman was expressly excluded from such activities as the pulpit ministry, she nevertheless found within her sphere Christian duties sufficient to occupy her whole life. All this in addition to her role as wife and mother.

Yet whatever her pursuits outside the context of the family, they were clearly to be subordinate to male activities. According to Dods, she was always to exist in a limited, well-defined sphere of action subordinate to the interests of one man instead of to the public. While it was the man's place to serve the state in a public capacity, it was the woman's place to serve the man. Although Dods, like his predecessors Godet and Fink, was forced to record the names of occasionally exceptional women, he likewise affirmed that whatever a woman's natural endowments might be there was a womanly mode of exercising them and a sphere designed in which to exercise them.

There is a touch of true paranoia in anti-feminist literature. Many sought to outline the dangers involved in present feminist agitation. One danger often cited was the damage that would accrue to feminine character. The Reverend John Milton Williams of Chicago, writing in *The Bibliotheca Sacra*, thought most women quick to recognize the difference between their own appropriate sphere and than of men and thought most found no disgrace in being denied suffrage privileges. He also thought that women were aware that the present drive to secure voting rights for women stood to do considerable damage to woman's character.

> Woman is not improved by any effort to make herself a man. She is most influential when most womanly, and farthest removed, in her habits, tastes, and aspirations, from anything coarse, masculine, or unwomanly. I submit, that civil office, a place on the bench, in the jury box, or in the police station, the role of politician competing with coarse men for office and place, is not woman's appropriate sphere or compatible with the ideal woman, and cannot be accepted without doing violence to the feelings of the modest, refined woman: nor is it compatible with the respect and deference we love to pay her sex.[32]

Cardinal Gibbons, in an article entitled "Relative Condition of Women Under Pagan and Christian Civilization" for the October, 1886 issue of *The American Catholic Quarterly Review*, offered a similar warning to women. While affirming that the Catholic Church proclaimed woman's equality in origin, destiny and participation in spiritual gifts, he hastened to add that equal rights were not identical with similar rights or the assumption of traditionally masculine pursuits by the nation's women. Woman was relegated to gentler avocations and activities which did not degrade her but secured to her "not equal rights so-called, but those supereminent rights that cannot fail to endow her with a sacred influence in her own proper sphere; for, as soon as woman trenches on the domain of man, she must not be surprised to find that the reverence once accorded her has been in part, or wholly, withdrawn."[33]

It was also true that such warnings carried with them the conviction that women in the movement were somehow corrupt. Name-calling was not absent from either feminist or anti-feminist argument. A man like Morgan Dix was so convinced that both the Bible and church tradition stood opposed to female equality he charged women in the movement not only of knowing this to be fact, but also rejecting it. This, in itself, proved "one reason why so many of the modern agitators for Woman's Rights, so called, are in the ranks of infidelity and free thought, ..."[34]

Anti-feminists were not only concerned about the irreparable damage the movement might do to female character, but also thought woman's incursion into the traditionally masculine fields damaging to the family structure and, ultimately, the entire social fabric. In 1870, D. R. Cady cautioned against women working outside the limits of scriptural pronouncements, for "we do not know the mischiefs which may follow if we transcend them."[35]

The same year, an interesting response came out of Eastern Pennsylvania. A book titled *A Reply to John Stuart Mill on the Subjection of Women* was published without mention of the author's name. Although he (I am assuming masculine authorship) does not argue from a religious basis per se, it underlies much of his argument. He labelled Mill's position, favorable to women, both unnatural and destructive of social institutions, as well as ignorant of or an outright challenge to the directives of St. Paul.

Christianity did not call for an equalizing of the sexes for this anonymous author. Instead it did quite the opposite: "For whatever Christianity and civilization have done for either man or woman, they have at least more distinctly fixed the peculiarities of the sexes. It is only when the savage and barbarous conditions of humanity are examined that there is even the semblence of equality or similarity between the sexes."[36] Such a travesty of divinely ordered distinctions as that proposed by Mill threatened all that was held sacred in the author's opinion. He warned that "if the existing bonds of society be so loosened, and the faith of humanity so shaken, in what had long been considered sacred and inviolable, that mankind are set adrift without any gods but expediency or necessity, evils may and will arise of which agitators seldom take any account."[37]

Possibly the most curtly worded statement in this area of concern came from the pen of J. M. Stevenson, who warned that to "destroy the order and harmony of the family, introduce anarchy there, and you have laid the mine which, if God prevent not, will in time hurl the whole frame-work of human institutions into hopeless ruin."[38]

The Chicagoan John Milton Williams, in his article for *The Bibliotheca Sacra*, devoted space to an extensive list of consequences if women should be allowed to transcend their appointed spheres. He denounced feminists who regarded suffrage as a panacea for their woes and summarily dismissed the entire movement as antithetical to woman's good sense. Such efforts as those now enjoined by women were to be considered "a revolt against marriage" and "more like a revenge than a reform." For Williams, feminists were essentially destructive in their demands.

> They have created in many an unreflecting woman unrest, and dissatisfaction with her divinely appointed sphere; lowered her estimation of the sacredness of her position as wife, and mother, and mistress of a home; thrown the apple of discord into thousands of otherwise happy families, and doubtless contributed to the alarming increase of divorces which appear on the records of our courts.[39]

Even worse, in Williams' estimation, suffrage for women would turn the home into a battleground. The strife of politics would divide family members and upset the serenity of the home, which Williams, like others, envisioned as a quiet retreat from the tensions of public life. He argued that woman "should remember that the sweet, well-ordered Christian home is the generic reform, including and superseding all others, and that it admits of no rival. Anything, everything, that vitiates or mars its influence or involves a neglect of its duties should be reprobated."[40]

Williams rested assured that only unscrupulous women would vote, and even those of the better class who availed themselves of the opportunity to vote would invariably vote as did their husbands. This made the whole effort for woman suffrage ridiculous in terms of its overall impact; the only thing it would accomplish presented a danger to society and women, for there would be a flooding of "the polls with a vast additional mass of corruption and illiteracy, while it would furnish very few opposing votes. Woman suffrage would aid reform, as the millstone about his neck would aid the swimmer."[41]

A single conclusion may be drawn from a study of anti-feminist writings: the most basic of assumptions was one which insisted that woman's present efforts to affirm and apply their equality was akin to an impossibility since nature and natural endowment could not be broached whatever female sentiment. A divinely-ordered natural hierarchy existed which allowed to women only a subordinate role. Their present demands to alter their role and function could only bring with it havoc, discord and the dangerous possibility of societal collapse. It is this basic assumption, together with the fear it engendered, which must be recognized as underlying all particular biblical arguments voiced by anti-feminists to be dealt with in the chapter which follows.

Notes

[1]Horace Bushnell, *Women's Suffrage: The Reform Against Nature* (New York: Charles Scribner, 1869), p. 24.

[2]*Ibid.*, pp. 75-76.

[3]*Ibid.*, pp. 81-82.

[4]John Todd, *Woman's Rights* (1867: rpt. New York: Arno, 1972), p. 14.

[5]Harriet Robinson, *Massachusetts in the Woman Suffrage Movement* (Boston: Roberts, 1881), p. 165.

[6]John Hooker, *The Bible and Woman Suffrage* (Hartford: Case, Lockwood and Brainerd, 1874), [Hooker originally delivered this as a lecture in November, 1869, shortly after the appearance of Bushnell's book.]

[7]Mary Dodge, *Woman's Wrongs: A Counter-Irritant* (1868; rpt. New York: Arno, 1972), p. 74.

[8]Frances E. Willard, *Woman in the Pulpit* (Boston: D. Lothrop, 1888), p. 120. [The article was originally published by Henry Van Dyke in *The Homiletic Review* (January, 1888) in response to an article by L. T. Townsend in the December, 1887 issue of the same journal.]

[9]Daniel Wise, *Young Lady's Counsellor* (New York: G. Lane and L. Scott, 1852), pp. 84-85.

[10]Morgan Dix, *Lectures on the Calling of a Christian Woman, and Her Training to Fulfill It* (New York: D. Appleton, 1883), pp. 17-18.

[11]*Ibid.*, p. 30.

[12]R. K. Hargrove, "Woman's Work in the Church," *The Methodist Review*, 43, No. 1 (March - April, 1896), 4.

[13]Charles Duren, "Place of Women in the Church, in Religious Meetings," *The Congregational Review*, 8, No. 39 (January, 1868), p. 27.

[14]Samuel Gilmore Anderson, *Woman's Sphere and Influence* (Toledo, Ohio: Franklin Printing and Engraving, 1898).

[15]J. N. Stevenson, "Place of Women in Assemblies for Public Worship," *Presbyterian Quarterly and Princeton Review*, 2 (January, 1873), p. 43.

[16]D. R. Cady, "The Biblical Position of Woman," *The Congregational Quarterly*, NS 2, No. 3 (July, 1870), 371.

[17]A. Hastings Ross, "The Silence of Women in the Churches," *The Bibliotheca Sacra*, 27, No. 106 (April, 1870), 339.

[18]Hargrove, *Op. Cit.*, p. 4.

[19]F. Godet, "The Ministry of Women," *The Contemporary Review*, 45 (January, 1884), p. 61.

[20]Anderson, *Op. Cit.*, pp. 11-12.

[21]Cyrus Cort, "Women as Preachers," *Reformed Quarterly (Church) Review*, 29 (1882), p. 130.

[22]R. A. Fink, "Women in the Church," *The Lutheran Quarterly*, 4 (April, 1874), p. 221.

[23]Marcus Dods, "Women in the Corinthian Worship," *The Lutheran Church Review*, 18, No. 3 (July, 1899), 504.

[24]Anderson, *Op. Cit.*, p. 6.

[25]Cady, *Op. Cit.*, p. 371.

[26]Anderson, *Op. Cit.*, p. 25.

[27]Linus P. Brockett, *Woman: Her Rights, Wrongs, Privileges and Responsibilities* (Hartford: L. Stebbins, 1869), p. 155.

[28]Wise, *Op. Cit.*, p. 86.

[29]Maria J. McIntosh, *Woman in America: Her Work and Her Reward* (New York: Appleton and Company, 1850), p. 23.

[30]Augusta Moore, "Women in the Church," *The Congregational Quarterly*, 16 (April, 1874), p. 283.

[31]Morgan Dix, *Op. Cit.*, p. 155.

[32]John Milton Williams, "Woman Suffrage," *The Bibliotheca Sacra*, 50 (April, 1893), p. 338.

[33]Cardinal Gibbons, "Relative Condition of Women Under Pagan and Christian Civilization," *The American Catholic Quarterly Review*, 11, No. 44 (October, 1886), 658.

[34]Dix, *Op. Cit.*, p. 23.

[35]Cady, *Op. Cit.*, p. 377.

[36]*A Reply to John Stuart Mill on the Subjection of Women* (Philadelphia: J. B. Lippincott, 1870), p. 29.

[37]*Ibid.*, p. 46.

[38]J. M. Stevenson, *Op. Cit.*, p. 59.

[39]J. M. Williams, *Op. Cit.*, pp. 335-36.

[40]*Ibid.*, p. 337.

[41]*Ibid.*, p. 341.

Chapter XIII

The Weight of Biblical Evidence

As adamantly as feminists argued that the Bible sanctioned
their reform, their opponents argued that the weight of biblical
evidence proved quite the opposite conclusion. The Bible deplored
such blasphemous ideas as those voiced by woman's rights advocates
and stood unquestionably against woman's present demand to enter
into public roles in society, whether in church or state.

The feminists had singled out prominent women in the Old
and New Testaments to sustain their thesis that women had previously assumed leadership roles quite in accord with divine will. Their
efforts did not go unnoticed by anti-feminists who saw them as wilful abuse of scriptural record. As early as January, 1868, Charles
Duren in his article for *The Congregational Review* charged that
conspicuous women of both Testaments, like Deborah, Huldah,
Anna, Miriam and the daughters of Philip the Evangelist, had been
misrepresented in the writings of nineteenth century feminists.
Rather than give these women prominence, he sought to discredit
their importance.

> . . . Deborah, though she was a very wise woman and judged
> Israel, did not go at the head of the army. Huldah was endowed
> with the prophetic gift; but she does not stand forth prominent
> in the civil and religious history of the Jews. Anna, though she
> devoted herself to the service of God in the temple, did not at
> all go beyond the bounds of female modesty and propriety.
> Miriam led the songs of her countrywomen after the triumph at
> the Red Sea. The daughters of Philip by no means stand forth
> in any public capacity. The female of the Corinthian church re-
> ceived spiritual gifts; but they appear to have been a kind be-
> fitting their sex; and they were enjoined to use them in a mod-
> est and unassuming manner.[1]

Two years later D. R. Cady published his article in *The Congregational Quarterly* which addressed the same issue. Like Duren, his response revolved about the concern for female propriety. Old Testament women—Miriam, Deborah, Huldah, Noadiah—never assumed public office nor sacrificed feminine virtue and decorum, whatever the skills they may have possessed. Their prominence lay not in public exercise, but in using their gifts within the confined sphere befitting to women.

> These are the most prominent instances in the Old Testament of the prophetic gifts being bestowed upon females, and, rightly considered, they seem to be in harmony with its general spirit as regards the position and province of woman. Neither of them set up as a public religious teacher. They were inspired of God, and we yield them honor. But even in their prophetic frenzy, they did not overstep the bounds of feminine decorum, nor break away from that sphere in which God had placed them.[2]

This concern with portraying biblical women as exceptional examples of piety though not public figures surfaces again and again in anti-feminist writing. They are commended as much for their modesty as they are for their spirituality. The Reverend Cyrus Cort in his article "Woman as Preachers" for the *Reformed Quarterly (Church) Review* provides a classic example of anti-feminist treatment of biblical women. After carefully noting the contributions of such women, he casually dismisses their public importance: "One thing is certain, however, that it (manner of exercising prophetic talents) was done in a comparatively private way without violating the strict rules regulating public worship in the temple, synagogue and Christian sanctuary."[3]

Several anti-feminists personally attacked feminist integrity and scholarship. F. Godet, in an article for the immensely popular *Contemporary Review*, flatly accused feminists of abusing sacred history in pursuit of their goals, making every woman mentioned in both Old and New Testaments wrongfully into a preacher. In what he thought to be a relevant aside, he recalled that the only individually designated false prophet of scriptural record was a woman—Jezebel (Revelations 2.20). For Godet, neither Deborah nor Huldah could have been, by any stretch of feminine imagination, construed as public ministers of the word of God, speaking openly in mixed public assemblies. Any feminist who thought or wrote differently suffered from gross ignorance of scriptural record and/or a notorious absence of exegetical skill.

J. M. Stevenson's article in the January, 1873 issue of *The Presbyterian Quarterly and Princeton Review* lent more support to this attempt to discredit feminine scholarship. Women had never exercised an official place in divine worship, according to Stevenson; and there was, in point of fact, no recorded instance of any woman addressing a religious assembly, either in the scriptures or in the "entire history of the [past] 4,000 years."[4] Although Stevenson was willing to admit that the Old Testament record did evidence rare cases wherein women, under supernatural inspiration, were called to act as prophets and that in one case a woman (Deborah) had indeed acted as a civil ruler of a nation, he offered reservations and qualifications even to these concessions. He quickly assured his readers that despite these noteworthy exceptions, women has never been allowed leadership roles in the conduct of religious worship. He concluded his article by instructing those of a mind to question his observations to consult his or her history texts.

The Old Testament offered no support for feminist arguments in the minds of their opponents. The only support they had gleaned from it was a result of prejudicial distortion of biblical texts; they had read into the texts what they desired and ignored that which might cripple their arguments.

The New Testament, too, had been ill-used by feminist scholars. Whereas feminists had found great support for female equality in the Christ event, anti-feminists remained convinced that it had not significantly changed matters. Jesus did not reveal an enlightened attitude toward women nor had the event itself lifted the Genesis "curse." Women clearly remained subordinate, and, as such, did not possess the right to public office of any kind. Nor had women ever exercised such a right in the early church.

Jesus, contrary to assertions made by a number of feminist

authors, had not sanctioned a public ministry for women. D. R. Cady went so far as to demand that feminist cite the actions and words of Jesus which justified their present claim that women were entitled to the position of public teacher. He, of course, was convinced that they could not cite one instance to uphold their argument.

Anti-feminists believed they could cite numerous examples which affirmed their conviction that Jesus denied to women a public ministry. Cady and others noted repeatedly that Jesus had not authorized a woman to serve as a disciple, a point which Cady thought a significant and telling omission on Jesus' part. This fact alone led Cady to conclude with a rhetorical question: "Does not Christ thus give silent but most emphatic and convincing testimony that she (woman) is not designed nor fitted for public station, but that her powers of influence and of usefulness, greater in many respects than those of man, are to be employed in more private ways?"[5]

Godet, too, saw Jesus as one who upheld, rather than toppled, the principle of woman's subordination. He not only did not give women a role in his public ministry, but allowed to them only the role clearly befitting a woman's proper sphere—ministering to him and his apostles. Godet found this role hardly the basis for nineteenth century woman's claim that she was entitled by sacred writ to a role in the public life of the church. It is unfortunate that the same thought echoes in the words of Augusta Moore in an article written for the April, 1874 issue of *The Congregational Quarterly*. As a woman anti-feminist she praised the wifely, motherly functions of women and saw in the scriptures but an enhancement of those functions.

The New Testament women that feminists had singled out as proof for woman's active role in early church life were similarly discounted by anti-feminist scholars. Philip's four daughters had not engaged in public speaking, and it was misleading to maintain this scripturally unwarranted belief, according to Cady.

Because they prophesied, we are not driven to the inference

that they preached or exhorted in the Church. But, on the
other hand, the indications given by the very language in which
they are referred to are, that they taught and labored in private
and unobstrusive ways, such as the Apostles sanctioned, such as
God in all the ages of the Christian Church has signally owned
and blessed, ...[6]

The point anti-feminists wished to make was that even if some
women did perform extraordinary functions in the early church,
such acts did not offer a sufficient basis for affirming that women
should enter into ministerial duties in the nineteenth century or any
other century. This view was expounded upon at great length by
Godet, Stevenson and Henry Van Dyke.

Van Dyke thought women who labelled these biblical figures
"pioneers of the liberation movement" given to vast overstatement
and, most certainly, faulty exegesis.

The fact that Mary Magdalene, to whom the Savior first appeared, was sent to announce his resurrection to the other disciples,
or that many women were present when the Savior preached
and when he gave his final instructions to the apostles, are
far-fetched, and little worth as proofs that women ought to be
ordained to the ministry.[7]

For Van Dyke, there was not a single recorded instance in
which women were ordained to any office in the church or took any
part whatsoever in its instruction or governance. All instructions
pertaining to preaching and church administration were directed to
men. The pastorial epistles spoke of wives of bishops and deacons
(I Timothy 3), never husbands of these officials. Such an absence of
direct instructions to women led Van Dyke to declare that scripture
was conclusive in its refutation of woman's present demands.

Bishop H. Vincent of the Methodist Episcopal Church reached
the same conclusions. In a symposium on "The Enlargement of
Woman's Sphere" for *The Independent* of New York in May, 1891
he presented his views.

Paul cannot mean to exclude women from activity in Christian work. He does not mean to say that she shall not in the domestic meetings of the church, prayer-meetings, class-meetings, fellowship meetings, and in the sanctuary of her own home, teach as did Lois and Eunice and Priscilla, and other saints of the Church. He is simply, in these letters, defining the character of the Christian ministry, and laying down laws for its regulation, and he provides that women shall not be officially recognized, appointed, and installed as ministers.[8]

Fellow Methodist Bishop, R. H. Hargrove, writing just five years after Bishop Vincent, concurred with his ecclesiastical colleague. Not only had Christ selected no woman as a disciple and Paul's instructions been meant for male bishops and deacons alone, but, for Hargrove, there could be not the slightest doubt that women were denied such offices. Paul had couched his words in language both particular and minute of detail which unmistakably intended to express divine directive on the matter.

Hargrove, too, questioned whether there had ever been an ecclesiastical order which included women. He conceded that deaconesses had appeared in the early centuries of the church, but he denied that there was any evidence to confirm their existence in the apostolic age itself. Thus the word "deacon" when applied to Phoebe in Paul's Letter to the Romans could not have indicated a formal order. According to Hargrove, the word had also been used to indicate the servants who had filled the waterpots at the marriage in Cana of Galilee, where Jesus had miraculously transformed the water into wine. Hargrove also noted that word was employed numerous times in the early Christian centuries without the slightest reference to an ecclesiastical order.

Hargrove, however, never bothered to explain why the same term applied to men in the service of the church warranted a completely different, more formal interpretation than when it was applied to women like Phoebe. Any formal, public ministry was beyond the bounds of feminine rights and duties, although he, like so many other anti-feminists, hastened to assure women that they could and undoubtedly had provided a necessary dimension to the cause of Christ through a private ministry of compassion and hospitality extended so graciously to those who labored publicly.

The question of Pauline sentiment, which runs so persistently through Hargrove's argument, really formed the core of New Testament exegesis against the woman's rights movement. To be even more precise, Paul's call for the silence of women in the church formed the very crux of the issue for anti-feminists, as it had for feminist scholars. The question was whether or not Paul in fact commanded woman's silence and subordination; the attendant question, whether such commands, if true, were still binding. The feminists shouted "no" to both questions; their opponents answered in the affirmative.

This affirmative response formed the backbone of anti-feminist arguments against the liberation of the female sex, despite repeated attempts by feminists to discredit it. Indeed, every anti-feminist of note introduced the damning words of Paul regarding woman's subject status. Much anti-feminist literature may be regarded as but commentary on selected Pauline texts (or those regarded as Pauline at the time).

Feminist opponents, like so many within the rights movement itself, began with a refusal to entertain any position which might in some way infer that Paul was guilty of contradiction. But, unlike their feminist counterparts, they concluded that the balance and intent of Paul's words effectively curtailed any belief positing an equality between the sexes; instead, he strengthened the argument for woman's continued subordination.

In dealing with the apparent contradiction between I Corinthians 11, wherein women are instructed to *pray and prophesy* with covered heads (veiled), and I Corinthians 14, wherein women are told to *keep silent* in religious assemblies, Godet chose to regard the Fourteenth Chapter as the one of greater importance. Corinthians 11.5-6 simply acknowledge extraordinary circumstances meriting exceptional behavior on the part of women. It was, according to Godet, never meant to encourage or initiate a formal practice within the church. Paul, in Godet's words, simply "recognized the fact that cases might arise, especially under the peculiar circumstances of the time, in which a woman in the assembly, stirred by a strong emotion, might break out suddenly either into prayer or into prophecy; . . . ."[9]

On the other hand, the context of I Corinthians 14, with its especial emphases on the gifts of prophecy and speaking in tongues and its insistence that such gifts were dependent upon the sudden action of the Holy Spirit, provided convincing, if not definitive, evidence for Godet. In a rather serpentine sentence in an article for *The Contemporary Reivew* he set forth his logic, which allowed him ultimately to conclude that the two passages in question were quite compatible.

> In such a state of things, it is easy to understand that the apostle did not wish to apply too rigorously the principle of the silence of women, and felt the necessity of leaving an outlet for the action of the Spirit and the overflow of the heart; while, by requiring that in these cases the speaker's face and head should be covered, so as to shelter her from any indiscreet gaze which might either flatter her vanity or arouse improper feelings in a part of her audience—for this, no doubt, is what is in his mind when he says that the woman should be covered "because of the angels," who invisibly attend the service, and ho would be grieved at such a profanation—he hopes to have taken all necessary precautions for avoiding any undesirable consequences of the concession.[10]

The logic may defy us today, but its real concern, to reconcile apparent contradiction in biblical materials, haunted nineteenth century biblical scholars. Anti-feminists devoted extensive articles to prove not only that Paul did not contradict himself, but also to prove that feminist reconciliations were in error. Cyrus Cort claimed that feminists "violate fundamental rules of scriptural interpretation and throw discredit upon the Apostolic teaching by striving to prove that St. Paul allows in one place what he repeatedly forbids in other places. distinct and positive passages must always rule the meaning of passages that are vague, indirect and doubtful in their meaning and application."[11] It is interesting to note that feminists used the selfsame argument, differing only in their assessment of which were the distinct and which were the vague passages. While anti-feminists used the Calvinist argument, apostolus unum improbando alterum non probat (in condemning one thing the apostle does not approve the other), feminists merely argued the reverse—Paul certainly would not later condemn that which he had formerly allowed.

However, some anti-feminists would argue this very point. The Reverend Stephen Knowlton, writing in 1867, and the Reverend Hastings Ross, in 1870, resolved the problem of contradiction by insisting that Paul had done exactly what the feminists had said he clearly would not have done. For Ross, Paul appeared to have clarified his thinking somewhere between writing I Corinthians 11 and I Corinthians 14; the second passage merely completed the intent of the first. While Paul had only condemned the manner of woman's speaking in I Corinthians 11, he later, in I Corinthians14, forbade the practice itself. What he allowed at one point, he later denied. Such, for Ross, did not mean that Paul was either vacillating nor contradictory in his views; it was merely a matter of Paul completing his thought.

For Reverend Knowlton, such a procedure was commendable. Paul's forbidding women to prophesy with head uncovered in I Corinthians 11 was a logical and kindly first step to his later renunciation of woman's right to any utterance in religious assemblies. Like a wise and experienced teacher, Paul had softened the blow and minimized the confusion by introducing one thing at a time.

The question of what the term "prophesy" actually encompassed was another question of major importance. Feminist exegetes consistently argued that the term when applied to women in I Corinthians 11 meant "to speak" and found its true meaning in Paul's own definition in I Corinthians 14.3—edification, exhortation or comfort to fellow believers. Scholars like Godet balked at such an interpretation, arguing that all persons who edify, support or console Christian brethren cannot be thought of as prophets. The argument advanced by feminists suffered serious logical fault. Godet thought it akin to saying that since all persons who row boats move their arms, therefore all persons who move their arms must be rowing boats. The logic was not only seriously deficient in Godet's estimation, but the resultant theological structure built upon it by deluded feminists would have troubled the mind of the great apostle himself.

St. Paul would have stopped his ears to hear the name of prophetesses given to women of all ages, whose public speaking may be excellent enough, but is certainly very different from his idea of prophecy, and who think themselves beyond the possibility of reproach because they wear—not indeed a veil, but—their bonnets. I think he would have said to them: "My sisters, you have learnt to perfection how to strain at a gnat, and how to swallow a camel.[12]

Yet, despite the ease with which Godet and others condemned feminist logic and their exegesis of the Corinthian passages, they themselves had not exhausted nor resolved the issue. The Bible repeatedly mentions women whom it clearly designates as prophets, e. g., Huldah, Anna, the four daughters of Philip the Evangelist. The book of Joel promised "your daughters shall prophesy," and the early church clearly thought Joel's promise fulfilled at Pentecost when men and women, moved by the Holy spirit, spoke in foreign languages. And it was equally clear that the church's history recorded still more instances of women engaged in prophecy. For instance, Justin Martyr, in his dialogue with the Jew Tryphon, mentioned women who possessed extraordinary gifts of the Spirit; and the early church historian Eusebius noted the case of the Philadelphian prophetess Potomania Amnias.

In response to this array of material citing the prophecy of women, Godet constructed a reply built upon two basic assumptions. First, none of the women prophets must be thought of as public figures. He pointed out that Huldah had been consulted in her home, not in a public assembly. Anna had spoken only in what should be regarded as private conversations; she had never addressed a religious assembly of any sort. Philip's four exceptionally-gifted daughters had only spoken within the confines of their father's home in Caesarea, and it was here that both Luke and Paul had heard their message. To argue that any of these female figures justified woman's right to a public ministry was totally ridiculous in Godet's mind.

Godet's second assumption stemmed from and was built upon the first: all prophecy was dependent upon a sudden and extraordinary influx of the Holy Spirit. Thus prophecy was not to be regarded as simply public speaking or preaching and certainly not indicative of an established office. The daughters of Philip, even if they had spoken in assemblies, "were at least true prophetesses, speaking under the influence of a special revelation, and the case is therefore provided for in the exceptional authorization granted by St. Paul in the eleventh chapter of his epistle."[13]

It was Godet's understanding that the promise in Joel approved of no public ministry for women, but showed still further that what was being dealt with was extraordinary manifestations of the Spirit, dependent upon direct revelations and readily conceded to all genuine prophets. Thus, the participation of women at the Pentecost event also fell into this category; Peter alone remained the public spokesman for the group. The same was true of Eusebius' mention of Potomania Amnias, and Eusebius had mentioned her precisely because such things were rare, an out of the ordinary occurrence. Such examples had never been recorded as if they were common practices among women, and would not have been but for their uniqueness.

Godet's position was not unique among anti-feminist theologians; his thoughts were reflected by numerous others. The Presbyterian J. M. Stevenson remained convinced that, whatever role these early prophetesses had filled, none had exercised their gifts in the official service of the New Testament church. But even if they had, Stevenson refused to believe that this provided an authority to the uninspired women who presently sought ministerial positions and, therefore, was of little worth in the present debate.

Hastings Ross, too, thought prophecy quite different from ordinary speaking or preaching and assuredly dependent upon an extraordinary influx of the Spirit for initiation. "Thus it is shown that in no one passage in the New Testament can either the verb προφητεύω, or the noun προφητης be proved to refer to or to include ordinary preaching or speaking; but, in almost every instance, both the noun and the verb expressly involve the idea of a supernatural influence or miraculous gift."[14]

In accord with his firm conviction that Paul had relented of his previously expressed liberality which allowed women to speak if veiled, Ross argued that I Corinthians 14 now forbade any further prophecy by women. The command for her silence in chapter 14 fell in the midst of Paul's demand that prophets speak in turn, avoiding undue chaos in the Corinthian assembly. Thus, since the issue was prophecy and women enjoined to remain silent, they were not to prophesy. The right, previously attested to, had summarily been condemned by Paul, who further admonished men to prophesy only within the limits of good order.

Augusta Moore, one of the most articulate of anti-feminist women, also claimed that Paul had soundly contravened woman's speaking. Agreeing with her feminist sisters that Mary Magdalene's message of Jesus' resurrection and the Samaritan woman's testimony of Jesus' divinity to fellow townspeople were examples of woman's informal preaching, she nevertheless admonished feminists to "remember that it was long after this the apostle issued his command, and that it hushed even these women in the churches. Because women may speak or preach on extraordinary occasions, does not prove that they may on ordinary ones, after they have been commanded to be in silence."[15]

Much of what was said by these convinced opponents of woman's right to speak echoed the words previously expressed by the Reverend Knowlton of West Medway, Massachusetts in an article for the October, 1867 issue of *The Congregational Quarterly*. In this work, Knowlton had forcefully stated his view that woman's prophetic insights had never been uttered in a public capacity. No female prophets had ever once offered public sermons to mixed religious gatherings, and they certainly should not be allowed to do so in the nineteenth century. Paul once again was cited as the condemning source, and the fourteenth chapter of I Corinthians again singled out as Paul's express words outlawing such behavior on the part of women.

Unlike other anti-feminists, however, Knowlton refused to entertain the belief that women had issued public statements prior to Pauline restriction. He could find no evidence whatever that women had ever exercised their prophetic gifts in any way thought contrary to the instructions of Paul advised in his Letter to the Corinthians.

One of the troubling words in the Corinthian passages was the Greek term " λαλεῶ"—to speak. It occasioned much debate in the feminist-anti-feminist controversy. Woman's rights advocates preferred to translate it "to babble" or "to prate," convinced that its use in I Corinthians 14 limited woman's speaking only when such speech was unintelligible or nonedifying. Their opponents thought otherwise.

Hastings Ross thought such an interpretation ignorant of the high standards of biblical scholarship. His 1870 article for *The Bibliotheca Sacra* contained the following important and relevant footnote:

> Of the two hundred and ninety-two times in which the word is used apart from the passage in question (I Corinthians 14. 34-35), only once can it be rendered "babble" without violence; and even there it is extremely doubtful.[16]

Stevenson's article three years later for *The Presbyterian Quarterly and Princeton Review* witnessed the same conviction. He contended that Paul had used the most generic word in the Greek language a word which covered all conceivable forms of speech. His intent was clearly an attempt to forbid women any vocal utterance in the religious assemblies of Corinth. Had he selected another word, the debate might have been quite different and the women granted a much stronger argument.

> Had he (Paul) used κηρύσσω, καταγγέλλω, ευαγγελίζω, all of which words express the idea of preaching then the prohibition would have referred to technical preaching. But λαλέω has no such limitation; it comprehends all forms of address. It is translated, to "utter," to "tell," to "talk," to "say," twenty-eight times, and 246 times to "speak."[17]

Like Ross, Stevenson felt that exegetes who insisted that the word be translated "to babble" biblical illiterates who foolishly challenged the majority opinion of biblical scholarship—all of which tended to support the opposite view from that adhered to by feminists.

The exegesis which would translate λαλεῖν "to babble," seems too puerile to call for any notice, when we consider that of the 292 times the word occurs in the New Testament, aside from the present passage, but a single instance occurs where it could, with any propriety, be so translated. The entire use of the word by the inspired writers is against the suggestion, and we know no reputable exegete who contends for such a translation of λαλεῖν .[18]

The following year yet another article appeared on the issue, this time in *The Congregational Quarterly*. Under the title "Speaking or Babbling," its author, not mentioned, discoursed at length about the translation of the crucial word " λαλεῖν ". Written in response to an earlier article for *The Congregational Quarterly* by Harmon Loomis (See Chapter Nine), it proceeded to discredit Loomis' exegesis. The author carefully reviewed the works of, what he considered to be, the best authorities in the field of biblical interpretation and consulted numerous Greek lexicons in his attempt to discern the classical meaning of the term. His conclusions, weighted by his extensive research, refuted scholars of Loomis' persuasion, who opted for the limited translation "to babble."

A study of these definitions shows that the use of the word is very wide, covering all utterances from a musical instrument up to an oration. Still its general sense was not to babble, but "to talk, to say." That it was sometimes or even frequently used for inconsiderate talk, as it sometimes was for the twitter of a bird, is most evident; but that it is to be translated, in any work of the classic Greek, from its own proper force, without regard to connection, to babble rather than to speak, needs proof, which has not yet been furnished. We should judge the contrary,—that, in any given passage, the connection must determine the meaning intended; that, if used of birds, dogs, locusts, monkeys, or musical instruments, its wide signification would admit of a rendering suited to the necessities of the context; but, if used of men and women, its general classic use would constrain the translation to speak, unless the context forbade it.[19]

The author was, of course, aware that Paul did not address the Corinthian congregation in classical Greek, but a later Greek which was the spoken language of common life. Still, the writer refused to believe, that, in the decline of the Greek language, the general meaning, "to speak," had been lost. In surveying the 290 plus times it had appeared in the New Testament, only once did it even remotely lend itself to a translation such as "to babble." If anything had been lost over the centuries, the author thought it more probable that one of its classical significations—to babble—had suffered that fate, while its more general classic use was retained.

These observations allowed the article's author to conclude that Paul's Greek congregations would not have expected him to speak in the now obsolete classical Greek sense of the word. He had undoubtedly addressed them in the common Greek of his own day, which had no such meaning as "babble" for the word under discussion.

With such reasonings and assumptions the author also secured the freedom to conclude that articles of the Loomis genre were little more than verbal nonsense. The word λαλεῖν meant intelligible speech: "That this is so is clear from its use, not merely " 'twenty-four times' " in I Corinthians 11, but from its use in two hundred and seventy other passages in the New Testament as well, in none of which other passages can there be a reasonable doubt that it means intelligent speech, except, perhaps, in I Corinthians 13.11."[20]

It was clear to this anonymous author that to translate any of these passages "to babble" was biblical license of the first order and an insult to their inspired author Paul. Paul, in his attempt to cure the abuse of the gift of tongues in the Corinthian church had chosen a verb which quite definitely included all forms of speech. In fact, he had selected the most unrestricted verb in the Greek language purposely, applying it not only to order the gift of speaking in tongues and the utterance of prophecy, but to counsel woman's silence. His intent was a comprehensive one, and feminist authors had twisted his original intent when they opted for a severely circumscribed translation. For the author of "Speaking and Babbling" any interpretation of the word which denied its general application was inconceivable.

> It will be hard to convince the world, without a better show of proof, that the sober-minded, inspired Apostle, while correcting the abuses which had crept into the Corinthian assembly, introduced into his own instruction an abuse of language which for eighteen centuries has subverted his real meaning. The thing is incredible.[21]

Godet's article appeared ten years later in the pretigeous *Contemporary Review*; and, while we cannot be certain that he had read the previous article in *The Congregational Quarterly*, we can be sure that he was familiar with biblical scholarship on this point. His position sustained what anti-feminists maintained was the acceptable view held by reputable scholars.

> Moreover, the word λαλεῶ has by no means the special sense attributed to it. It is used twenty-four times in this chapter alone (I Cor. 14), as applied either to the gift of tongues (vs. 2, 4, 5, 6, etc.), or to prophecy (vs. 3, 29, etc.), or to speaking in ectasy (v. 18), or to speaking with the understanding (v. 19); and yet, after all this, when this very word—which, as we have seen, fills the whole chapter—is used to express an act forbidden to women, suddenly it takes a quite new and peculiar meaning—that of chattering and asking questions—a meaning which could only be imparted to it by special and decisive indications in the context![22]

The question of context was a vital aspect of the debate as well. Feminists had discounted the Pauline passages on the basis that they were uttered in the midst of a particular set of circumstances and thus restricted by time and parochial concerns. Anti-feminists again refused to entertain such logic. Cyrus Cort spoke for many when he insisted that Paul was a liberal and if there was to be any departure from the traditional, he would have done so. It was clear then that "woman preaching and praying in promiscuous assemblies is a modern and unscriptural innovation and a perversion of Apostolic and Christian usages. As such it can only be injurious in its ultimate results."[23] To argue a parochialism was absurd; no age could outgrow or be absolved from the principles of faith and practice established by the apostle Paul.

The same sentiments were expressed by the Lutheran scholar, F. P. Mayser of Lancaster, Pennsylvania in an article for *The Lutheran Church Review*. Although written late in the century, the article maintained earlier arguments. In outline form, Mayser presented reasons for denying women a right to office or vote in the church. His denial rested ultimately on Paul's command for woman's silence in the church, a demand which Mayser insisted was all-inclusive. Paul's directive encompassed every function wherein women might want to teach, usurp authority or establish control. Extraordinary exceptions found in the Old and New Testaments could not be made the rule, and even women possessed of the necessary intellect and skill could not transgress the Pauline principle, no matter how much they might desire to do so.

Mayser reasoned that the principle itself was grounded on divine order and therefore not subject to modificaiton or abandonment. "It was a fundamental principle which he (Paul) maintained, and which cannot be changed for the sake of expediency, nor by the progress of civilization, the moral culture, or the higher intellectual and social position which woman may occupy in later days,"[24] according to Mayser.

Fellow Lutheran Theodore E. Schmauk, writing the same year for the same denominational journal, provided a less rigid interpretation. Indeed, Schmauk, an astute biblical scholar in his own right, proved sympathetic to woman's present plight and more generous in his evaluation of feminine exegeses. Yet he cannot be ignored as one who stood in opposition to women on this crucial issue.

While he argued forcefully for woman's right to decision within the legislative functions of the church, i.e., her right to vote in assembly, his sympathies did not overshadow or cause abandonment of his strong conviction that woman had no right to any official office in the church. Like Mayser, his firm resolve in the matter stemmed from his interpretation of the Pauline commands. Paul's prohibitions rested not upon circumstance as so many feminists were want to argue, but upon the apostle's convictions regarding the priority of man in creation and the repudiation of this priority by the Corinthian and Ephesian women.

Yet, even here Schmauk sought to soften the blow. He willingly acknowledged that exceptions might be made and quoted both Luther's and Calvin's consent to allow women to preach when no qualified male was available for the task. Nevertheless, Schmauk considered the general intent of Paul's words still valid, and he insisted they be unconditionally adhered to by all conscientious Christians. Time and circumstance, whatever their merits, had neither dulled nor erased Paul's admonitions.

> The principle laid down by the Apostle is as binding today as it ever was. The married woman is to show in public that she is bound to a husband and that she reverences him. She is not to speak or act independently of his will or on her own motion in such cases where either common consent and usage of the virtuous or he himself personally does not give her permission. Neither she nor any other woman is to speak or act in public if, even with good motives, her activity becomes a disgrace.[25]

Mayser echoed the words of Hastings Ross, written almost thirty years earlier. Ross, addressing himself to the issue of woman's silence in the Corinthian church, had maintained that Paul's task had been one of eliminating what had become pure havoc in the assemblies of that church. Since women had been primarily responsible for the chaos, Paul had prohibited women from speaking in *all* religious meetings. Furthermore, Paul had not confined his prohibition to a particular church or country, any present custom or other temporary consideration; he had effectively muzzled women in church assemblies forever.

The command was prefaced, for Ross, upon woman's earlier disobedience in the Garden and the resultant "curse." This being the case, Paul's reason for subjecting women to silence was unshakable; her silence was as permanent and extensive as the race itself. To argue that customs had changed and therefore Pauline precepts were somehow nullified and no longer binding upon nineteenth century womanhood was "as relevant as to talk about the changes of the moon, and not a whit moreso,"[26] claimed Ross. Paul's commands covered *all* meetings of the church where both sexes were in attendance; to argue otherwise was to fly in the face of divine directive.

Other anti-feminists shared the Mayser-Ross thesis against parochial application. In 1873, Stevenson maintained that "Woman's place in public worship, as determined by the history of scripture, Church and the unequivocal command of God, based upon unchangeable reasons, is not that of a teacher or leader, but that of an unofficial worshipper."[27] Such a view had been sanctioned by most distinquished scholars for the past 1500 years, according to Stevenson, and any who argued that changing times altered its application ignored the fact that the essential relationship between the sexes could not be altered. It had been established by divine decree; it was a basic law of creation that man was the official head of woman.

A year later, Augusta Moore's article again lent support to male anti-feminist argument. She rejected feminist belief, arguing instead that Paul's prohibition of woman's speaking in church extended beyond business meetings today and beyond the activities of the Corinthian church in the first century, A. D.

> Most meetings of Christians in those days were held in private and secluded places; so Sabbath ministrations in the church *building* could not have been intended, as many seem to think they were. And the word εκκλησία means "assembly," including any and every church meeting for religious communion and worship.[28]

Godet, too, addressed the issue, in 1884. For Godet, Paul's appeal to Genesis, with its general principle of woman's subordination to man, proved that Paul did not ever contemplate a time when his command would be justly treated as obsolete.

It is clear from anti-feminist treatment of the argument from parochialism that the question of woman's silence was intimately bound to the question of woman's divinely ordered subjection. Time and time again it is the latter assumption which allows their unwillingness to affirm that time and/or circumstance might have altered or invalidated Pauline regulations.

Knowlton matter-of-factly declared in 1867 that Paul had ordered the silence of women on no other basis but that of her creation. Thus, women were called upon to observe the same silence in the nineteenth century as they had been called upon to observe in the first century. Man was created first; women second, and it was as simple as that. Woman was created for man; the reverse was incorrect. God had determined woman's subordination from the very beginning of time, a supposed fact which allowed Knowlton to insist, "Here we have not a local and temporary, but a universal and permanent, fact; and it is on this fact that Paul unequivocally bases the precept in question. Whether we understand why this should be a reason for such a restriction or not, that this, and not an Eastern custom, was the reason, seems to me clear beyond a question."[29]

Hastings Ross accepted the same premise, and his 1870 article for *The Bibliotheca Sacra* is built upon the conviction that Paul's command for woman's silence proceeded from a recognized law apparent in her creation. For Ross, the most convincing verses for this view were those found in I Timothy 2.13-14, wherein Paul, their assumed author, acknowledged Adam's priority in creation and woman's priority in sin. This allowed Ross to declare that "the priority of Adam in the creation, and the fact that Eve was deceived, and was first in the transgression, are reasons, however explained, which no times, or dispensations, or anything else, can change."[30]

The anonymously authored article "Speaking or Babbling," which sought to prove that women were forbidden any form of speech in religious assemblies, insisted that ultimate justification for the restriction was not simply supplied by exegetical study of the Greek term " $\lambda a \lambda \epsilon \acute{\omega}$," but rather by woman's divinely ordered status. It was this fact alone which had prompted Paul's command for silence in I Corinthians 14.34-35. As such, it was without limitation by time or circumstance, an unalterable and universally applicable precept dependent upon sex and the divine decrees of creation.

> Right or wrong, their sex and the law are the reasons given by Paul for enjoining silence on women in the churches, not the unintelligibility of their utterances, not their light and inconsiderate words, not the fact that somebody else has a revelation, not that two or more are talking at the same time,—none nor

all of these,—but because they are women and not men. Their
sex is at bottom the ground of the silence required.[31]

Similary, Godet, too, aligned with previous anti-feminist
scholarship in its attempt to join the issue of woman's silence to
the assumption of her subordinate position in creation. He reasoned
that the apostle had stated plainly that a woman was denied participation in church gatherings precisely because of the position
assigned to her by the Creator, a position of subjection and dependence. To challenge Paul's command for woman's silence was
thus to seriously attack God's divine intention for women. Woman
as secondary in creation, together with her deception by the satanic
serpent of the Genesis myth, confirmed for Godet the justice of
Paul's decision to gag women in church assemblies. Paul had realized
that woman still harbored the defects and weaknesses of Eve and
remained unfit for leadership and responsibility.

> She is, in general, to do nothing which implies authority over
> the man, remembering that her existence, inasmuch as it is of
> later origin, is complementary to his,—and remembering, more-
> over, the facility with which she opened her heart and imag-
> ination to the tempter and made herself the instrument of the
> fall of man. It is to be observed that in these last words St. Paul
> does not say "Eve, but the woman;" (reference is to I Timothy
> 2) by which he evidently means to imply that this readiness
> to be dazzled is proper to the whole sex. The fine qualities of
> woman, the depth of her feelings, the vivacity of her imagin-
> ation, the ardour of her devotion, make her more accessible
> than man to the fascinations of error, and hence she must
> submit to be guided rather than herself attempt to guide.[32]

Neither Schmauk nor fellow Lutheran F. P. Mayser neglected
the selfsame argument; both thought the subjection hypothesis valid
for rejecting woman's right to speak in church. Although Schmauk
once again proved to be more liberal in his views than Mayser, he
nevertheless went to great lengths to spell out for his readers the
theory of woman's subjection to man. The consequences of its
application were easily discovered; in appearance, public behavior
and action woman was always to show that she was bound to the will
of her husband in all things.

Mayser, on the other hand, was a good deal more curt in his outlined argument against woman's right to speak publicly. Man was the head of woman, and woman, always the subordinate of man, could not execute any sort of authority or rule over man without acting in defiance of God's explicit demands and contrary to his specific design for the created order. Biblical texts verified this, and Mayser cited numerous passages, including Genesis 3.6 and I Corinthians 11.3, 8-9, to sustain his contention. The Christ event had not altered the subject status of women according to Mayser. Not only had it not removed them from their subordinate roles in society, but it had confirmed their subordinate status. Once again, Mayser cited a series of biblical texts which he thought supportive—I Corinthians 11.3, 9; I Corinthians 14.34; I Timothy 2.11-12.

In summary, the anti-feminists, relying primarily on Pauline materials, presented a somewhat more united front than did their feminist opposition. Their arguments were biblically conservative, shrinking back from a form critical approach and distaining of the brazen liberalism displayed by their opponents. Their arguments, however construed and whatever the difference in emphases, remained remarkably similar. They, unlike their feminist counterparts, betrayed a definite fear of challenging the traditional lest all topple in ruins about their heads. One might reasonably assume that such adherence to time-honored beliefs oftentimes forced them to sacrifice truth, compassion or both.

Their roles as apologetes for the traditional allowed them to discredit the best in feminst scholarship as well as the worst. Chained to a biblical literalism, they found feminist attempts to raise significant exegetical questions but a reflection of their scholarly inexpertise and hardly worthy of response. One is even given the impression that they might not have responded if they had not seen such interpretations as a clarion call of danger ahead. The biblical exegesis might be faulty, but the very persistence of the women was real and threatening. Their only recourse was to point out alleged errors and once again admonish the women to stay in their God-appointed, biblically-directed place or face certain social and moral destruction.

Notes

[1]Charles Duren, "Place of Women in the Church, in Religious Meetings," *The Congregational Review*, 8, No. 39 (January, 1868), 26-27.

[2]D. R. Cady, "The Biblical Position of Woman," *The Congregational Quarterly*, NS 2, No. 3 (July, 1870), 372.

[3]Cyrus Cort, "Women as Preachers," *Reformed Quarterly (Church) Review*, 29 (1882), p. 127.

[4]J. M. Stevenson, "Place of Women in Assemblies for Public Worship," *Presbyterian Quarterly and Princeton Review*, 2 (January, 1873), p. 45.

[5]Cady, *Op. Cit.*, p. 373.

[6]*Ibid.*, p. 376.

[7]Henry Van Dyke in Willard's *Woman in the Pulpit* (1888), p. 124.

[8]Bishop John Vincent, quoted in Love's *St. Paul and Woman* (1894), pp. 16-17. [The reader is also referred to the article, "The Englargement of Woman's Sphere," *The Independent of New York* (May, 1891).]

[9]F. Godet, "The Ministry of Women," *The Contemporary Review*, 45 (January, 1884), p. 50.

[10]*Ibid.*

[11]Cort, *Op. Cit.*, p. 125.

[12]Godet, *Op. Cit.*, p. 52.

[13]*Ibid.*, p. 60.

[14]A. Hastings Ross, "The Silence of Women in the Churches," *The Bibliotheca Sacra*, 27, No. 106 (April, 1870), 345-46.

[15]Augusta Moore, "Women in the Church," *The Congregational Quarterly*, 16 (April, 1874), p. 282.

[16]Ross, *Op. Cit.*, p. 342.

[17]Stevenson, *Op. Cit.*, p. 48.

[18]*Ibid.*, pp. 48-49.

[19]"Speaking or Babbling," *The Congregational Quarterly*, 16 (October, 1874), p. 577.

[20]*Ibid.*, p. 583.

[21]*Ibid.*, p. 584.

[22]Godet, *Op. Cit.*, p. 53.

[23]Cort, *Op. Cit.*, p. 124.

[24]F. P. Mayser, "Shall Women Vote in Church," *The Lutheran Church Review*, 18, No. 3 (July, 1899), 483.

[25]Theodore E. Schmauk, "St. Paul and Women," *The Lutheran Church Review*, 18, No. 3 (July, 1899), 521.

[26]Ross, *Op. Cit.*, p. 341.

[27]Stevenson, *Op. Cit.*, p. 54.

[28]Moore, *Op. Cit.*, p. 279.

[29]Stephen Knowlton, "The Silence of Women in the Churches," *The Congregational Quarterly*, 9, No. 4 (October, 1867), 331.

[30]Ross, *Op. Cit.*, p. 341.

[31]"Speaking or Babbling," *Op. Cit.*, p. 585.

[32]Godet, *Op. Cit.*, p. 55.

Chapter XIV

A Measure of Success

As can be seen in convention deliberations and the century-long debate between feminists and anti-feminists, theological issues played a prominent role in the controversy. Never far from the surface, theological considerations often provided the bases for feminist and anti-feminist arguments alike. It is equally apparent that the theological positions of the contending parties determined for thousands their adherence or nonadherence to the woman's rights movement.

It is, of course, impossible to determine the theological victor even today. Many of the arguments voiced so forcefully by nineteenth century feminists and their opponents remain a vital part of contemporary debates. Yet to view the nineteenth century controversy as an arduous struggle with no firm results is to perpetrate an injustice. A review of the century reveals definite advances, which I have conservatively and cautiously pronounced "a measure of success." The caution is occasioned by the conviction that much of what the nineteenth century woman hoped to achieve was and is not yet realized. Whatever successes were attained by the end of the century, they cannot be used to overshadow and obscure the disappointments and failures. Indeed, the feminists themselves saw the century's end not as a time to relax their efforts, but to renew them.

By 1900, the feminists were already pausing to review over a half-century of struggle. Reviews were mixed. Despite concerted efforts, the women had not attained constitutional recognition. Nor had they succeeded in having the word "male" stricken from the Fourteenth Amendment, thereby allowing women the privileges of citizenship now granted to Black men. And they had not secured the all-important Sixteenth Amendment which would extend them true citizenship rights of their own.

However, the women did have cause for celebration, limited as it might be. They had successfully broken down several barriers and entered upon professional fields previously closed to them, e. g., education, medicine, law, politics and, to some extent, the pulpit ministry. They had achieved numerous legislative and judicial triumphs, particularly in the areas of property rights and favorable divorce settlements for women. Their persistence had also brought their concerns to the nation's attention and into the very chambers of the national legislature, where it occupied legislators' time and energies for over a half-century before suffrage rights were granted in 1920.

Other successes were also apparent. While the following is not to be regarded as a detailed nor comprehensive record of woman's successes by 1900, it does show major discernible trends favorable to women. It also reveals the primary indicators upon which women relied in order to optimistically speculate about possible future victories. At the same time, its intention is to grant the reader some insight into the feminists' self-appraisal of their half-century of effort.

Women had memorialized and petitioned Congress in the interests of woman's rights from a very early date in the history of the movement, and an evaluation of their progress in this regard may be the most appropriate place to begin an assessment. For the most part the assessment remains bleak.

Women had "lobbied" continuously to have the word "male" removed from the Fourteenth Amendment which secured citizenship and franchise privileges to Black males. They failed; and, when in December, 1866, a resolution before the Senate attempted to secure suffrage rights for women of the District of Columbia, all the memorials and petitions with which the women again beseiged Congress again proved futile. Their requests were spurned, and the measure soundly defeated. Still they continued their fight for the extension of suffrage to women, lobbying for it in the territories and in the states where the question was an issue before local legislatures and against efforts to repeal it once it had been granted such as the Edmunds Law sought to do in Utah.

On March 15, 1869, they succeeded in having the Sixteenth Amendment introduced in Congress by Representative Julian of Indiana in the House and Senators Pomeroy of Kansas and Wilson of Iowa in the Senate. Defeated at that time, the women kept the amendment alive, reintroducing it repeatedly in subsequent years. Yet each time it was introduced, it was rejected. Not until passage and ratification of the Nineteenth Amendment in 1920 would the women meet with success.

Despite the actual legislative defeats however, a growing number of congressmen spoke valiantly on behalf of the amendment and the woman's cause. Among them were Senator A. A. Sargent of California and Senator Blair of New Hampshire. The former, after arguing determinedly for extension of suffrage to women in the Territory of Pembina in 1874, took it upon himself to reintroduce the ill-fated Sixteenth Amendment in January, 1878. The latter also pleaded the women's case in the United States Senate, and he, too, introduced the Amendment once again in December of 1886. Although both attempts resulted in failure, the senators, by virtue of their reputations and persuasive talents, won senatorial colleagues to the women's cause.

The women themselves did not let such discouragements noticeably affect their efforts. In fact, wedged between these various rejections were minor, though significant triumphs, which spoke volumes and allowed optimism. By 1870, women had been granted congressional committee hearings on the subject of suffrage for women. Thus, their voices, as well as their memorials and petitions, were heard in the halls of Congress.

The women took full advantage of this opportunity to present their demands and reason their case in person. Most leaders of the movement spoke before the Senate and House Judiciary Committees, the Senate Committee on Privileges and Elections or the Select

Committee on Woman Suffrage. While it is impossible to name all who addressed these various congressional committees, any listing reads like a Who's Who among woman's rights advocates. Susan B. Anthony and Elizabeth Stanton were, of course, the major spokeswomen and regular addressers of both House and Senate committees. Others who distinguished themselves on particular occasions were Dr. Mary Walker of Washington, Mary Tillotson of New Jersey and Mrs. N. Cromwell of Arkansas in 1878 with the introduction of the A. A. Sargent resolution, and Sara Andrews Spencer who spoke against the bill proposing the disenfranchisement of the women of Utah.

Since one of the purposes of this work is to investigate the extent to which theology informed and influenced the woman's rights movement in the nineteenth century, its prominence in these presentations is noteworthy. Aside from the obvious call for equality before the law, the women also sought to reverse centuries of ideological thinking based upon theological presuppositions. Such necessitated a reliance upon theological argument.

One of the first formal addresses before the Judiciary Committee of the House of Representatives was delivered by Isabella Hooker in January, 1871. After assuring her listeners that the divinely ordained doctrines of personal liberty and personal responsibility were relavent to the matter at hand and had proven a propelling power in American government itself, she concluded with a powerful statement on behalf of woman's right to participate in national decision making.

> Much more, how can you grow into the stature of perfect men in Christ Jesus our Lord, how can you become perfect legislators, except your mothers are instructed on these subjects you are called to legislate upon, that they may instruct you in their turn! . . . In past ages this woman, in the providence of God we will say, has been shut out from political action, for, so long as the sword ruled and man had to get his liberty by the sword, so long women had all she could do to guard the home, for that was her part of the work—and she did it bravely and well, you will say. But now men are not fighting for their liberty, with the gun by the door and the Indians outside. You are

> fighting for it in halls of legislation, with the spirit of truth, with spiritual weapons, and woman would be disloyal to her womanhood if she did not ask to share these heavy responsibilities with you.[1]

Elizabeth Cady Stanton further illustrates this theological bent in woman's rights addresses before congressional committees when she spoke before the Senate Committee of the Judiciary in 1872. Refuting the belief that the country's forefathers had ever intended to withhold the right to vote from women, she again reiterated the damage done by solely male-interpretation.

> Women did vote in America at the time the Constitution was adopted. If the framers of the Constitution meant they should not, why did they not distinctly say so? The women of the country, having at last roused up to their rights and duties as citizens, have a word to say as to the "intentions" of the fathers. It is not safe to leave the "intentions" of the Pilgrim fathers, or the Heavenly Father, wholly to masculine interpretation, for by Bible and Constitution alike, women have thus far been declared the subjects, the slaves of men.[2]

Many more instances might be cited to show that women did not ignore the theological question when speaking to the nation's legislators, but saw it as a vital and integral part of their presentations. Yet a great deal more insight is gained as to its importance with the realization that it proved an equally vital ingredient in arguments voiced against their proposals.

Women were deliberatley and continuously met with theologically-based opposing arguments by some of the nations's leading legislators. One of the best examples provided occurred in 1866 on the occasion of the resolution to give women in the District of Columbia the elective franchise, an occasion wherein numerous amateur theologians blossomed in the United States Senate.

On December 11, 1866, Senator Williams of Oregon rose from his Senate seat to speak in opposition to woman's vote in the District. His opposition stemmed not from political convictions, but rather from a conviction that God himself stood opposed to such a measure. He informed his senatorial colleagues that woman's interests were amply provided for by a voting male populace; but, even more important, was his warning that if women were to secure independent political power, the consequences might prove terrifying. His alarm was prompted by his theological understandings of God's intention for the created order and the relationship between the sexes.

> When God married our first parents in the garden, according to that ordinance they were made "bone of one bone and flesh of one flesh;" and the whole theory of government and society proceeds upon the assumption that their interests are one, that their relations are so intimate and tender that whatever is for the benefit of the one is for the benefit of the other; whatever works to the injury of the one works to the injury of the other. I say, sir, that the more identical and inseparable these interests and relations can be made, the better for all concerned; and the woman who undertakes to put her sex in an antagonistic position to man, who undertakes by the use of some independent political power to contend and fight against man, displays a spirit which would, if able, convert all the now harmonious elements of society into a state of war, and make every home a hell upon earth.[3]

Fellow senator Frelinghuysen of New Jersey was of the same mind. Maintaining that God had stamped upon woman a milder, gentler nature which disqualified her for the battles of public life, Frelinghuysen informed the Senate that the very structure of the Christian religion stood opposed to the resolution now before them.

> Mr. President, it seems to me that the Christian religion, which has elevated woman to her true position as a peer by the side of man from which she is taken; that religion which is a part of the common law of this land, in its very spirit and declarations recognizes man as the representative of woman. The very structure of that religion which for centuries has been being built recognizes that principle, and it is written on its very doorposts. The woman, it is true, was first tempted; but it was in Adam that we all died. The angel, it is true, appeared to Mary; but it is in the God-man that we are all made alive.[4]

The argument that since male figures governed life and death thus assuring leadership solely to the male may seem somewhat illogical today. However, at the time Frelinghuysen spoke it was not without influence, and, in some circles, quite popular in the debate to discourage woman's participation in public life.

Another reason cited in the 1866 debate revolved about the general assumption that woman did not possess innate abilities which qualified her to assume authoritative roles. Senator Davis, yet another of the Senate's amateur theologians, took the floor to argue this very point. His words, opposed to both woman suffrage and Black suffrage, claimed that God had provided male and female with different faculties and attributes which adapted them to differing roles in life. The woman's place in the destinies of nations was to act as "high and officiating priestess" at "the domestic altar." A woman's native qualities fitted her for domesticity, which Davis envisioned in all its ideality. His portrait of woman suffered from an equal amount of idealism and idolatry.

> The domestic altar is a sacred fane where woman is the high and officiating priestess. This priestess should be virtuous, she should be intelligent, she should be competent to the performance of all her high duties. To keep her in that condition of purity, it is necessary that she should be separated from the exercise of suffrage and from all those stern and contaminating and demoralizing duties that devolves upon the hardier sex—man.[5]

This particular position, which argued a high calling for women in the area of domesticity, appeared to be quite popular in the United States Congress among opponents of woman suffrage. It would be voiced again and again as measures came before the House and Senate designed to secure for women electoral franchise or extension of rights in public life.

It was argued most adamantly in May, 1874 when a bill before the Senate called for the extension of suffrage privileges for women in the territory of Pembina. Among the senatorial theologians who surfaced in the debate was Senator Bayard of Delaware. Long an opponent of granting women the right to vote, he rose to speak against the amendment before the assembly, which had been introduced by one of the most formidable champions of the woman's cause in the U. S. Senate—Senator Aaron Sargent of California.

According to Bayard, the resolution which lay before them was in violation of the revealed laws of religion and in utter disregard for divine law itself. This being the case, he reasoned, its passage by the Senate would destine American society, and particularly American family life, to corruption and disorder.

> I frankly say, Mr. President, that which strikes me most forcibly is the gross irreverence of this proposition, its utter disregard of the Divine will by which man and woman were created different, physically, intellectually, and morally, and in defiance of which we are now to have this poor, weak, and futile attempt of man to set up his schemes of amelioration in defiance of every tradition, of every revelation, of all human experience, enlightened as it has been by Divine permission.[6]

Not all theologically-reasoned arguments under congressional view came from males however. When in 1878 the Senate Committee on Privileges and Elections had the Sargent version of the Sixteenth Amendment under advisement and study, it received a pointed letter from Madeleine V. **Dahlgren** of the Anti-Suffrage Society. The letter, proceeding from a foundational argument decidedly theological, bears a striking resemblence to Senator Davis' statements of 1866. Dahlgren, insistent that women as wives and mothers had duties to perform of a high and sacred nature, labelled the vote for women an unnatural right and liable to produce overwhelmingly adverse effects for women and society. She thought God's law opposed to such unnatural innovations.

> We cannot without prayer and protest see our cherished privileges endangered, and have granted us only in exchange the so-called equal rights. We need more, and we claim, through our physical weakness and your courtesy as Christian gentlemen, that protection which we need for the proper discharge of those sacred and inalienable functions and rights conferred upon us by God. To these the vote, which is not a natural right (otherwise why not confer it upon idiots, lunatics, and adult boys) would be adverse.[7]

Her decision to place all of womankind together with idiots and lunatics is both unfortunate and informative. Although it was, no doubt, an attempt to emphasize the native incapacities of women for exercise of elective franchise and their need for protection as the weaker sex, it shows equally well the severely depressed view some women held of themselves and their abilities.

Not all senators nor their constituents were as bluntly against woman's rights as Senators Williams, Frelinghuysen and Davis, and many went on record in favor of the woman's cause. Not only did they introduce and support passage of the Sixteenth Amendment, but they also proved to be champions for woman's equality in heated senatorial debates. One occasion of note occurred in 1886 with the issuance of a minority report by the Senate Committee on Woman Suffrage. The report delivered by John W. Stewart of Vermont and signed by Senators E. B. Taylor, W. P. Hepburn, L. B. Caswell and A. A. Ranney reviewed the injustices perpetrated against women and clearly annunciated her created equality.

> The history of woman is for the most part a history of wrong and outrage. Created the equal companion of man, she early became his slave, and still is so in most parts of the world. In many so-called Christian nations of Europe she is today yoked with beasts and is doing the labor of beasts, while her son and husband are serving in the army, protecting the divine right of kings and men to slay and destroy. In the farther East she is still more degraded, being substantially excluded from the world Man has not been consciously unjust to woman in the past, nor is he now, but he believes that she is in her true sphere, not realizing that he has fixed her sphere, and not God.[8]

The report stimulated an animated debate on the floor of the Senate. Despite the admirable effort of Senator Blair of New Hampshire, who spearheaded the drive to state the woman's case,[9] the Sixteenth Amendment, under consideration at the time, was once again set aside.

The measure of success for the woman's movement on the national level therefore did not rest upon the passage of major legislation in their behalf, but on the recognition of their right to state their position and the willingness of a growing number of congressmen to support it. While the national legislation they sought would not be forthcoming for twenty more years, the feminists of 1900 were far from discouraged. The trend appeared to be in their favor, and thus defeats produced heightened persistence and greater resolve. Untiringly they would ultimately keep the issue before the national legislature for almost sixty years.

While they thought it supremely important to win their case on the national level, they did not neglect state and local legislative bodies. Here, too, similar battles were fought and proved somewhat more successful. By 1900, definite progress had been made and was duly reported by the women. In the February, 1897 issue of the *Chautauquan* an article appeared written by Vina J. Lee entitled "Where Women Vote." Essentially a review of voting privileges secured by women in the various states, it reported: "For a majority of the states—not less than twenty-five or thirty states—have given women suffrage of one kind or another. The most common form is the power to vote at school elections."[10] While such a privilege as voting at school elections may appear today to be so minimal as to be unworthy of mention, it was for nineteenth century women most often the necessary first step to gain extended franchise rights. It served as a weathervane of future possibility and, indeed, probability.

The Lee article also noted that three states had already granted women little or no restriction with regard to the vote. In Wyoming women had voted with the male populace since 1870, and the right had been retained with ratification of its state constitution in 1890. The women of Utah also possessed the ballot, although the right had been suspended for a time by the Edmunds Law. But, in 1895 with the ratification of Utah's state constitution, women once again had been granted full suffrage rights. Not only had Utah reinstated the elective franchise for women, but, shortly thereafter it had elected its first woman senator, Martha Hughes Cannon. Then, in 1893, the third state, Colorado, voted in favor of suffrage for women; and, by 1897, three women already served in the Colorado Assembly.

Other states had granted only limited suffrage rights to women, but again they were significant. In Kansas, women voted in municipal elections, and several Kansas towns had woman mayors. Nebraska had a female prosecuting attorney in Brown County and, like Kansas, had witnessed the introduction and defeat of a state constitutional amendment for general woman's suffrage. In Washington, the women had voted in the territory for five years before the Supreme Court rescinded the right; and it, too, had a defeated constitutional amendment for woman's suffrage on record. So also did the states of South Carolina and New York.

Suffrage privileges were allowed to women on issues of taxation or election of school officers in Arizona, Colorado, Delaware, Idaho, Illinois, Indiana, Kansas, Kentucky, Massachusetts, Michigan, Minnesota, Montana, Mississippi, Nebraska, New Hampshire, New Jersey, North Dakota, Ohio, Oklahoma, Oregon, South Dakota, Texas, Utah, Vermont, Wisconsin and Wyoming. The fact that so many states were now willing to grant even these meager concessions proved heartening to feminists.

However, state and local efforts reflected setbacks and failure as well. A number of states repeatedly defeated amendments for general suffrage. Washington women not only lost their suffrage rights by Supreme Court action, but women in New York lost even the right to elect school officers. It was nullified by judicial act in 1893. In Massachusetts feminine attempts to secure the right to vote in municipal elections met with a resounding "no" in the state legislature. In Pennsylvania women were accorded only the right of petition, while in Arkansas and Missouri women secured only the privilege of signing or refusing to sign petitions for liquor licenses. In Texas only the right to sign petitions for school officers was granted the state's women, and in Louisiana women could only vote on the question of running or not running railroads through parishes.

The limited advances may signal little cause for rejoicing while the failures may merit cause for disappointment and discouragement. Yet the women did not view it as such; instead, every advance, no matter how minor, became a reason for optimism and every failure produced a commitment to try harder. Once again their optimism was fueled by the fact that leading legislator were willing to argue in their behalf.

Senator George Hoar of Massachusetts not only championed their cause in the halls of the United States Congress, but in his native Massachusetts as well. He even went so far as to write an article in one of the nation's leading magazines, *The Century Magazine.* Attesting to the mushrooming ranks of woman's rights advocates, he sought to ascertain the root cause of the controversy—the theological presuppositions regarding woman's nature. In his words, what needed to be dealt with was "a misunderstanding of the true nature of men and women, and a misunderstanding of the true nature of government. It is the same misunderstanding and prejudice that the advocates of freedom have encountered from the beginning of time."[11]

At the National-American Woman's Suffrage Association Convention in 1892, another assessment of woman's progress was made. The speaker was Susan B. Anthony. Reflecting on the question of what had been gained by women in the past forty years, she mentioned among other things women speaking from pulpits in the nation's churches, women serving as alternate delegates to the National Republican Convention and New York Governor Roswell P. Flower's recommendation that women serve as delgates to the approaching New York Constitutional Convention. But her concluding statement is even more telling: "Wendell Phillips said what he wanted to do on the abolition question was to turn Congress into an anti-slavery debating society. That is what we have done with every educational, industrial, religious and political body—we have turned them all into debating societies on the woman question."[12] For Susan B. Anthony, too, the measure of success lay in their ability to force recognition of the issue and stimulate debate and support on the part of the nation's leading figures.

In this attempt, Anthony's assessment is not misleading nor an understatement. The fourth volume of the six-volume *History of Woman Suffrage*, published in 1902, lists in its appendices an impressive list of woman suffrage supporters. While acknowledging that the lists themselves are incomplete, the authors maintained that they did give an adequate reflection of the extent to which woman suffrage had gained respectibility and, thus, verbal backing from prominent political figures. Listed are no less than ninety-four senators or former senators, four speakers of the House of

Representatives, eighty-eight former or present members of the House, seventy-seven governors, two Supreme Court justices, four vice presidents and four presidents—Abraham Lincoln, Rutherford B. Hayes, James Garfield and Theodore Roosevelt.

The political arena was not the only area in which women in 1900 registered a measure of success. The growing numbers of women entering a variety of professional fields previously denying them entrance also attested to the undeniable fact that woman's persistence and tenacity over the past decades was now reaping rewards. Institutions devoted exclusively to the education of females for service in a myriad of professions proliferated. At the same time, growing numbers of previously all-male educational facilities were now opening, or had opened, their doors to women scholars. Most notable in the latter regard were medical schools, and medicine became the first real profession open to women. By 1900, Carrie Chapman Catt reported that forty-nine medical schools in the United States and Canada now admitted women, with but nine of these separate women's colleges.

The century had also evidenced numerous personal success stories, far too many to mention here except in a cursory way. Women like Harriet Hosmer, Margaret Foley and Anne Whitney had distinguished themselves as artists. Myra Bradwell of Chicago, Belle Mansfield and Ellen Mussey had attained recognition in the legal field. Mary Booth, editor of *Harper's Bazar*, Martha Field, President of the Woman's International Press Association, Kate Tannatt Woods of *The Ladies Home Journal*, and Sarah J. Lippincott, Washington correspondent for the *New York Tribune* were admired and recognized as leading journalists. In medicine there were such notable women as doctors Emily and Elizabeth Blackwell; Dr. Susan Edson, physician to President Garfield; Dr. Anita N. McGee, assistant United States surgeon in the Spanish-American War; Dr. Ann Preston, Dean of Medical College and founder of Woman's Hospital in Philadelphia; and Dr. Marie F. Zakrzewska, founder of the New England Hospital for Women and Children. In the field of education numerous women gained personal recognition and success. Among them were Elizabeth Peabody, Emma Willard and Martha Foote Crowe, Dean of Northwestern University. In literature were names like Louisa May

Alcott and Harriet Beecher Stowe. In astronomy Maria Mitchell commanded respect from the entire scientific community. Social work areas evidenced the contributions of several distinguished women—Jane Addams of Chicago's Hull House; Florence Kelly, Illinois' chief state factory inspector; Abby H. Gibbons, President of the Woman's Prison Association; and Frances E. Willard, President of the Woman's Christian Temperance Union and an untiring advocate for social reforms. Indeed, by 1880, women could declare that no less than eighty-seven different women had obtained patents from the United States Patent Office.

These outstanding personal successes on the part of individual women led Carrie Chapman Catt to comment in 1900:

> Although woman in the "learned professions" still had difficulties to overcome in addition to those which confront man, it is evident that these are growing fewer every year. Basing one's judgment upon the rapidity with which conditions have changed in the last fifty years, a prophecy may be ventured with safety that in a few years the professional woman and professional man will stand before the world with equal chances of success or failure. The constantly increasing demand of women for work, the gradual decrease of prejudice against the woman worker, and the improved standard of qualification have opened nearly all occupations to women, and all the professions, learned and otherwise, within the last fifty years.[13]

The woman's assault on the pulpit was also of major importance in gauging the success of woman's efforts. And here, as elsewhere, success was mixed with defeat. *The History of Woman Suffrage* lists of 1902 record only twenty names in its list of woman ministers supportive of woman's rights. More revealing of defeat rather than success is the fact that of the twenty, only five are not Unitarian or Universalist (nine of the former, six of the latter). Both denominational groups had from their beginnings allowed women access to the pulpit. Of the remaining five, only two can be considered members of mainline Protestantism—Annis F. Eastman, a Congregationalist, and Anna Howard Shaw, an ordained minister of the Methodist Protestant Church. Antoinette Brown Blackwell, who might have increased the latter number to three, had long since left the Congregational denomination for a Unitarian pulpit.

These few statistics and others prompted Carrie Chapman Catt to interpretation and comment, this time in her book *The Nineteenth Century: A Review of Progress*. Her words betray a guarded optimism.

> There are now eighteen denominations, including Friends and the Salvation Army (which do not require ordination), that permit women to preach. Several hundred women are occupying regular pulpits. Those churches whose government is determined by large representative bodies, such as the Methodist Episcopal Conference and the Presbyterian Assembly, have never granted ordination to women. The denominations in which ordination may be secured at the request of a single congregation are those in which women ministers are most numerous. The so-called liberal denominations—Unitarian and Universalist—have ordained the largest number of women in proportion to their total membership. Among the churches which have ordained women are the Unitarian, Universalist, Congregational, Baptist, Free Baptist, Methodist Protestant, Free Methodist, Christian, and United Brethren.[14]

The Reverend Anna Howard Shaw gave a more complete review in an article for the *Chautauquan* in 1898. She began her review with an optimistic prediction, which bears mention in that it most assuredly reflects the sentiments of others in the movement as well. As one of the leaders of the woman's movement, Shaw's words are always one of the most accurate guides for determining the women's sentiments and self-assessment. With confidence she wrote, "Judging from the rapid increase of the past ten years it is safe to say that the dawn of the twentieth century will see not less than two thousand women preaching the gospel in the United States."[15]

According to Shaw, the United Brethren could rightly claim the distinction of having ordained the first woman to the ministry, for Lydia Sexton had been ordained to the ministry of that denomination in 1851 and served it continuously for almost forty years. The second woman ordained was Antoinette Brown, whose

ordination had been secured only with difficulty. Brown, an exceptional student and graduate of Oberlin College, was refused ordination by the Congregational Church until 1853. In fact, she was
not even acknowledged on Oberlin's graduation lists until forty
years after she had graduated.

Her ordination, when finally achieved, was a source of inspiration to many. Harriet Hunt, who attended her ordination service,
wrote of how deeply moved she had been by the ceremony: "I felt
a strong desire to attend on this occasion; the subject of woman in
the ministry had occupied much thought, and the more I pondered
it, the more convinced I was that her love nature and the strength
of the religious element in her, fitted her peculiarly to bind up the
broken heart, to sympathize with the penitent, to strengthen the
weak, to raise the fallen, and to infuse hope and trust in the Divine."16

At the time of Reverend Shaw's data collection in 1898, of
all the Protestant bodies the Congregationalist led the field with no
less than thirty women ordained to the ministry of that denomination. Such a figure, if correct, shows the severe limitations of the
listing found in *The History of Woman Suffrage*, which records only
the most prominent of the thirty—Reverend Annis Eastman, Associ-
ate Pastor in Elmira, New York.

Shaw also notes that the Regular Baptists could only boast
of three woman ministers—Mary Jones in Washington state, 1882;
Frances E. Townsley in Nebraska, 1885; and Edith Hill Booker in
Kansas, 1894. She was also careful to note that all three of these
women had secured their ordinations only after overcoming wide-
spread antagonism. In the case of Townsley ordination was granted
only after twelve years of service as an evangelist.

Freewill Baptists were a good deal more receptive to the
prospect of ordaining women to the ministry, having ordained seven-
teen and licensed nine others to serve that denomination by 1898.
The first to be licensed, although not officially ordained, was Clarissa
H. Danforth in 1815. Seventy-one years passed before any women
was privileged to serve as a fully ordained minister in the denomination. That distinction was first granted to Anna Bartlett in 1886.

The Christian Church had only ordained six women, a fact that Shaw found puzzling. So few women actively serving the denomination seemed particularly strange since the denomination itself appeared to have no real prejudice against the service and ordination of women ministers.

Shaw, in many ways one of the foremost realists in the woman's movement, also took occasion to mention denominational bodies who maintained a fierce obstinacy on the issue. Both the Presbyterian and the Methodist Episcopal Church were singled out as denominations who stubbornly refused to ordain women.

The Presbyterian Church not only still denied ordination to women, but also prohibited them from speaking in its pulpits. The latter restriction, which quite often appeared to be violated, led to one of the most sensational ecclesiastical trials in the nineteenth century.

The trial was that of the Reverend Isaac M. See, pastor of the Wickliffe Presbyterian Church in Newark, New Jersey in 1877. On October 29, 1876, the Reverend See had opened his pulpit to two temperance women, Mrs. L. S. Robinson and Mrs. C. S. Whiting. His act drew the condemnation of the Reverend E. R. Craven of the Third Presbyterian Church of Newark who promptly brought a formal charge before the Newark Presbytery. He accused See of being in violation of biblical dictate as recorded in I Corinthians 14.34-37 and I Timothy 2.13 and asked that the Presbytery censure See for his behavior. So adamant was Craven on the issue that he spoke a full four hours on the subject in his attempt to convince the body of See's wrongdoing.

When the Reverend McIllvaine introduced a resolution advocating that the charge be dismissed by common consent of the parties involved and the Reverend See affectionately counselled to adhere more rigidly to the standards of the Presbyterian Church in the future, both See and Craven protested. Dr. See refused on the basis that what was at issue was ultimately a question of divine will and added, "I believe myself to be not guilty of the charge, but I admit the specifications."[17] To consent to McIllvaine's resolution was, for See, to consent to guilt, something he could not do.

Debate, thus, continued at length, with numerous clergymen rising to quote scripture or Presbyterian tradition and regulation against See. Not all spoke against him, however, and one cleric even admitted that he had himself offered his own pulpit for temperance lectures by female speakers. But support was not strong enough, and, when the vote was tallied, See was found guilty of violating scripture. The vote was 16 to 12.

The case was finally appealed to the General Assembly after yet another defeat at the Synod of New Jersey. This body, the major governing body of the Presbyterian Church, also voted not to sustain the appeal. Only 85 voted to sustain the appeal, 71 voted to sustain it in part, and 201 voted not to sustain.[18] The Reverend See had clearly lost his case and, in the process, had dramatically exposed the ecclesiastical barriers to woman's right to speak from Presbyterian pulpits.

Despite such a sensational refusal on the part of the Presbyterian Church, Shaw would note that Presbyterian Grace Briggs had recently graduated as head of her class at Union Theological Seminary and that fourteen other women were pursuing theological study at the same institution. This fact alone allowed Shaw to suppose that it would be but a short time before the ban imposed by the Presbyterian Church would be revoked. It might have shocked her if she had been told that Presbyterian women would have to wait almost sixty years before they would attain the right to ordination.

The Methodist Episcopal Church also continued to refuse women ordination; it would finally grant full ordinational rights to women in 1956, within two weeks of the Presbyterian Church. However, it had licensed women to speak, until 1880 when preaching licenses were prohibited women by action of the General Conference. They would be reinstated in 1919.

In 1898, at the time Shaw was writing, Methodist Episcopal women could only distinguish themselves as missionaries, evangelists and social workers, which they did effectively and in surprisingly large numbers. Thus, although women like Frances E. Willard longed for ordination, she had to content herself with social reform movements and the presidency of the W. C. T. U. Even though she proved a remarkable champion of social reforms and devoted an extensive amount of time to these areas, she never ceased to accost the barriers which prevented the ministry of women in Methodism.

Any investigation of the Methodist Episcopal stance on female ordination would be incomplete without mention of the case of Anna Oliver and Anna Howard Shaw. In 1880, both Oliver, a graduate of Boston University, and Shaw, also a graduate of Boston, presented their request for ordination to Bishop Andrews of the New England Conference. Their request was readily denied, and an appeal was carried to the next General Conference meeting held in Cincinnati. Here, not only were their requests denied, but both women saw their licenses to preach suspended, a privilege Shaw had held for eight years and Oliver for four years.[19]

That was only the beginning of tragedy for Oliver. While Shaw immediately secured ordination in the Methodist Protestant Church despite some strong objection, Oliver returned to her ministry of a Brooklyn church. The church itself was $14,000 in debt, a debt which Oliver could not lift. Beyond this she was often attacked in print by James M. Buckley, a devout opponent of women in the ministry and editor of the *Christian Advocate*. In the words of her life-long friend Anna Howard Shaw, "She was attacked by that influential Methodist paper, the *Christian Advocate*, edited by the Rev. Dr. James M. Buckley, who declared that he would destroy her influence in the church, and so with that great organ behind him he attacked her. She had that to fight, the world to fight and the devil to fight, and she broke down in health. She went abroad to recover, but came home only to die."[20]

Shaw's review in the *Chautauquan* also made mention of denominational bodies which had never denied women the right of ordination or which, not requiring formal ordination, had never closed their pulpits to women speakers. In the first category were the Universalists and the Unitarians; in the second groups like the Salvation Army and the Society of Friends. The Universalists listed fifty ordained women and nine licensed preachers at the time of Shaw's article, while the Unitarians could boast twenty-eight ordained women ministers. Other churches and sect groups frequently allowed women to supply Christian leadership and speak from their pulpits. Because formal ordination was not required by these groups, statistics are difficult to acquire. Shaw claimed that the Society of Friends alone enrolled approximately 350 women as preachers by the turn of the century.

While Shaw's review appears to struggle for optimism at times and while she undoubtedly saw in the cited statistics a reason to expect future successes, she tempered her article with the blunt admission that even these figures might cloud the issue somewhat. She realistically conceded that ordained women still were not accepted on the same basis or scale as men and that many denominations ordaining women still viewed the practice as "a tacit acknowledgment of weakness."[21] With this observation in mind, she concluded her article with a well-constructed word of warning: "So long as they are permitted to officiate only in small and poor parishes; so long as many denominations continue to oppose their preaching as contrary to the Scriptures and antagonistic to the best interests of the Church; and so long as its greatest possible insignificance all that women do in this office—just so long will their real value as pastor and preacher remain unknown."[22]

The pulpit, of course, was not the only area providing success for women in Christian service, and nineteenth century feminist appraisers did not neglect this fact. As early as 1869 women began to serve on local church committees, state and national religious associations and as ordained deaconesses. They increasingly organized, officered and managed their own missionary associations for their respective denominations. All this when in 1809 their subscriptions to newspapers or charities required their husbands' signatures and when in 1840 they still could not legally serve as treasurers of their own sewing societies. In light of such facts, the women had come a long way in 1900.

Two women had even successfully served as chaplains to state legislatures—Phebe Hanaford in the Connecticut Legislature and

Lorenza Haynes in Maine's House of Representatives. It was also true that, by 1900, numerous women speakers had spoken from the nations pulpits apart from the question of ordination or formal ministry. In fact, a national woman's convention in a city often provided the occasion for pulpit addresses by various women in convention attendance, ordained or otherwise. On Sunday mornings these women eagerly occupied pulpits open to them in the city wherein the convention was being held. While it is equally true that the churches extending invitations to convention attendees were most often Unitarian or Universalists, Methodist, Congregational and Baptist churches were not above opening their pulpits to a woman's rights advocate.

One such occasion occurred at the National-American Woman's Suffrage Convention held in Washington, D. C. in 1894. At that time, Carrie C. Catt occupied the pulpit of the Peoples Church, Ellen B. Dietrick the pulpit of All Souls Church, while the Reverend Anna Shaw preached to a large, attentive audience at Metzerott's Music Hall, taking for her text "Let no man take thy crown." The following year witnessed no less than six convention delegates in Washington's pulpits—Shaw, Clara Colby, Meriwether, Yates and Howland.

Although only two years have been noted, such activities must not be thought exceptional. They would become the rule as the nineteenth century drew to a close. In fact, even ecclesiastical antagonists of the calibre of Stanton and Gage found ample opportunity to voice their convictions from the nation's pulpits. Although one cannot deny that many denominations rigidly enforced their restrictions against women speaking from their pulpits, a growing number of pulpits did become open to the women, even when the denomination itself stood opposed to the actual ordination of women. Once again, feminists noted this freedom for pulpit address among their successes.

The efforts of feminists throughout the nineteenth century were valiant, even heroic at times. They had succeeded, and they had failed. How the failure or the success was weighted was often determined by perspective or whether or not it could be used as an indicator of future possibilities. This approach assured women that their hopeful attitude was not unmerited.

Personal stories, too, suffered mixed reviews. Some, like Anna Oliver, had died knowing only rejection and disappointment. Others, like those cited who had successfully gained recognition in various professional fields, breathed an air of eager optimism.

Evaluations were graded and scaled differently by different women in the movement, and rightly so it would appear. Yet, I think, none would disagree with my own cautious evaluation that they had achieved a remarkable, though limited, measure of success.

Notes

[1] Isabella Hooker, *Remarks of Mrs. Hooker Before the Judiciary Committee of the House of Representatives* (Washington: n. p., 1871), p. 30.

[2] Stanton address to U. S. Senate Committee of the Judiciary, January 10, 1872, *HWS*, II (1881), 512.

[3] Senator Williams before the U. S. Senate, December 11, 1866, *HWS*, II (1881), 109.

[4] Senator Frelinghuysen before U. S. Senate, December 11, 1866, *HWS*, II (1881), 135.

[5] Senator Davis before U. S. Senate, December 11, 1866, *HWS*, II (1881), 145.

[6] Senator Bayard before U. S. Senate, May, 1874, *HWS*, II (1881), 576.

[7] M. Dahlgren letter to Senate Committee on Privileges and Elections, January, 1878, *HWS*, III (1886), 102.

[8]Minority report of Senate Committee on Woman Suffrage, 1886, *HWS*, IV (1902), 83.

[9]*Congressional Record—Senate*, Part I, 49th congress, second session, 18 (December 8, 1886), 34-38.

[10]Vina Lee, "Where Women Vote," *The Chautauquan*, 24, No. 5 (February, 1897), 589.

[11]Senator George Hoar, "The Right and Expediancy of Woman Suffrage," *The Century Magazine*, 48, No. 4 (August, 1894), 605.

[12]Susan B. Anthony at N-A. W. S. A. Convention, 1892, *HWS*, IV (1902), 605.

[13]Carrie Chapman Catt, "Women in the Industries and Professions," *The Nineteenth Century: A Review of Progress in The American Woman: Who Was She?* ed. Anne F. Scott (Englewood Cliffs, N. J.: Prentice Hall, 1971), pp. 48-49. [The original article was published by G. P. Putnam and Sons of New York in 1901.]

[14]*Ibid.*, pp. 47-48.

[15]Anna Howard Shaw, "Women in the Ministry," *The Chautauquan*, 18 (1898), p. 489.

[16]Harriet Hunt, *Glimpses and Glances* (1856; rpt. New York: Source Book, 1970), p. 304.

[17]Dr. Isaac See, quoted in *HWS*, III (1886), 486.

[18]*Ibid.*, p. 488.

[19]Anna Oliver, *Test Case on the Ordination of Women* (New York: Wm. N. Jennings, 1880).

[20]Anna Howard Shaw at N-A. W. S. A. Convention, 1893, *HWS*, IV (1902), 207.

[21]Anna Howard Shaw, "Women in the Ministry," *Op. Cit.*, p. 493.

[22]*Ibid.*, p. 496.

Conclusion

The nineteenth century had proven to be an eventful century for America, one filled with acute restlessness, eager enthusiasm and an almost overwhelming optimism, which even the Civil War did not check. Indeed, it might be said that the century's numerous problems brought the nation's optimists to the fore.

Westward expansion, urbanization and growing industrialization introduced new tensions and greater complexity to American life. To the social and economic problems surrounding the issue of slavery were added the equally troubling problems created by a great influx of immigrants, products of continental revolutions and famine in Ireland. Although such proved disruptive, it also provided occasion for rethinking the American dream.

Humanitarian reforms swept the United States, sustained by a fierce individualism, inherent belief in the idea of progress and an ever-expanding field of knowledge. Innovation and experimentation became the order of the day, as traditional beliefs and institutions were repeatedly challenged. New theories and ideas were introduced, rejected and replaced by even newer, more daring approaches.

It was in the midst of this fast growing society bent upon reforming and perfecting all its social institutions that women sought to develop, define and articulate their places and roles. They fought and defended their right to participate in all humanitarian reforms— temperance, peace, prison reform, anti-slavery, etc.—insisting that they too had a vested interest in the welfare of their society. So successful were they in their insistence and persistence that they often (if only in numbers alone) came to dominate certain social reform movement. At the same time and essentially for the same reasons, they demanded entrance into professions previously inaccessible to them—medicine, law, the ministry. It was their ambitions and convictions which also caused them to seek admittance to institutions of higher education and full access to knowledge formerly reserved for males alone. In time, many of the nation's male colleges became coed, while new female institutions were founded with curricula both quantitatively and qualitatively better than previous decades. Behind all efforts for equal education, the right to professional careers and the right to participate in the reform of American society, however, was the all-encompassing demand for true citizenship, legally, economically and politically defined. Such a demand necessitated the rejection of a theologically-based ideology which supposed the undesirability, if not the impossibility, of its being realized.

The woman's rights movement must, thus, be viewed as not only a complex movement in and of itself, but also as an important fragment of an even more extensive movement for reform which gripped the hearts and minds of nineteenth century Americans. One would do little, if any, injustice to the women's movement if one were to insist that the women had simply taken prevalent ideas of the time and applied them logically in the interests of their sex.

Their growing recognition of the validity and scope of their reform is significant. To a great degree, it accounts for their inability to avoid the question of the role of religion and the attendant questions of theological prejudice towards women.

Religion, of course, was a live issue in the nineteenth century even apart from the interest shown in it by feminists, and American Christianity at the time was certainly not immune to the experimentation and innovation which began to dominate the social scene. Nor was it deaf to the cry for social perfectibiltiy.

The religious atmosphere of America in the nineteenth century was electric. Revivalism permeated both urban areas and frontier America. Sects, with queer and unique theologies sprang up everywhere—Shakers, Mormons, Millerites, Transcendentalists, and Spiritualists to name but a few. It was an age of utopian dreams often linked to religious beliefs. Religious communes proliferated, all seeking greater social and spiritual perfection. The century itself would end on the high note of the Social Gospel Movement, which sought and eagerly awaited a socially realized Kingdom of God. Add to this picture of intense religious concern the fact that impressive numbers of women joined religious communes, alined with utopian communities and participated in proliferating sect groups, where they often commanded positions of leadership, and much is already said about the religious awareness of American women and their receptivity to theological liberalism and innovation.

Thus it was that when women formally organized their drive to have their social and spiritual existence and equality recognized, they were not only greatly influenced by socially accepted reform rhetoric, but also quickly determined that religion provided one of the most vicious obstacles in their path. Unable to ignore it, it drew their attention and energies. Forced by this recognition, their own committedness and the consciousness and temper of the age, they brought the entire issue to the forefront of their crusade.

With theological questions continuously before them in conventions, their awareness understandably increased; and with it, their ability to deal intelligently and forcefully with the implications derived and/or sustained by the entrenched traditionalism of contemporary biblical scholarship. Although it is true that much of feminist theology was developed before the first woman's right convention was held in 1848, convention debates and discussions reveal a growing maturity on the part of woman scholars. They sophisticated, broadened and deepened their theological insights and resolve, reworking and building upon the foundations laid down by earlier, pre-convention feminists.

The convention of course served a variety of purposes, not the least of which was its ability to function as a vital educational forum for the dissemination of belief and idea. So effective was the convention in this regard that many die-hard skeptics, upon hearing women voice their new-found theologies, were forced to relent and admit, however reluctantly, that feminist theology was not without validity and integrity. Preconceived prejudice evaporated before the barrage of insight presented by feminist theologians, who refused to compromise what they felt to be God-given rights now denied them.

Conventions were not the only weapons used by the women. Efforts to address religious prejudices, either derived from traditional theology or socially-conditioned mindsets, led a significant number of persons within the movement into in-depth studies of both theology and history. Some entered seminaries in order to familiarize themselves with Greek and Latin, languages which would facilitate their efforts to counter arguments presented by accomplished theologians who affirmed the traditional in biblical exegeses. Others perused church history texts and ecclesiastical tomes in hopes of exposing the injustices suffered by women and thereby recall women from ecclesiastical obscurity.

All in all, the nineteenth century proved an era of tremendous and far-reaching scholarship for women. Woman learned to think, to organize ideas and to articulate her thoughts in convincing and forceful arguments. Although this is true in all areas of knowledge, it is most assuredly true for the women who ventured into the areas of biblical studies and theology. By the end of the nineteenth century we can speak of truly educated women, biblically literate and commendable theologians.

Previous centuries had honored the exceptional woman who through circumstance or a rare display of persistence had stood above the commonality of her sex. The nineteenth century, however, revealed the exception to be the rule as vast numbers of women stated their desire and sought the means to rise above their previous commonality.

While the attainment of practical goals awaited realization beyond the cutoff date of this work—1900, much had been accomplished by these stubborn and courageous feminists of nineteenth century America. They could not yet vote, but they had made impressive inroads into the political, economic, educational and legal spheres of national life. And although they did not flood America's pulpits by 1900 by any stretch of the imagination, they had laid the theological groundwork which allowed women of the twentieth century to push for just such an event. Indeed, their theology is as vital today in the ongoing debate for ecclesiastical recognition and spiritual equality as it was in the nineteenth century.

Nineteenth century feminists had learned some important lessons in their attempts to tackle centuries of accumulated religious prejudice. Although it is impossible to delineate each and every lesson which must have been learned, it is just as impossible to ignore the most important ones.

First, the women had learned that traditional theology was not sacrosanct. Traditional theology had not exhausted all alternatives of biblical translation and interpretation. By realizing this the women were freed to acquire skills enabling them to present alternatives which did not depreciate womankind nor retain them in abject positions of subordination. Instead, they found they could rescue women from their second class spiritual citizenship while still acknowledging the integrity of the biblical record. Not only that, but they could develop their theologies in full accord with acceptable exegetical methods, even though it must be admitted that they proved extremely receptive to the new historico-critical methods which were aborning.

Secondly, women discovered that they had unjustly suffered deprivations and degradations at the hands of the church, a revelation which women then sought to expose and reverse. Maintaining that women had been criminally excluded from ecclesiastical life by the male desire to dominate it, feminists now affirmed a God-given right to equal participation in the life of the church. Tracing her outcast status to church council issuances of restrictions upon her sex and theologies which promoted attitudes and practices demeaning to the female sex, she now ridiculed the faulty assumptions which undergirded them. Her insights on these matters were shrewd enough so that they could not be easily shrugged off by prominent church historians. Indeed, they succeeded in formulating some penetrating, albeit embarrassing, questions.

Thirdly, woman found that she did possess a history which affirmed her worth, a worth which was sustained both biblically and socially. In the Old and New Testaments she discovered women who, when delivered from dusty obscurity, played decisive and important roles in the life of Israel and in the life of the early Christian church. In the annals of church history she found equally impressive women who supplied the energies and ideas which helped shape Christendom. Although feminists realized that many female names were never recorded in history texts, the few that did exist were sufficient to produce a renewed pride in being female.

Fourth and lastly, their growing knowledge of themselves as women and as a force in history brought with it a new sense of self-confidence. Women affirmed their abilities to meet their male counterparts on intellectual battlefields and proved themselves no mean opponents. They wrote, studied, spoke with new conviction and growing self-assurance. Women proved to others, and more importantly to themselves, that they were capable of organizing and directing practical reforms, as well as their own lives. They could vanquish those arguments which claimed woman an intellectual inferior incapable of rational thought; their words and actions proved quite the opposite conclusion.

Whatever the lessons learned by nineteenth century women and whatever their value for the women of succeeding generations, they must not be accorded a completeness. The lessons, like the practical goals envisioned by American women in the nineteenth century, are far from tried in their in fullest implications. Thus, a conclusion to this work can only reiterate this fact and share with the women of the nineteenth century the optimistic hope that one hundred years from now, when an historian sits down to write a similar history of twentieth century feminism, he or she will be able to write a more effortless conclusion.

A Selected Bibliography

Primary Sources

Books and Pamphlets:

Anderson, Samuel Gilmore. *Woman's Sphere and Influence*. Toledo, Ohio: Franklin Printing and Engraving, 1898.

Baldwin, George C. *Representative Women*. New York: Blake man and Company, 1855.

Beecher, Catherine. *An Essay on Slavery and Abolition with Reference to the Duty of American Females*. Philadelphia: Henry Perkins, 1837.

Beecher, Henry W. *Woman's Influence in Politics*. Boston: R. F. Wallcut, 1860.

Branagan, Thomas. *The Excellency of the Female Character Vindicated*. 1808; rpt. New York: Arno Press, 1972.

Brockett, Linus P. *Woman: Her Rights, Wrongs, Privileges and Responsibilities*. Hartford, Connecticut: L. Stebbins, 1869.

Bushnell, Horace. *Women's Suffrage: The Reform Against Nature*. New York: Charles Scribner and Company, 1869.

Child, Lydia Maria. *The Progress of Religious Ideas Through Successive Ages*. 4th ed. 3 vols. New York: James Miller, Publisher, 1855.

Clarke, Adam. *The Holy Bible Containing the Old and New Testaments, The Text Carefully Printed from the Most Correct Copies of the Present Authorized Translation including the Marginal Readings and Parallel Texts with a Commentary and Critical Notes Designed as a Help to a Better Understanding of the Sacred Writings.* London: Joseph Butterworth and Son, 1825. I.

Cobbe, Frances Power, *Duties of Women.* 8th American ed. Boston: George H. Ellis, 1881.

Crocker, Hannah Mather. *Observations on the Real Rights of Women, with Their Appropriate Duties, Agreeable to Scripture, Reason and Common Sense.* Boston: n. o., 1881.

Davis, Almond H. *The Female Preacher or Memoir of Salome Lincoln.* 1843: rpt. New York: Arno Press, 1972.

Diaz, Abby Morton. *Only a Flock of Women.* Boston: D. Lothrop Company, 1893.

Dietrick, Ellen Batelle. *Women in the Early Christian Ministry.* Philadelphia: Alfred J. Ferris, 1897.

Dix, Morgan. *Lectures on the Calling of a Christian Woman, and Her Training to Fulfil It.* New York: D. Appleton, 1883.

Dodge, Mary. *Woman's Wrongs: A Counter-Irritant.* 1868; rpt. New York: Arno Press, 1972.

Emerson, Ralph W., et. al. *Memoirs of Margaret Fuller Ossoli.* Boston: Roberts Brothers, 1881.

Foster, John O. *Life and Labors of Mrs. Maggie Van Cott, The First Lady Licensed to Preach in the Methodist Episcopal Church in the United States.* Cincinnati: Hitchcock and Walden, 1972.

Fuller, Margaret. *Woman in the Nineteenth Century.* 1855; rpt. New York: W. W. Norton and Company, Inc., 1971.

Gage, Matilda J. *Woman, Church and State*. Chicago: Charles H. Kerr and Company, 1893.

Garrison, Wendell Phillips and F. J. Garrison. *William Lloyd Garrison: The Story of His Life as Told by His Children*. 4 volumes. New York: Houghton Mifflin and Company, 1894.

Godwin, Mary Wollestonecraft. *A Vindication of the Rights of Women*. 1972; rpt. New York: E. P. Dutton and Company, 1929.

Grimke, Angelina. *Appeal to the Christian Women of the Southern States*. New York: n. p., 1836.

Grimke, Angelina. *Letter to Catherine Beecher, in Reply to an Essay on Slavery and Abolitionism, Addressed to A. E. Grimke, Revised by the Author*. 1838; rpt. New York: Arno Press, 1969.

Grimke, Sarah. *Letters on the Equality of the Sexes and the Condition of Women*. 1838; rpt. New York: Burt Franklin, 1970.

Hale, Sarah Josepha. *Woman's Record, or Sketches of All Distinguished Women, From the Creation to A. D. 1854*. 1855; rpt. New York: Source Book Press, 1970.

Hanaford, Phebe A. *Daughters of America or Women of the Century*. Augusta, Maine: True and Company, 1882.

Harper, Ida Husted. *The Life and Work of Susan B. Anthony*. 2 vols. Indianapolis: Bowen-Merrill Company, 1899-1908.

Hays, George P. *May Women Speak? A Bible Study by a Presbyterian Minister*. Chicago: Woman's Temperance Publication Association, 1889.

Hooker, Isabella. *Remarks of Mrs. Hooker Before the Judiciary Committee of the House of Representative, January, 1871*. Washington, D. C.: n. p., 1871.

Hooker, John. *The Bible and Woman Suffrage*. Hartford: Case, Lockwood and Brainerd, 1974.

Hunt, Harriott K. *Glances and Glimpses: or, Fifty Years Social, Including Twenty Years Professional Life*. Boston: J. P. Jewett and Company, 1856.

Johnson, Helen Kendrick. *Woman's Progress Versus Woman Suffrage*. New York: New York State Association Opposed to the Extension of the Suffrage to Women, 1904.

Lee, Luther. *Woman's Right to Preach the Gospel; a Sermon Preached at the Ordination of the Reverend Miss Antoinette Brown, at South Butler, Wayne County, New York, September 15, 1853*. Syracuse, New York: The Author, 1853.

Love, William Deloss. *St. Paul and Woman*. New York: Fleming H. Revell Company, 1894.

McIntosh, Maria J. *Woman in America: Her Work and Her Reward*. New York: D. Appleton and Company, 1850.

Milburn, William Henry. *The Pioneer Preacher*. New York: Derby and Jachson, 1858.

Miller, Leo. *Woman and the Divine Republic*. Buffalo: Haas and Nauert, 1874.

Oliver, Anna. *Test Case on the Ordination of Woman*. New York: William N. Jennings, Printers, 1880.

Palmer, Phoebe Worrell. *Promise of the Father: of A Neglected Speciality of the Last Days Addressed to the Clergy and Laity of all Christian Communities*. New York: W. C. Palmer Jr., 1872.

Phillips, Wendell. *Speeches, Lecture and Letters*, 1st series. 2 vols. Boston: Lee and Shepard, 1892-94.

Phillips, Wendell. *Speeches on Rights of Women.* Philadelphia: Alfred J. Ferris, 1898.

Reply to John Stuart Mill on the Subjection of Women. Philadelphia: J. B. Lippincott, 1870.

Roberts, Benjamin T. *Ordaining Women.* Rochester, New York: Earnest Christian Publishing House, 1891.

Shaw, Anna Howard. *The Story of a Pioneer.* New York: Harper and Brothers, 1915.

Stanton, Elizabeth C., et. al. *The Woman's Bible.* 2 vols. in one. 1895-98; rpt. New York: Arno Press, 1972.

Stanton, Elizabeth E. *Eighty Years and More.* 1898; rpt. New York: Schocken Books, 1973.

Todd, John. *Woman's Rights.* 1867; rpt. New York: Arno Press, 1972.

Willard, Frances E. *Glimpses of Fifty Years: The Autobiography of an American Woman.* Chicago: Woman's Temperance Publication Association and H. J. Smith and Company, 1889.

Willard, Frances E. *Woman in the Pulpit.* Boston: D. Lothrop Company, 1888.

Wise, Daniel. *Young Lady's Counsellor.* New York: G. Lane and L. Scott, 1852.

Articles:

Anon. "The Eligibility of Women Not a Scriptural Question." *The Methodist Review*, 73, March, 1891, pp. 456-63.

Anon. "The Ground of Woman's Eligibility." *The Methodist Review*, 73, May, 1891, pp. 287-91.

Anon. "Speaking or Babbling." *The Congregational Quarterly*, 16, October, 1874, pp. 576-87.

Cady, D. R. "The Biblical Position of Woman." *The Congregational Quarterly*, 12, July, 1870, pp. 370-77.

Congressional Record, 18, Part I, 49th Congress, 2nd session, December 8, 1886, pp. 34-38.

Cyrus, Cort. "Women as Preachers." *Reformed Quarterly (Church) Review*, 29, 1882, p. 123f.

Davies, J. Llewelyn. "Christianity and the Equality of the Sexes." *The Contemporary Review*, 46, August, 1884, pp. 224-34.

Dods, Marcus. "Women in the Corinthian Worship." *The Lutheran Church Review*, 18, July, 1899, pp. 498-504.

Donaldson, J. "The Position of Woman Among the Early Christians." *The Contemporary Review*, 56, September, 1889, pp. 433-51.

Duren, Charles. "Place of Women in the Church, in Religious Meetings." *The Congregational Review*, 8, January, 1868, pp. 22-29.

Fink, R. A. "Women in the Church. *The Quarterly Review of the Evangelical Lutheran Church*, 4, April, 1874, pp. 220-33.

Gibbons, 'Cardinal.' "Relative Condition of Women Under Pagan and Christian Civilization." *The American Catholic Quarterly Review*, 11, October, 1886, pp. 651-65.

Gilbert, George H. "Women in Public Worship in the Churches of Paul." *The Biblical World*, 2, July, 1893, pp. 38-47.

Godet, F. "The Ministry of Women." *The Contemporary Review*, 45, January, 1884, pp. 48-63.

Goodenow, W. S. B. "Voice of Women in the Church." *The New Englander*, 36, 1877, pp. 115-31.

Hargrove, R. K. "Woman's Work in the Church." *The Methodist Review*, 43, March-April, 1896, pp. 3-14.

Hoar, George F. "The Right and Expediency of Woman Suffrage." *The Century Magazine*, 48, August, 1894, pp. 605-13.

Knowlton, Stephen. "The Silence of Women in the Churches." *The Congregational Quarterly*, 9, October, 1867, pp. 329-34.

Lee, Vina J. "Where Women Vote." *The Chautuaguan*, 24, February, 1897, pp. 589-91.

Livermore, Mary A. "Woman Suffrage." *The North American Review*, 143, October, 1886, pp. 371-81.

Loomis, Harmon. "Women in the Church, May They Speak in Meetings?" *The Congregational Quarterly*, 16, April, 1874, pp. 264-78.

Love, William Deloss. "Women Keeping Silence in Churches." *The Bibliotheca Sacra*, 35, January, 1878, pp. 1-44.

Lyttelton, E. "Women's Suffrage and the Teaching of St. Paul." *The Contemporary Review*, 69, May, 1896, pp. 680-91.

Mayser, F. P. "Shall Women Vote in Church." *The Lutheran Church Review*, 18, July, 1899, pp. 479-86.

Moore, Augusta. "Women in the Church." *The Congregational Quarterly*, 16, April, 1874, pp. 279-84.

Ross, A. Hastings. "The Silence of Women in the Churches." *The Bibliotheca Sacra*, 27, April, 1870, pp. 336-59.

Schmauk, Theodore E. "St. Paul and Women." *The Lutheran Church Review*, 18, July, 1899, pp. 505-24.

Schmauk, Theodore E. "The Epistle of Timothy and the Woman Question." *The Lutheran Church Review*, 18, July, 1899, pp. 525-36.

Schmauk, Theodore E. "A History of Authority, and of the Right to Rule, in Christian Society, in its Bearings on the Woman Question." *The Lutheran Church Review*, 18, July, 1899, pp. 543-53.

Shackford, C. C. "Woman, Historic and Prehistoric." *The Monthly Review and Religious Magazine*, 43, January, 1870, pp. 54-65.

Shaw, Anna Howard. "Women in the Ministry." *The Chautauquan*, 18, August, 1898, pp. 489-96.

Spalding, J. L. "Has Christianity Benefitted Woman?" *The North American Review*, 140, May, 1885, pp. 399-410.

Stanton, Elizabeth C. "Has Christianity Benefitted Woman?" *The North American Review*, 140, May, 1885, pp. 389-99.

Stevenson, J. M. "Place of Women in Assemblies for Public Worship." *The Presbyterian Quarterly and Princeton Review*, 2, January, 1873, pp. 42-59.

Torrey, Charles W. "Woman's Sphere in the Church." *The Congregational Quarterly*, 9, April, 1867, pp. 163-71.

Williams, John Milton. "Woman Suffrage." *The Bibliotheca Sacra*, 50, April, 1893, pp. 331-39.

Collections and Edited Works:

American Woman: Who Was She? Ed. Anne Firor Scott. Englewood Cliffs, N. J.: Prentice Hall, Inc., 1971.

Eminent Women of the Age: Being Narratives of the Lives and Deeds of the Most Prominent Women of the Present Generation. Eds. James Parton, et. al. Hartford, Connecticut: S. M. Betts and Company, 1869.

Feminist Papers. Ed. Alice S. Rossi. New York: Columbia University Press, 1973.

History of Woman Suffrage. 6 vols. Eds. Elizabeth C. Stanton, et. al. New York: Fowler and Wells and Susan B. Anthony, 1881-1922.

Letters of Theodore Weld, Angelina Grimke Weld and Sarah Grimke. Eds. Gilbert H. Barnes and Dwight L. Dumond. New York: Appleton-Century, Crofts and the American Historical Association, 1934.

Transactions of the National Council of Women. Ed. Rachel Foster Avery. Philadelphia: J. B. Lippincott, Co., 1891.

Up From the Pedestal: Selected Documents From the History of American Feminism. Ed. Aileen Kraditor. Chicago: Quadrangle, 1968.

Other:

Proceedings of the Woman's Rights Conventions Held at Seneca Falls and Rochester, N. Y., July and August, 1848. 1870; rpt. New York: Arno Press, 1969.

Proceedings of the Woman's Rights Convention Held at Akron, Ohio, May 28 and 29, 1851. 1851; rpt. New York: Burt Franklin, 1973.

Secondary Sources

Anthony, Katharine. *Margaret Fuller: A Psychological Biography.* New York: Harcourt, Brace and Company, 1921.

Beard, Mary R. *Woman as Force in History: A Study in Traditions and Realities.* New York: Macmillan Company, 1946.

Blackwell, Alice Stone. *Lucy Stone: Pioneer of Woman's Rights*. Boston: Little, Brown and Company, 1930.

Burnett, Constance Buel. *Five for Freedom*. New York: Greenwood Press, Publishers, 1968.

Daly, Mary. *The Church and the Second Sex*. New York: Harper and Row, 1968.

Flexner, Eleanor. *Century of Struggle, the Woman's Rights Movement in the United States*. Cambridge: Belknap Press of Harvard University Press, 1959.

Hare, Lloyd C. M. *The Greatest American Woman: Lucretia Mott*. New York: Negro Universities Press and American Historical Society, 1937.

Lerner, Gerda. *The Grimke Sisters From South Carolina: Pioneers for Woman's Rights and Abolition*. 1967; rpt. New York: Schocken Books, 1971.

Lutz, Alma. *Susan B. Anthony: Rebel, Crusader and Humanitarian*. Boston: Beacon Press, 1959.

Peck, Mary Gray. *Carrie Chapman Catt*. New York: H. W. Wilson, 1944.

Sherwin, Oscar. *Prophet of Liberty: The Life and Times of Wendell Phillips*. New York: Bookman Associates, 1958.

Additional Resources

Primary Resources

American Sisterhood: Writings of the Feminist Movement From Colonial Times to the Present. Ed. Wendy Martin. New York: Harper-Row, 1972.

Anon. *Bible on Women's Public Speaking.* Louisville, Kentucky: Baptist Book Concern, 1895.

Anon. "St. Paul and the Woman Movement." *The Westminster Review*, 131, February, 1889.

Anon. *The Woman's Book.* New York: Charles Scribner's Sons, 1894.

Anon. "Woman's Place in Church Work." *The Review of Reviews*, 5, April, 1892.

Austin, George Lowell. *The Life and Times of Wendell Phillips.* Boston: B. B. Russell and Company, 1884.

Beecher, Catherine. *The Evils Suffered by American Women and Children: The Causes and the Remedy.* New York: Harper, 1846.

Beecher, Henry W. *Wendell Phillips.* New York: Fords, Howard and Hulburt, 1884.

Birney, Catherine H. *The Grimke Sisters, Sarah and Angelina.* Boston: Lee and Shepard, 1885.

Blake, Lillie Devereux. *Woman's Place Today: Four Lectures in Reply to the Lenten Lectures on "Woman" by the Rev. Morgan Dix*. New York: J. W. Lovell, 1883.

Bloomer, C. Chamberlain. *Life and Writings of Amelia Bloomer*. Boston: Arena Publishing, 1895.

Bottome, Margaret. "Women in the Church—A Symposium." *Homiletic and Pastoral Review*, 21, 1891.

Bowles, Ada C. "Women in the Ministry." In *Woman's Work in America* by Annie Nathan Meyer. New York: H. Holt, 1891.

Broadus, John Albert. *Should Women Speak in Mixed Public Assemblies?* Louisville, Kentucky: Baptist Book Concern, 1890.

Burnap, George W. *Lectures on the Spheres and Duties of Woman and Other Subjects*. Baltimore: John Murphy, 1841.

Butler, Josephine. "Woman's Place in Church Work." *Christian Literature*, 6, 1892.

Chaney, G. L. "Ministry of Woman." *Monthly Religious Magazine*, 44, 1870.

Charteris, A. H. "Work of Women in the Church." *Presbyterian Review*, 9, 1888.

Child, Lydia Maria. *Brief History of the Condition of Women, in Various Ages and Nations*. 2 vols. 5th ed. New York: C. S. Francis and Company, 1854.

Child, Lydia Maria. *Letters From New York*. 2nd series. New York: C. S. Francis and Company, 1845.

Child, Lydia Maria. *Letters From New York*. 2nd series. New York: C. S. Francis and Company, 1845.

Child, Lydia Maria. *Letters*. Harriet W. Sewall, compl. Boston: Houghton, Mifflin, 1883.

Cox, William M. "The Social and Civil Status of Women." *Presbyterian Quarterly*, 9, 1895.

Craigie, Mary E. *Christian Citizenship*. New York: National, n. d.

Crusader and Feminist: Letters of Jane Grey Swisshelm, 1858-65. Ed. Arthur J. Larsen. St. Paul: Minnesota Historical Society, 1934.

Davis, Paulina W. *History of the National Woman's Rights Movement*. 1871; rpt. New York: Source Book, 1970.

Douglass, Frederick. *Life and Times*. Boston: Dewolfe, Fiske, 1895.

Duniway, Abigail Scott. *Pathbreaking: An Autobiographical History of the Equal Suffrage Movement in Pacific Coast States*. 1914; rpt. New York: Schocken Books, 1971.

Eliot, William G. *Lectures to Young Women*. 4th ed. Boston: Crosby, Nichols and Company, 1854.

Feminism: The Essential Historical Writings. Ed. Miriam Schneir. New York: Random House, 1972.

Gale, Martha. *Woman's High Calling*. Boston: Congregational Publishing Society, 1876.

Hallowell, Anna Davis. *James and Lucretia Mott: Life and Letters*. Boston: Peter Edes of Thomas and Dnerews, 1884.

Harriet Martineau's Autobiography. Ed. Maria Weston Chapman. Boston: Houghton, 1877.

Higginson, Thomas W. *Margaret Fuller Ossoli*. 1890; rpt. N. Y.: Greenwood Press, 1968.

Higginson, Thomas W. *Women and the Alphabet*. New York: Houghton Mifflin and Company, 1900.

Holland, F. M. "Our Clergywomen." *Open Court*, 5, 1892, pp. 3121-23.

Humphreys, John F. "Woman's Work in the Church." *Homiletic Review*, 25, 1893.

Letters and Journals of Thomas W. Higginson. New York: Negro Universities Press, 1969.

Life and Letters of Frederick Douglass. Ed. Philip Foner. New York: International Publishers, 1950-55.

Mansfield, Edward D. *Legal Rights, Liabilities and Duties of Women*. Salem: John P. Jewett and Company, 1845.

Miller, James Russell, *Women's Ministry and Other Papers*. Philadelphia: J. B. Lippincott, 1875.

Moody, Helen. *The Unquiet Sex*. New York: Charles Scribner's Sons, 1898.

Needham, Elizabeth C. *Woman's Ministry: A Spiritual Exposition of Woman's Place in the Church of God*. New Ed. Chicago: Revell, 1895.

Niccolls, Samuel J. "Work of Women in the Church." *The Presbyterian Review*, 10, 1899, pp. 267f.

Phelps, E. S. "Pulpit of Woman." *Atlantic Monthly*, 26, 1870, pp. 1lf.

Proceedings in the Trial of Susan B. Anthony. Rochester, New York: Daily Democrat and Chronicle Book Print, 1874.

Seebach, M. R. "Women: Shall They Preach?" *Lutheran Quarterly*, 33, 1903.

Selected Articles on Woman Suffrage. 3rd ed. Edith M. Phelps. New York: H. W. Wilson Company, 1916.

Stanton, Theodore and Harriet S. Blatch. *Elizabeth Cady Stanton as Revealed in Her Letters, Diary and Reminiscenes.* New York: Harper and Brothers, 1922.

Stephenson, P. D. "The Woman Question." *The Presbyterian Quarterly*, 13, 1899, pp. 206-28; 685-724.

Swisshelm, Jane Grey. *Half a Century.* 1880; rpt. New York: Source Book Press, 1970.

Warren, W. F. "Position of Women in the Church." *Methodist Review*, 56, 1896.

Washburn, George. *Women: Her Work in the Church.* New York: Sanford, Cushing, 1868.

Willard, Frances E. "Women as Preachers." *Our Day*, I 1888, p. 21; 286.

Willmarth, J. W. "Woman's Work in the Church." *Baptist Review*, 10, 1888.

Writings of Margaret Fuller. Ed. Mason Wade. New York: Viking Press, 1941.

Secondary Resources

Anthony, Katherine. *Susan B. Anthony: Her Personal History and Her Era.* New York: Doubleday, 1954.

Breckinridge, Sophronisba P. *Women in the Twentieth Century.* New York: McGraw Hill, 1933.

Bullough, Vern L. *The Subordinate Sex: A History of Attitudes Toward Women.* Urbana, Illinois: University of Illinois Press, 1973.

Callahan, Sidney. *The Illusion of Eve.* New York: Sheed and Ward, 1965.

Catt, Carrie C. and Nettie R. Shuler. *Woman Suffrage and Politics: The Inner Story of the Suffrage Movement.* New York: Charles Scribner's Sons, 1923.

Clarke, Mary S. *Bloomers and Ballots.* New York: Viking, 1972.

Coolidge, Olivia. *Women's Rights: The Suffrage Movement in American 1848-1920.* New York: E. P. Dutton, 1974.

Cromwell, Otelia. *Lucretia Mott.* Cambridge: Harvard University Press, 1958.

Culver, Elsie Thomas. *Women in the World of Religion.* Garden City, New York: Doubleday, 1967.

Degler, Carl N. *Out of the Past.* New York: Harper and Row, 1958.

Dorr, Rheta Louise. *Susan B. Anthony: The Woman Who Changed the Mind of a Nation.* New York: Frederick A. Stokes and Company, 1928.

Earhart, Mary. *Frances Willard: From Prayer to Politics.* Chicago: University of Chicago Press, 1944.

Gamble, Eliza Burt. *The Sexes in Science and History.* New York: G. P. Putnam's Sons, 1916.

Gilman, Charlotte Perkins. *His Religion and Hers: A Study of the Faith of Our Fathers and the Work of Our Mothers.* New York: The Century Company, 1923.

Grimes, Allan P. *The Puritan Ethic and Woman Suffrage.* New York: Oxford University Press, 1967.

Hays, Elinor Rice. *Morning Star: A Biography of Lucy Stone, 1818-1893.* New York: Harcourt, 1961.

Higginson, Mary Potter. *Thomas Wentworth Higginson.* New York: Houghton Mifflin Company, 1914.

Hoppin, Ruth. *Priscilla, Author of the Epistle to the Hebrews*. New York: Exposition Press, 1969.

Irwin, Inez H. *Up Hill With Banners Flying: The Story of the Woman's Party*. Penobsoot, Maine: Traversity, 1964.

Irwin, Inez H. *Angels and Amazons: 100 Years of American Women*. Garden City, New York: Doubleday, Doran and Company, Inc., 1933.

Julia Ward Howe and the Woman Suffrage Movement. Ed. Florence H. Hull. 1913; rpt. New York: Arno Press, 1969.

Kraditor, Aileen S. *Ideas of the Woman Suffrage Movement, 1890-1920*. New York: Columbia University Press, 1965.

Langdon-Davies, John. *A Short History of Women*. New York: Viking Press, 1927.

Ludovici, L. J. *The Final Inequality*. New York: Norton and Company, 1965.

Lutz, Alma. *Created Equal: A Biography of Elizabeth Cady Stanton*. New York: John Day Company, 1940.

Lutz, Alma. *Crusade for Freedom: Women in the Anti-Slavery Movement*. Boston: Beacon Press, 1968.

Lutz, Alma. *Emma Willard*. Boston: Beacon Press, 1964.

O'Connor, Lillian. *Pioneer Women Orators*. New York: Columbia University Press, 1954.

Other Half: Roads to Women's Equality. Eds. Cynthia F. Epstein and William Goode. Englewood Cliffs, N. J.: Prentice-Hall, 1971.

Riegel, Robert E. *American Feminists*. Lawrence, Kansas; University of Kansas Press, 1968.

Ross, Ishbel. *Sons of Adam, Daughters of Eve: The Role of Women in American History.* New York: Harper-Row, 1969.

Sinclair, Andrew. *The Better Half: The Emancipation of the American Woman.* New York: Harper and Row, 1965.

Smith, Page. *Daughters of the Promised Land: Women in American History.* Boston: Little, Brown and Company, 1970.

Stearns, Bertha. "Reform Periodicals and Female Reformers." *The American Historical Review,* 37, July, 1932, pp. 678-699.

Thorp, Margaret Farrand. *Female Persuasion: Six Strong Minded Women.* New Haven: Yale University Press, 1949.

Victory: How Women Won It: A Centennial Symposium of the National-American Suffrage Association. New York: H. W. Wilson Company, 1940.

Wilson, Forrest. *Crusader in Crinoline.* Philadelphia: J. P. Lippincott Company, 1941.

INDEX